THE ULTRA RICH

Books by Vance Packard

THE HIDDEN PERSUADERS

THE STATUS SEEKERS

THE WASTE MAKERS

THE PYRAMID CLIMBERS

THE NAKED SOCIETY

THE SEXUAL WILDERNESS

A NATION OF STRANGERS

THE PEOPLE SHAPERS

OUR ENDANGERED CHILDREN

THE ULTRA RICH

THE ULTRA RICH

HOW MUCH IS TOO MUCH?

VANCE PACKARD

LITTLE, BROWN AND COMPANY
Boston   Toronto   London

FIRST EDITION

Library of Congress Cataloging-in-Publication
Data

Packard, Vance Oakley, 1914–
  The ultra rich.

  Includes index.
  1. Wealth — United States. 2. Millionaires —
United States. 3. Millionairesses — United States.
I. Title.
HC110.W4P24   1989   332'.0973   88-23071
ISBN 0-316-68752-9

10 9 8 7 6 5 4 3 2

Designed by Jacques Chazaud

*Published simultaneously in Canada
by Little, Brown & Company (Canada) Limited*

PRINTED IN THE UNITED STATES OF AMERICA

To Nell Harris Fernandez

"When I think of the degree of my wealth
I find it unbelievable, ungraspable."

— Leonard Stern, pet food maker, after his
net worth was reported at $500 million.[1]
By 1988 his estimated net worth
had almost tripled, to $1.4
billion.

CONTENTS

SECTION I

Trends Regarding Great Private Wealth

1. Our Dreams and Apprehensions about Big Wealth   *3*
2. The Explosion of Personal Fortunes   *13*
3. On Encountering Rich People   *30*

SECTION II

How They View — and Cope with — Their Wealth

A. Ways of Viewing Wealth

4. Wealth as an Extension of Self   *43*
5. Wealth as a Problem to Be Escaped   *71*
6. Wealth as an Ego Prop   *85*
7. Wealth as a Way to Keep Score   *95*
8. Wealth as a Challenge for True-Blue Capitalists   *108*
9. Wealth as an Incidental Aspect of Life   *117*

B. Ways of Using Wealth

10. Seeking to Live It Up   *135*
11. Trying Elite Playgrounds and Pastimes   *163*

12. Living High but Craving Something Else   *178*

13. Maintaining a Just-Folks Life-style   *192*

14. Playing the Power Game   *208*

15. Venturing for More Than Money   *213*

16. Demonstrating Social Responsibility —
     How Benevolent Are They, Really?   *221*

     C. Ways Family Dynamics Shape Treatment of Wealth

17. The Yearning for — and Problems of —
     Family Dynasties   *241*

18. The Fragmenting Effect of Modern Family Forms   *256*

     D. How They Protect Their Wealth

19. Protective Strategies While Still Alive   *275*

20. Strategies for the Hereafter   *285*

21. A Tycoon Who Would Crack Down
     on the Super-Rich   *294*

SECTION III

Conclusions

*How Should Today's Society Treat Vast Accumulations
of Private Wealth?*

22. The Lowering Rationality and Increasing
     Consequences of Great Private Fortunes   *305*

23. On Curbing a Moneyed Aristocracy   *320*

24. On Encouraging the Wealthy to Shift Priorities   *332*

     REFERENCE NOTES   *339*

     INDEX   *349*

ACKNOWLEDGMENTS

I wish to express my appreciation first of all to the thirty-odd persons of great wealth who, in my visits with them, gave me their thoughts about coping with their money.

There were others who supplied valuable information on how the rich protect their money, on possible solutions to curbing the accelerating concentration of wealth, and on other matters of interest. In particular I express my appreciation to these individuals:

Former Commissioners of the U.S. Internal Revenue Service: Mortimer Caplin, Sheldon S. Cohen, and Don Alexander.

Academicians with special knowledge on constitutional problems: Carl S. Shoup, Professor Emeritis of Columbia Law School; Lester Thurow of the MIT Sloane School of Management; Oliver Oldman of the Harvard Law School; James D. Smith who was serving at the Institute for Social Research, University of Michigan; Richard W. Lindholm, economist at the University of Oregon.

U.S. Government officials: Robert Anthony, attorney for the Securities Exchange Commission; Mel Thomas of the Congressional Joint Tax Committee; David Parish of the Individual Branch, IRS; Marvin Schwartz of the IRS; Eugene Steuerle who played a role in shaping the 1987 tax reform bill; Pat Oglesby of the Joint Committee on Taxation, U.S. Congress.

Tax attorneys specializing in estate planning: Jerry McCoy of Washington, D.C.; Jonathan Blattmachr of New York and San Francisco; Earl Colson of Washington, DC.; and others.

People giving guidance in specific areas: Roy Brady, chief of statistics, Value Line; Gerald Gold, vice president of Prudential Bache; James Mills of Home Facts, Inc. in Reston, Va.; David Kahan of the Center on Budget and Policy Priorities; Herman Kogan and Daryl Feldmier, noted Chicago newspapermen; Nancy Smith, Dallas society columnist; and Louis Kelso of Kelso and Company. I received valued help from Randall Packard, Cindy Packard Richmond, Andrew Greenwood, and Robert Crowell.

Finally I am considerably indebted to two other people: First, in New York City, reporter Denise Lynch, who helped supply background information on many of the wealthy people whom I visited, synchronized many of the appointments, and supplied a vast amount of helpful information; in Washington D.C., reporter Joann Stern, who helped considerably in obtaining information on strategies the rich use to protect their wealth and on problems in taxing wealth directly. She also made advance trips for me to Palm Beach and Dallas.

TRENDS REGARDING GREAT PRIVATE WEALTH

CHAPTER 1

OUR DREAMS AND APPREHENSIONS ABOUT BIG WEALTH

An Introduction

"I know of no country, indeed, where the love of money has taken a stronger hold on the affections of men."

— ALEXIS DE TOCQUEVILLE,
famed French visitor, 1835

Something extraordinary has been happening to our reward system at the higher levels. This book is an effort to explore the implications for our society of the increasing accumulation of wealth in the hands of the rich. The concentration of private wealth recently reached its highest point in a half century. This raises economic, social, and human questions.

Is this concentration of wealth implicated in a number of our economic problems? Can these people of enormous wealth be justified in social terms? Do we need them? And what does the wealth do to the individuals themselves as their fortunes run into the hundreds of millions, and billions, of dollars?

How do they think about, and cope with, their wealth? What do they plan to do with it, if anything? Does social responsibility enter significantly into their thinking?

One of the more enlightening parts of the research for this exploration involved visits with thirty extremely rich people. They lived in sixteen states. Their average net worth was around $330 million at the time I started my visits in 1985. One was a billionaire.

By the time I had completed this report two years later, their average wealth had risen 28 percent to $425 million; and four additional people I had visited were listed as billionaires by *Fortune*.[1] Presumably the recent economic turbulence has lowered the average wealth of the thirty but probably not back to the $330 million they had when I visited them. Many have vast holdings in real estate. Only four had most of their wealth tied to a publicly traded stock at the time of the October 1987 crash. Of those, only one held stock that lost value over the full year of 1987.

One surprise was how few fit our media-induced concepts regarding life-styles and characteristics of the very rich. They turned out to comprise a remarkably varied and instructive group. Several were colorful. A few were peculiar. Some were astonishingly frank.

One of the richest men in Texas confessed disappointment that all four of his sons were either incapable of, or uninterested in, carrying on the family business.

While in the Kansas City area one evening I was talking with a local tycoon, dressed in a bathrobe, and his wife (who is company treasurer) in their enormous hilltop home. He mentioned that their net worth in the last three weeks had increased by $43 million.

A Rockefeller heiress said there was no way she could justify all the wealth she has.

One male centimillionaire remarked with chagrin that he had inadvertently married a lesbian more interested in him as a stud and life supporter than as a life companion.

An immigrant in the construction business told of an interesting provision in his will: None of his children can ever receive from trusts more money in any one year than the salary of the president of the United States (a mere $250,000). At such a rate it would take an heir one hundred years to receive $25 million, which is about where substantial fortunes begin.

The major question that emerged from this inquiry was whether fortunes in the $50 million to $8 billion range can be justified in today's America. This question becomes particularly pertinent given the fact that the great bulk of such fortunes are passed on to heirs. Should we consider such people fabulously rich or just excessively rich? Are they "ultra" rich in the dictionary sense of going beyond "due limit"?

This book will, I hope, provide a quizzical look at the wealth accumulation system as it operates in U.S. society, with some glimpses at other western societies, and inquire about possible changes.

Americans have always had a hard time deciding what they think about the accumulation of vast individual fortunes. The first point made in the Declaration of Independence is: "We hold these truths to be self-evident, that all men are created equal, that they are endowed by their Creator with certain inalienable rights, that among these are life, liberty and the pursuit of happiness."

Pursuit of happiness has generally come to include the opportunity to rise above the crowd by successful pursuit of personal wealth. But where does that leave equality? It has generally come to mean the right to an equal start in life, an equal opportunity to make the climb.

As a goal in life, equality has for most Americans never had the deep-down appeal of pursuit of happiness through wealth, even among large numbers of underprivileged. At times in our history severe cleavages have developed between rich and nonrich because the rich seemed to be becoming excessively wealthy or powerful; the general public has called for corrective action to ease the sense of conflict.

The American Revolutionary War was not as much an

uprising against a hereditary class of economic royalists as it was against the hereditary political power of King George. Two of the signers of the Declaration of Independence, John Hancock and Charles Carroll, were enormously wealthy by the standards of the day. The French Revolution was much more clearly a wrathful economic uprising, via the guillotine, against a hereditary rich class that dominated the underclasses.

Still, during and after the American Revolution many estates were broken up. As our new nation sought to get started, some leaders such as John Adams were concerned that the revolutionary mood might get out of hand and threaten the social order. Rambunctious affairs such as Shays Rebellion fired their anxiety. But the predominant concern of the Founding Fathers was in the other direction — that precautions needed to be taken to prevent a hereditary wealthy class from taking charge. There was talk of need of a "citizen leader." Some were uneasy about George Washington taking over as the first president not only because he was a general and seemed to enjoy a bit of pomp but because he was a man of substantial wealth. A lot of it came from his wife, Martha. He owned great tracts of land. When he died it was discovered that he was one of the richest men in the land.

After George Washington there was no president of conspicuous wealth for a full century.[2] Wariness about coming under the domination of an economic elite almost certainly was a factor. In fact the only really wealthy presidents we have ever had — Theodore Roosevelt, Franklin D. Roosevelt, and John F. Kennedy — all had strong credentials as champions of the common man.

The hazard of concentrated wealth was clearly on the minds of several of America's foremost Founding Fathers. Thomas Jefferson, while visiting pre-revolutionary France, was alarmed by the grave consequences for French society of the fact that property there was "absolutely concentrated in very few hands." In late 1785 he wrote James Madison of his deep concern and counseled that America's legislators could not "invent too many devices for subdividing property" to ensure the democratic and productive capacities of the emerging nation.[3]

John Adams concluded that the balance of power in the new nation would be strongly affected by the way property and land were distributed. He wrote: "If the multitude is possessed of the balance of real estate, the multitude will have the balance of power and ... the multitude will take care of the liberty, virtue and interest of the multitude in all acts of government."[4]

The new nation was barely a third of a century old when there arose considerable restlessness in the land because of fear that the rich — particularly a regional aristocracy consisting of old families of New England — were gaining altogether too much power in the nation. Thomas Skidmore, in proclaiming the formation of the Working-Men's Party in 1829, charged that great wealth had become an instrument "which is uniformly used to extort from others their property." He charged that "it ought to be taken away from its possessors on the same principle that a sword or a pistol may be wrested from a robber."

Andrew Jackson, well-to-do himself, eased tensions for a while by sweeping out of the "west" to take over the White House.

That did not fully settle the matter. In 1838 Daniel Webster, the grand orator from New England, took the floor of the Senate to deplore the constant clamor about "the pernicious influence of wealth." The complainers, he contended, would choke the fountain of emerging industry and "dry up all streams."

At about this time the famous visitor from France, de Tocqueville, took measure of the American character. Despite the wariness of a rich elite, he felt there was scant evidence of a real equalitarian mood in the land. In his *Democracy in America* he said he knew of no country where a profounder contempt is expressed for the theory of the permanent equality of property.

However, he saw in the growth of the new manufacturing concerns — which seemed to require workers to obey and entrepreneurs to command — the possible seeds of a new aristocracy. If it came it would not be an aristocracy of landed gentry who took a caring attitude toward people occupying their land but a more harsh commanding elite. He cautioned "friends of democracy" to keep their eye on this threat. (Several decades later the threat did become real in the form of the "robber barons" of big industry.)

Meanwhile, in the years leading to the Civil War there was in the republicanism movement a pervasive hostility to wealth and privilege in the land as a possible source of corrupting power. For many, one of the satisfying upshots of the Civil War was that the southern power elite based on plantations built with the help of slave labor received a major setback.

In the latter part of the nineteenth century there was in a number of states considerable political corruption. This was reflected in the fact that several enormously wealthy men bought their way into the U.S. Senate in order to assure favorable legislation for their projects. The outcry convinced ambitious people of wealth that they ought to use less blatant means. They began financing surrogates.

The deep personal aspiration for wealth that de Tocqueville perceived as a part of the American character got ample demonstration in the late nineteenth century in the sensational success of preacher-author Horatio Alger. He churned out about 135 rags-to-riches books. A major theme was that any poor boy could become a millionaire.

Meanwhile, the industrial revolution was finally starting to create really vast undertakings: steel mills, intercontinental railroads, oil fields and coal mines, giant plants to make farm machinery, enormous textile mills and meat-packing plants. Fortunes of then great enormity were being made. Often there was collusion among the moguls creating these enterprises in seeking advantages through monopolies, trusts, and interconnection of directorates. At one point the interests of J. P. Morgan, the superbanker, had 341 directors in 112 corporations.[5] There were cries that the robber barons were exploiting workers. For the first time it was common to read newspaper accounts of violent clashes between strikers and hired strike-busters. Exposés appeared by such excellent "muckraking" authors as Upton Sinclair and Ida Tarbell. At about the same time the cool, sardonic Thorstein Veblen, author of *The Theory of the Leisure Class,* observed that when individual wealth gets above "a certain rather indefinite average," a mood develops that works toward a "leveling policy."

Republican President Teddy Roosevelt was repelled by what seemed to be a growing plutocracy. A man who loved a battle, he came out swinging as a "trust buster" and a critic of great inherited wealth. He largely started the movement that produced the Sherman Antitrust Act, and as president he sought through taxation to break up great concentrations of inherited wealth. In a tax message to Congress he contended: "The prime object should be to put a constantly increasing burden on the inheritance of these swollen fortunes which it is certainly no benefit to this country to perpetuate."[6]

Cries to sock the rich were heard well into the twentieth century. Senator Williams of Mississippi in 1913 proclaimed: "I think the time will come some day when there must be a limitation put upon the amount that may be inherited or left to any one person to destroy the power that great fortunes transmit from generation to generation."[7] A mild federal income tax was introduced in 1913 and an inheritance tax became law in 1916.

During the 1920s a lot of people were becoming rich and the general populace hoped that greater prosperity would prevail generally. This hope proved largely to be in vain. One explanation is offered below.

Following the 1929 crash, a new era of examining the evils of great wealth developed. Some blamed the big rich for getting us into the mess known as the Great Depression. Economist John Kenneth Galbraith, in looking back on that era in his 1972 book *The Great Crash,* argued that the depression occurred partly because wealth had become so concentrated that ordinary people were running short on money to buy the vast amount of goods that industry could turn out.

U.S. senator Huey Long, a gifted rabble-rouser from Louisiana, became a challenging national figure with his battle cries of "Share the wealth!" and "Every man a king!" before his assassination in 1935.

During the New Deal of Franklin D. Roosevelt a host of bills were enacted not only to stimulate the economy but to try to make the economy perform more fairly for the poor and for working-class people. He lashed out at "economic royalists," pushed into law steeper graduated income taxes and, at the high levels of wealth, stiffer estate taxes. In calling for such taxes in his message to Congress in June 1935, he contended that the generation-to-generation transfer of great fortunes "by will, inheritance or gift" was not consistent with either the ideals or the sentiments of the American people. Furthermore, he stated that there was no way to justify great accumulations of wealth on the basis of conceivable family security.

The new taxes scared many of the really rich such as the Fords into locking up tens of millions of dollars in foundations bearing their name and into working to create protections from taxation. During World War II the tax rate on persons of great wealth soared to more than 90 percent of newly accumulated income and in fact President Roosevelt talked of a need to put a flat cap on incomes for the duration of the war.

In the third quarter of the twentieth century, despite a sizable recession around 1973, a more permissive attitude developed toward the very rich. Sociologist G. William Domhoff still believed there was too much conspiring among the people of great wealth. In 1979 he spelled out his concerns in *The Powers That Be: Processes of Ruling Class Domination in America.* While quarreling with Marxist theory, he tended to see political and economic problems in modern America as being rooted in conflicts and compromises between a ruling class and the working class.

But in general there was a decline in cautionary books about the rich, such as the earlier *Lords of Creation* and *The Power Elite.* Books about the rich became primarily informational (examples: Jacqueline Thompson's *The Very Rich Book* in 1981, Harry Hurt III's *Texas Rich* in 1981, Kit Konolige's *The Richest Women in the World* in 1985, and Michael Patrick Allen's *The Founding Fortunes* in 1987).

By the 1980s the public attitude toward great fortune builders was absolutely benign. Americans saw the evidence of spectacular wealth accumulation in the annual listing that *Forbes* magazine began making of the 400 richest Americans. Great fortunes were being assembled not by a handful of people but by large numbers of people. By and large Americans were back to equating wealth and success, and seeking to get in on the action. *Money* magazine (March 1984) ran an article pronouncing that now being rich "happens to be in fashion." It cited no less an authority than President Reagan, who made the comment that "What I want to see above all is that this remains a country where someone can always get rich."

And he helped the process mightily. In the Blue Room of the White House he replaced the portrait of Thomas Jefferson with that of Calvin Coolidge, who, as far as I can find, is not on any historian's list of major U.S. presidents. But Mr. Coolidge did not make waves and he did say, "The business of America is business."[8]

Mr. Reagan made a crusade of easing restraints on the entrepreneural rich individuals and their companies. The 1981 tax law he pushed through Congress made it possible for the rich to pass their money to their spouses without any tax at all and to pass more than half a million dollars on as gifts without tax. The maximum tax brackets were reduced substantially. He passed out word that under him the antitrust enforcers would not equate bigness with badness. In 1986 a law calling for tax simplification, which he sponsored, was passed. It eliminated some protections that had been built in for the rich, but the heart of it was that the centimillionaire and the dentist would shortly both be in the same maximum income tax bracket of around 28 percent. Regressive taxation was replacing progressive taxation.

Many ordinary Americans aspired to make at least a little killing in this permissive, high-debt environment, and they were encouraged to go for big ones by their own state governments. The governments had changed lottery betting from being an illegal sin to an approved source of revenue-raising. They were offering sucker odds since they kept about half of all the money that people bet, but they worked to sustain excitement by letting the prizes get bigger and bigger until they became hard to grasp in ordinary life terms. Their offers sounded somehow fabulous.

New York State, with prizes in the tens of millions of dollars, called its lottery "The American Dream Come True." Illinois was the first state to get to $40 million as a first prize. The winner, a young printer, said he planned to use some of his winnings to pay off a few bills and to buy an engagement ring for his girlfriend. And he planned to keep his printing job. Other big U.S. winners said they planned to buy a new car or take a trip to Hawaii or buy a better house. Their dreams and imagination, it turned out, were not up to the sizes of the prizes. They continued to think just of ways to make life more comfortable or enjoyable.

Several states began mapping out a real super-revenue-raiser — a megalottery that could offer $100 million in top prizes every week of the year.

By the late 1980s there was some uneasiness about the stupendous national debt and deficits in foreign trade and other evidences of a precarious economy.

But money was churning. And to many people the intriguing news was that some people were making incredible amounts of money.

CHAPTER 2

THE EXPLOSION OF

PERSONAL FORTUNES

"To turn $100 into $110 is work. To turn
$100 million into $110 million is inevi-
table."

— Billionaire EDGAR BRONFMAN
of Seagrams Co.[1]

Each year Americans are re-
quired to disclose their income for that year but they are
never asked to reveal how rich they really are in terms of
net worth. Only after one dies do taxing officials try to figure
out what the "estate" of an obviously rich person is worth.
By then the clever ones — or their clever lawyers — usually
have unloaded much of their wealth by a variety of strategies, which we will get to later.

Until the past decade little was generally and reliably
known about personal wealth, especially if held in private

companies. Public companies are required to file proxy statements if a person or family owns more than 5 percent of their stock. Thus one might read in fine print in the Value Line Investment Survey of an Akron trucking company named Roadway Services, which most of us have never heard of: "Roush family controls about 30% of common." That figure for 1986 when multiplied out comes to $540 million worth of stock.

From time to time business magazines would try to compile a list of the richest Americans and typically would list a few dozen worth more than $50 million. Early in this decade, as indicated, the business journal *Forbes* undertook a really massive search for superrich people and it has since published its latest findings each fall. These findings startled many people.

In 1982, for example, the cutoff point for inclusion in its list of the 400 richest American individuals was a net worth of $93 million. By 1987 the cutoff point had advanced to $225 million. Between 1985 and 1987, the number of billionaires jumped from fourteen to forty-nine. Four of these were entitled to a new phrase in our language — "multi-billionaires."

Because of the difficulty of tracing wealth, the *Forbes* list is not infallible and does not pretend to be. But it does present a solid picture of the recent explosion of enormously wealthy people in this country. A California chain operator I met did not deny *Forbes* had been about right in pegging his wealth at $200 million but he was sore because the publication had not included a couple of fellows he knew who were richer than he was.

Many of the more astounding accumulations of wealth in terms of single-year earnings were being made by wheeler-dealers of finance. I refer particularly to financiers who were putting together takeover deals or mergers, and to investment fund managers. *Financial World* in June 1987 reported that the five top money-makers in the financial community in 1986 had been rewarded for their year's work by an average of $88 million. Only one of them was yet in the *Forbes* 400. That person was Michael Milken, known as the Junk Bond King. As a senior vice-president at Drexel Burnham Lambert, he made very creative use of junk bonds to help raiders achieve takeovers. *Forbes* pegged him as worth $600 million in 1987. That's not bad for an ambitious forty-year-old vice-president.

This explosion of wealth has been occurring at all levels from simple millionaires to billionaires. Dr. Thomas Stanley, marketing professor at Georgia State University, who has been studying millionaires for a dozen years, announced in 1985 that 100,000 new millionaires were being created each year and that by 1987 their total number would reach 1,000,000. The Statistics of Income *Bulletin* of the Internal Revenue Service, using estate figures of deceased persons, which tend to understate, was more conservative in its estimate of total number of millionaires but said the number of millionaires had doubled between 1976 and 1982. And one of the SOI division's officials advised me in 1984 that the number of individuals worth $5 million had more than doubled between 1976 and 1981. Note that these great increases in individual wealth all occurred before 1982 when the stock-buying public began placing a higher valuation on companies.

When you learn of individuals worth hundreds of millions, or billions, it is awesome to try to grasp the amounts involved.

The wealth of the 400 individuals cited by *Forbes* equals the savings that all Americans have in commercial banks. And that wealth of the 400 is considerably greater than the annual federal budget deficit which has created so much difficulty for the nation. Or take a personal example. The richest man in Arkansas, Sam Walton of Wal-Mart stores, had a net worth in 1987 that was several billion dollars more than his state government's annual budget. He dropped a billion or so in net worth on Black Monday of October 1987 but he shrugged it off as a technical paper loss.

This explosion of personal prosperity is not shared by the 90 percent of Americans who are not "rich." The Federal

Reserve Board, in one accounting, labeled people in the top 10 percent as the "Rich," the "Very Rich," and the "Super Rich." The starting point for being merely "Rich" in 1983 was $419,000 per household. Below the "Rich" were the 90 percent labeled "Everybody Else." During the preceding twenty years the net worth of the merely "Rich" had grown 47 percent faster, in constant dollars, than that of "Everybody Else."[2]

In 1963 "Everybody Else" owned 36 percent of the nation's economic pie. By 1983 "Everybody Else's" share of the pie had dropped to 32 percent. The chairman of the Congressional Joint Economic Committee, David Obey, in commenting on this drop said: "It is . . . disturbing that the 90% of American families who are not on the top end of the economic totem pole appear to have suffered a loss of almost 10% in their share of national net worth. . . . This trend runs counter to the belief of our citizens that wealth is being more equitably distributed."[3]

In 1987, figures compiled by the U.S. Labor Department showed U.S. workers earning less in real terms than they had earned six years earlier.

And Barbara Ehrenreich, a research fellow at the Institute for Policy Studies, has reported finding that starting around 1977 there was a "sharp reversal of the equalizing trend that had been under way since shortly after World War II." Felix Rohatyn, the noted investment banker and civic leader, was quoted in the report as observing: "A democracy, to survive, must at the very least appear to be fair. This is no longer the case in America."[4] The report added as an example that today a young family with a median income can no longer afford to buy a medium-priced house.

Longer-term studies have also been done on changes in the share of the nation's wealth held by its richest citizens. One report, made to Congress in 1976 by economist James D. Smith, then of Penn State, covered the half century from 1922 to 1972. Its focus was on changes in the share of total wealth held by the top half of one percent of the population.[5]

Another longer-term analysis has been assembled by economist Ravi Batra of Southern Methodist University. It covers 173 years of American economic history, from 1810 to 1983. Its focus was on changes in the share of total wealth held by the top one percent of the population.[6]

For the half century that the two studies overlap they show an essentially similar pattern. Both show a big surge upward in concentration of wealth between 1922 and 1929, which was the peak year of the whole span of both. They both show a relatively stable picture of barely average concentration of wealth for the quarter century between 1945 and 1970.

Batra's longer span shows that for the whole 1810–1983 period the *average* amount of the nation's wealth concentrated in the top one percent of the population was 27.5 percent.

The latest reading Batra had, for 1983, came from a 1986 estimate provided by the Joint Economic Committee of Congress. It showed that the concentration of wealth in the top one percent of the population had increased dramatically since 1969. In fact it had reached 34 percent — or more than a third of our nation's wealth held by just one percent of the population. This figure was just two percent short of the 36 percent set in 1929, when — was it coincidence? — the nation's whole economy began trembling.

These two analyses suggest the possibility that a high concentration of wealth in relatively few hands may be not only unfair, as Mr. Rohatyn stated, but may perhaps be unwise national policy. (We'll examine this proposition later.)

But let us get back into the stratosphere with the people of our primary focus, the immensely rich. The explosion of growth into the thousands of individuals finding themselves worth more than $50 million does not necessarily mean we have been blessed with a great increase in brilliant entrepreneurs. Changes in the national and world economies alone can account for most of the explosion of private wealth. For example:

1. With swift transportation possible, great mass markets for products opened up both nationally and internationally.

2. There has also been a great growth, as indicated, of enterprises which — unlike those in basic industry — can explode quickly in size. I refer especially to the multitude of chain operations for providing goods and services. Explosions also have been possible in filling the vacuum-like niches created by the computer revolution. (Here scientific brilliance, at least, has helped the process.)

3. Within the past two decades there has been a dramatic tightening in the amount of desirable land available for commercial or residential use. Prices have consequently soared. This fact alone has created hundreds of large fortunes.

4. The Reagan Revolution, while running up an enormous public debt, contributed massively with its taxing and other policies to creating an environment helpful to fortune-builders.

5. For well-to-do Americans who had surpluses of wealth to invest, it didn't take brilliance to double, triple, or quadruple their investment in a half-dozen years in the U.S. securities market. Money generated by heavy deficit spending by the government, money flowing in from foreign investors, and money flowing out of ever-larger pension funds were all put into competition for available shares of U.S. corporations, which ran up their value.

Who are these super-wealthy people? Where are they? How did they acquire their enormous net worths? *Forbes* found that more than half of its 400 richest Americans come from six states: New York, California, Texas, Florida, Illinois, and Delaware (du Pont country). In 1985 quite a few states had no individual entries among the 400, including Maine, Mississippi, Montana, and the Dakotas.

Nearly half of the very wealthy on the list got their money — or a big head start — from inheritance. Fifty-nine made their fortunes solely or primarily from real estate operations. About three dozen more include land or real estate among their major assets. New York realtor and billionaire Harry Helmsley called real estate attractive because: "You don't have to do anything. You just have to sit. The values go up." James Mills, a consultant to realtors, told me it is easy to run $20,000 of your own money up to tens of millions of dollars' worth of buildings just by manipulating mortgage money.

A substantial number of fortunes are based on oil or manufacturing. The surprises, however, were that a fourth of all the great fortunes today are based on chain operations or media empires (which often involve chains). You can explode quickly with a hot chain because it requires relatively small expenditure for production facilities, managerial and research backup, and you can readily expand or contract the chain to meet demand. Media holdings are attractive because they often involve a sort of franchise — or corner — on assured markets. Of the twenty-six billionaires *Forbes* discovered in 1986, eight were operating chains of some sort — merchandising or media.

Another surprise is that a number of people we assume are immensely rich are mostly not by today's standards. We have long believed that the heads of great corporations — say, the chief executive officers of our largest corporations — are at the top of our reward system. Actually most are lucky if they have $8 million to their name. This is true even though the pay and bonuses of the nation's top chief executives rose about four times faster than the wages of average people during the decade ending in 1987 — and about thirty times faster than corporate profits — according to a study by Sibson and Company reported in the *New York Times* (April 27, 1988).

Only those who were able to make a killing by exercising long-term options to buy their company's stock at some long-ago price far lower than the current price are really rich by today's standards. This option largely accounts for the fact that "total compensation" of many chief executive officers soared during the surge in stock prices in the mid-1980s, especially if they managed to take their profits before the October 1987 crash in stock prices. For example in 1987 the president of Waste Management received $950,000 in pay and bonuses and $13 million in "long-term compensation," presumably by exercising stock options.

Each spring *Business Week* publishes an "Executive Compensation Scoreboard." Its reports of May 5, 1986 and May 2, 1988, for compensation in the preceding year show the change in just two years of the "total compensation" for the chief executives of seven of the nation's most enormous industrial corporations. These figures include, as indicated, not only salary and bonus but also any long-term compensation.

	1985	1987
General Electric	$1,614,000	$12,631,000
DuPont	$2,002,000	$5,948,000
Exxon	$3,561,000[a]	$5,464,000
Ford	$1,692,000	$3,730,000[b]
General Motors	$1,782,000	$2,180,000
Procter & Gamble	$1,003,000	$1,444,000
IBM	$736,000	$841,000
Average for the seven	$1,770,000	$4,605,000

[a] Mostly from options.
[b] Mostly bonus.

In short, total compensation almost tripled in two years due in most cases to taking advantage of a general stock price boom that had relatively little to do with corporate profits.

The low IBM figures are of particular interest since IBM long had a reputation of being the most profitable major company in history, and the "most admired." By today's logic of personal fortune building one of the richest men in America today should be Thomas J. Watson, Jr., since only a few decades ago his father built IBM into a great worldwide company. No Watson has ever been in the *Forbes* 400 and the Watson family in general is not considered really rich.

For many years Mr. Watson, Sr., had virtually total power in the building of IBM. He was nationally famous for being a benevolent dictator who made every employee toe the line in dress and body fat. He acquired companies. A long-time official of IBM tells me that at many points he could have cut himself in for, say, 12 percent of IBM's stock (which 12 percent would be worth $10 billion at this writing).

In fact, however, when he died his estate was worth $5 million.[7] For a dramatic contrast, a display of how our reward system for business executives runs on two tracks, take the case of William Millard (whom we will visit). In just a few years he ran his chain of ComputerLand stores up to the point that in 1984 *Forbes* put his net worth at $600 million. (It has changed since.) A major factor in his success was that he had a good arrangement with IBM for selling its smaller computers.

To get back to Mr. Watson, I suspect that a matter of personal philosophy was involved. I used to watch the old gentleman at our church in New Canaan, Connecticut, take notes of the sermons with a little gold pencil. He conceived of his role as one of stewardship, not profit-making. Such an attitude is becoming exceptional in business. On August 19, 1984, the lead article in the business section of the *New York Times* was entitled: "The Age of 'Me First' Management." It began: "It doesn't take a revolutionary to figure out that something is amiss in American business today; that a 'me-first, grab what you can' extravagance increasingly appears to be cropping up among the nation's top executives." Since the big money simply is not there if you are working for pay, many seek roles where they can get a part of the action through a stake in ownership or commissions or percentages in deal-making.

While many entrepreneurs or investors have been adding tens of millions of dollars a year to their net worth, and while chief executive officers of major corporations were adding mere millions a year, the man most in charge of trying to make the whole U.S. economy work was being paid $89,000 per year. That man, until 1987, was Paul Volker, head of the Federal Reserve Board, often called the second most powerful man in America. His piddling pay came from us, the taxpayers. To make ends meet in high-cost Washington, his wife took a job as a bookkeeper. He was described as living "like a struggling graduate student in an apartment furnished mainly with castoff furniture from his daughter Janice. He uses green milk crates for an end table."[8]

A group of people starting to pull into the big rich at least in terms of annual gross earnings are entertainment stars.

The only entertainer to make the *Forbes* 400 in 1985 was Gene Autry, seventy-eight-year-old former singing cowboy who phased out his movie career three decades ago. His $150 million was largely based on holdings in real estate, a radio chain, and music publishing.

Another entertainer who would have scored big on the list if he was an American is British rock star of Beatle fame, Paul McCartney.

After Bob Hope was listed in the 1983 issue of *Forbes* as worth $200 million, he issued a challenge to the magazine: "If my estate is worth over $50 million I'll kiss your ass. I mean it."[9] So the publication set off to make a more thorough examination with hired appraisers. The problem was that the bulk of his wealth was in about eighty parcels of real estate, mostly many thousands of acres of raw land in Southern California, and hence difficult to assess. The magazine concluded that his estate was conservatively worth at least $119 million. If so, both had been wrong. No ceremony was requested. Mr. Hope was in his early eighties and was still making lots of extra money by doing TV shows and commercials for such companies as Texaco. Being on stage — or adding to wealth — apparently was a compulsion.

Among entertainers under seventy-five years of age one of the biggest winners seemed to be another rock star, Michael Jackson. The 1984 *Forbes* put him among the up-and-comers with $70 million. Recording and performing star Bruce Springsteen appeared to be comparably wealthy.

In September 1987 *Forbes* took a separate look just at entertainers and found ten who seemed assured of making at least $20 million in 1987 alone. The top money-maker was TV comedian Bill Cosby, who is not only an actor but an author, a show-business entrepreneur, and a very highly paid endorser of products. Its estimate was that he would gross $57 million. The movie comedian Eddie Murphy apparently would make $27 million, and Sylvester Stallone, master of acting violence, would make $23 million. Five of the top ten, including Springsteen, were rock or pop singers. One of the surprises was the estimate that cartoonist Charles Schulz, who has built a worldwide enterprise around his "Peanuts" characters, would make $30 million.

A *People* magazine survey in 1986 indicated however that the top total net worth star in the current generation of entertainers might presently be Barbra Streisand. While currently making $5 million a picture, she had lifetime earnings of nearly $100 million. And she probably has kept a lot of it. She has skinflint habits of hitching rides to the theater to avoid cab fares, clipping grocery coupons, and sending out recycled Christmas cards. A hairdresser claimed she was very slow in paying bills.[10]

By 1986 one-time TV entertainers who had turned to production were well up among the really rich: they had made the *Forbes* 400 richest Americans list, with net worths in the hundreds of millions. Talk-show host Merv Griffin made it big (more than $200 million) by developing *Wheel of Fortune.*

The best-paying sport, if one can stay at the top and take the battering, apparently is boxing. A CBS commentator put the lifetime earnings of the world champion Larry Holmes at $45 million. Lifetime earnings may or may not equal present net worth. His main investments are in stores and hotels. By 1988 the most recent heavyweight champion, Mike Tyson, had about the same net worth.

Stars in other sports featuring individual players tend to get small payoffs. Tennis and golf stars for example are pretty far down among sports stars in terms of payoff while playing. John McEnroe, Ivan Lendl, and Jimmy Connors by 1985 had *lifetime* earnings of only $5 million. No golfer had made that much, lifetime, from play, even by 1987. In that year the *New York Times* put Jack Nicklaus first in earnings, lifetime, with $4,959,000, with Tom Watson, Ray Floyd, Lee Trevino, Tom Kite, Lanny Wadkins, Hal Irwin, Ben Crenshaw, and Andy Bean following down, in order, to $2.5 million, lifetime.

Among team sports, baseball seems clearly to offer the biggest rewards. In 1988 the major league teams had seventy-three players making at least $1 million a year. A *New York Times* analysis (April 1, 1988) showed that the number making at least $2 million a year doubled from five to ten in one year. The highest paid was Ozzie Smith of the Cardinals with $2,340,000. The other nine in the $2 million class were Dale Murphy of the Braves, Eddie Murray of the Orioles, Jim Rice of the Red Sox, Rick Sutcliffe of the Cubs, Dan Quisenberry of the Royals, Fernando Valenzuela of the Dodgers, Gary Carter of the Mets, Don Mattingly of the Yankees, and Mike Schmidt of the Phillies.

Two of the superstars of basketball also made on the court about $2 million a year in the mid-1980s. They were Larry Bird of Boston and Kareem Abdul-Jabbar of Los Angeles. Football stars are lucky to make a million a year on the field.

But for some sports stars, pay for competition is only a part — often a small part — of their total earnings. If they are personable, there are major earnings from endorsements and appearances. The number-one capitalist in the sports world appears to be Jack Nicklaus. He is much involved in doing TV commercials for products having nothing to do with golf. He has long been greatly in demand to do designed-by Nicklaus golf courses. And he is heavily into real estate investment. In 1986 the *Miami Herald,* in a listing of rich Floridians, put Jack Nicklaus of North Palm Beach at $100 million.

In earlier periods the really great entrepreneurial fortunes tended to be made by investing in "basic" industries such as steel, transit, meat-packing, auto-making. Today high-tech industry has certainly become basic and accounts for about a dozen spots in the top 400. But a lot of the new big rich have built their fortunes in peripheral or seemingly even trivial areas. For example the 1985 *Forbes* listing of the wealthiest 400 Americans cited these twenty-odd titans of wealth:

- a maker of devices that warn speeding autoists or truckers of radar traps ahead;
- a manufacturer of teddy bears;
- a Coca-Cola bottler (in 1984 there were two Coca-Cola bottlers);
- a builder of country clubs;
- a maker of products for pets;
- a maker of running shoes;
- four men in the candy-making business;
- two men in the pizza business;
- three publishers whose main money-makers were *Penthouse, Hot Rod,* and *National Enquirer*;
- a man who sells almost any product he feels can be presented as a "bargain";
- two casino operators;
- several corporate raiders;
- three cosmetic marketers;
- a producer of rental trailers;
- a publisher of yellow pages for phone books;
- two owners of a giant door-to-door or telephone selling service;
- a marketer of greeting cards.

If these pursuits seem peripheral, perhaps we can surmise that in these puzzling economic times it is on the periphery of the economy rather than in basic industry that many entrepreneurs are finding the more spectacular rewards.

America appears to have many more centimillionaires per capita than any other country (with Canada possibly an equal and also The Netherlands. Canada has vast resources and The Netherlands historically has been deep in international trading.) One obvious advantage to American entrepreneurs is that they have such a vast marketplace.

In October 1987, *Fortune* magazine, in a survey of the whole world's individual billionaires, credited the U.S. with forty-seven. If you exclude national rulers, the U.S. had more billionaires than all the rest of the world's nations taken together. The analysis found six billionaires in West Germany, five in Canada and The Netherlands, four in Japan, three in England, four in Italy, one in France. In all of Latin America it found only one noncriminal centimillionaire. He was a Brazilian. And it found no billionaires in thirteen European countries.

An analysis of the October 1987 *Fortune* report on the world's richest individual billionaires shows these nonruling private individuals as the richest persons in the fifteen countries of the world that then had billionaires:

1. United States — Sam Walton (discount stores), $8.7 billion
2. Canada — Kenneth Thomson (newspapers, department stores, real estate), $5.5 billion
3. England — Gerald Grosvenor, the Sixth Duke of Westminster (inherited lands), $4 billion
4. The Netherlands — Godfried Brenninkmeyer (clothing store chains, etc.), $3.4 billion
5. West Germany — Friedrich Karl Flick (steel, autos, insurance), $2.8 billion
6. Japan — Yoshiaki Tsutsumi (railway inheritance), $2.5 billion
7. Hong Kong — Li Ka-Shing (trading conglomerate), $2.5 billion
8. Indonesia — Liem Sioe Liong (Chinese immigrant banker), $2 billion
9. Saudi Arabia — Suliman Saleh Olayan (oil, banking, real estate), $2 billion
10. Italy — Raul Gardini (sugar, chemicals, food), $1.9 billion
11. France — Liliane Bettencourt (beauty products), $1.5 billion

12. Egypt — Osman Ahmed Osman (builder), $1.5 billion
13. Taiwan — Y. C. Wang (plastics), $1.5 billion
14. Brazil — Sebastiao Ferraz de Camargo Penteado (construction, mining, ranching), $1.2 billion
15. Singapore — Lee Seng Wee (banking, rubber, pineapple), $1 billion

There are occasional major collapses of individual fortunes, but as Mr. Bronfman said, big money customarily grows and grows. That is true especially if it is inherited and hence typically put by astute estate managers into diversified portfolios and land. The most exposed are new rich whose money is largely tied up in a single company, or entrepreneurs caught in a badly collapsing industry, or people of great wealth who seem to enjoy grand-scale gambling such as the Hunt brothers of Texas. (We'll get to them later.) Clint Murchison, Jr., of Texas, once enormously rich, was eventually besieged by creditors. His troubles were due to gambling too much on highly speculative ventures, family quarrels over money, and his own near incapacitation while facing his troubles by an affliction in the brain affecting body movement.[11]

Of the 400 people in the 1982 *Forbes* list, only five were dropped from the 1983 listing because of "serious financial setback." All five were reported still "enviably rich."

The du Ponts, long prominent in U.S. enterprises starting with the manufacture of gunpowder, offer interesting cases in point. Together they are certainly America's wealthiest "family," with net assets above $10 billion. No one in the family holds any significant position in the DuPont company. None of them has been a flaming entrepreneurial success elsewhere. Yet in 1982 there were twenty-nine du Ponts on the *Forbes* 400 list. By 1985 the number of du Ponts on the list had grown to thirty-three. Of the thirty-three, nineteen were women; and of the thirty-three only nine had du Pont as a last name. When they have New Year's Day reunions, they have frequently worn nametags. Each family is said to be furnished periodically with a printed update showing who is who in the clan, who has divorced whom, and so forth.

One of the new du Pont entries to the *Forbes* richest 400 list was of particular interest. That was Lammot du Pont Copeland, Jr., or "Motsey," who years earlier sought to become a major entrepreneur on his own with numerous ventures. He claimed he fell under the influence of some unscrupulous associates. At any rate, in 1970 he filed the largest personal bankruptcy case in history, listing liabilities of $59 million. There were about a hundred creditors. After a few years, a settlement approved by a federal referee provided that he pay remaining creditors about twenty cents on the dollar over a ten-year period. He meanwhile had assets substantially protected in a number of inviolate trusts and continued to live, at least until the final settlement, in a stately mansion outside Wilmington.[12] By 1985, presumably helped by new inheritance, his net worth was so high that he was on the *Forbes* list of the 400 richest Americans, with a net worth at $150 million.

None of this citing of curious ways that some modern great fortunes are built is meant to denigrate the importance of the entrepreneurial spirit in maintaining national economic well-being. It is indeed crucial and badly needed.

But we should not forget that the merchant and the farmer also are entrepreneurs often with their necks stuck way out.

And when they try to face off creditors they don't have multiple corporations, trusts, and a battery of lawyers to protect them from real destitution.

Several business acquaintances pointed out to me that for every spectacular success in venture capitalism there are a number of people who fail or falter. Hence, they feel, even the sky should be no limit to dollar-measured success for the entrepreneur willing to take risks. Some were offended that I even raised the question "How much is too much?" Is that valid? Or is there now some point or level in the accumulation of enormous wealth by families where society reasonably should inquire whether personal fortunes have gotten beyond proper limit and that some top portion of the wealth should be put more clearly to social purpose?

For clues to an answer we will now inspect the life circumstances and thinking about wealth of the ultra rich by visiting some whose fortunes are so vast that, for many, they are hard to comprehend.

CHAPTER 3

ON ENCOUNTERING

RICH PEOPLE

"From now on I am going to be real quiet."

— Florida centimillionaire, explaining why he could not risk an interview

My accumulation of impressions about very rich people did not begin with research for this book. As a writer and public speaker I inevitably had, over the years, some interesting glimpses of them.

In 1960, for example, a national magazine asked me to do a report on the new rich of that period. So I did a quick visit to five states and dropped in on about twenty people, all but one at their offices, to ask them how they made their money. That was about it. Being very rich in those days could mean $10 million. There were a few turndowns, but in general there was not the wariness and low-profile compulsion that is widespread today, especially at the new high levels of wealth. Very few of the twenty I visited then were worth even $50 million, which was an awful lot of money in those days. Two of the encounters remain particularly vivid in my mind.

William Zeckendorf was a legendary New York builder of the period. A tall, portly, amiable man, he saw me at his "home" on the Greenwich, Connecticut, waterfront. He was living in a four-room converted stable while preparing to build a suitable house on the beach. His land included the estate where the daughter of the fabled investor Hetty Green had built one of the more monumental mansions in all of Connecticut. It had more than forty rooms.

Mr. Zeckendorf seemed pleased to explain how he had expanded the thirty-five-acre estate into one twice as large, seventy acres, without buying a single additional acre. With dredges and other great machines he had filled in thirty-five acres of his inlet. As my eyes roamed his enlarged landscape I couldn't see the original grand Green mansion and inquired about it. He pointed back to a hilltop and said: "It was up there. I used it for fill."

Also memorable was my visit with Mr. and Mrs. John D. MacArthur who were well on their way to becoming among America's first billionaires. When I saw them they were just unknown centimillionaires (i.e., anyone worth more than $100 million). They built their fortune selling insurance, sometimes door to door, on the installment plan.

Their national headquarters was far from the financial district of Chicago, out in a drab section of northwestern Chicago. The entrance seemed to have been that of a small town bank of 1920 vintage. Inside you could easily see where walls had been broken through into surrounding buildings. Thousands of people were at work. I finally found the MacArthurs on a third floor. Mrs. MacArthur, a trim, taciturn lady, was secretary to the corporation and had a cubbyhole office outside Mr. MacArthur's small office.

He was a genial, rumpled, blunt-speaking man who, after greeting me, put his feet back on a plain old desk. I was directed to a plain maple chair. "Bricks and mortar don't sell insurance. People do," he said, waving to the dilapidated furnishings. The view from his window was of a gasoline station and Little Joe's Restaurant.

After we had talked awhile he called in his wife, explaining, "She sees that things get done." Mrs. MacArthur complained she was bone-weary from a trip to Florida to close a deal for a vast real estate development there and had not had time to shop for supper. She guessed it would have to be hamburger loaf.

Another centimillionaire I encountered much later, around 1975, was Joseph Hirshhorn, who lived some miles from us in Connecticut. Mr. Hirshhorn was the uranium king, worth hundreds of millions of dollars, who had taken to being a grand-scale art collector. Buying high-cost or first-class art is a favorite way for very rich people to demonstrate they are also people of culture and deserve grade-A social attention. Mr. Hirshhorn had worked out a dandy deal with the federal government. His vast collection could be housed in a museum with his name on it right on the Washington Mall, near the monuments to other great Americans such as Washington, Lincoln, and Jefferson.

My wife, Virginia, is an artist and he asked us to lunch mainly to show her his collection before it was shipped off to Washington. There were acres of large sculptures out on the great lawn surrounding his house in Greenwich. A helicopter hovered overhead lifting the more massive pieces up to take them to railroad flatcars destined for Washington.

Mr. Hirshhorn, a roly-poly man, took us on a tour of sculptures. Midway through our tour, his wife (a former member of his staff) called to say that lunch was ready.

He hollered: "We'll be there in five minutes."

She hollered back, "No, come now or the cook will be upset." The centimillionaire, cowed by his cook, aborted our most interesting tour.

So much for prelude. I think I have managed to indicate that my early encounters with the extremely rich had left me more intrigued than awed.

Only in the last few years did I start seeing the very rich

as anything but curiosities. The great surge in their numbers and the growing immensity of their holdings within the past decade, however, brought them increasingly to my attention. They seemed to represent a noteworthy change in national life that deserved watching. And finally, I decided they were worth a full-scale exploration. As I thought about this phenomenon, a lot of questions came to mind.

What was all this hard-to-comprehend personal wealth saying about the drift of our society and our economy?

Was this concentration of a significant share of the national wealth in the hands of a few thousand people creating distortions in the ability of the rest of our 270 million citizens to afford the good life?

Was it locking up billions in nonproductive or low-productive investments poorly suited to generate ongoing expansion of economic activity?

Was it — or was it not — creating significant new wealth that the possessors were using, abusively, to get their way?

Was the growing gap between the immense fortunes and the conceivable wants of the families involved so great that some kind of economic craziness was setting in?

Had conspicuous display by grand-scale spending lost much of its appeal as a source of gratification because of the new conditions and hazards of modern life — and the almost hopeless challenge of spending so much money?

Had the increase in marital instability undermined the feasibility of trying to perpetuate family dynasties?

Do people of great wealth at least pay their fair share of taxes?

And what on earth were these enormously rich people doing with all their money?

I assembled stacks of research and contacted numerous authorities. The subject was interesting and provocative. At the same time I knew that at some point I would have to go into action to get to know these people better. What was myth and what was real? How did they fit into our changing society? What did they think about themselves, their money, and their roles? How were they coping with their wealth?

Thus it was that I set forth to try to check out the data

against real-life people in various regions of the nation by direct encounter.

Although vast wealth, to my mind, starts at around $30 million I decided to try to confine my visits to real heavyweights, and to ask to visit with them in their home settings. I wrote only to people who had been cited in business publications as being centimillionaires or billionaires (or whom I knew were this wealthy on good authority). In two cases I knew they might not yet be centimillionaires themselves but were youngish members of an immediate family that had many hundreds of millions of dollars.

My hope was to see about thirty people. So I started writing letters, eventually about a hundred. The people were chosen primarily to provide a diversity of regions, a sampling of the main ways that people become immensely rich today, a difference by sex. Within that framework, a few were approached because something about them particularly interested me. I heard they were doing something innovative or socially useful with much of their money. Thus the selection I approached was skewed at least a little toward people who were doing something socially constructive. (I submit that as proof that my approach was curious, not hostile.)

But I knew very little about most of the people I first approached except that they fitted into the above framework.

I assumed I would encounter considerable aloofness and wariness, and I did as I prepared to send off letters. Usually just getting a prospect's phone number or home address took quite a bit of digging. The major part of this sleuthing was performed by my remarkable associate Denise Lynch. She made several hundred long-distance calls. The chief protective aide of San Francisco's Gordon Getty (of the Getty billions) seemed startled that she had even gotten as far as him, the aide. I had hard going in Dallas until I spent $40 for a very slim volume, *The Dallas Social Directory*. Even that did not include some of the town's major centimillionaires. In New York City one female prospect could only be reached through a long-time male business associate. Ms. Lynch reached a few by playing games with telephone operators to get them unwittingly to divulge unlisted numbers or addresses.

Many were wary because of fear of robbery or kidnapping, and for good reason in many cases. One of the du Ponts I approached, Willis Harrington du Pont, had been tied up along with his wife by robbers at their Florida home. He was apologetic, but probably wouldn't have seen me anyway. People who are known primarily for their inherited wealth often have some sense of guilt and seek to avoid publicity. Among the approximately one hundred I originally approached, slightly more than half had substantial inherited wealth, a percentage that has shown up in other studies of the very rich. However, among the finalists I actually saw, slightly more than half turned out to be self-made.

As for kidnapping, Allen Paulson, airplane maker of Savannah, agreed to see me even though his son had fought off and killed a kidnapper.

David Packard, the California billionaire of Hewlett-Packard, invited me to see him but by the time I arrived (after a 250-mile trip) he had changed his mind and begged off. Family security was one of the concerns he stressed.

One morning at seven A.M., just as I was awakening, I got a call from the wealthiest man in Florida at the moment. He was the building materials tycoon in a building-booming state, with net assets reported at more than $300 million. Although eighty years old he had been on the job an hour. He was cordial and said he would enjoy talking with me but he had a real problem. Not only did he have children but grandchildren and great-grandchildren. After his name appeared on the *Forbes* 400 list that fact got into the Florida papers and was broadcast over the airwaves and his life had been made miserable.

"I couldn't believe it — and don't want to start it up again. I got hundreds of letters and phone calls from people wanting money. And a lot of people started driving slowly past our house."

He said the Miami area seemed to be attracting most of

the "bums of the world" and he was scared of kidnapping and burglary. From now on he was going to be "real quiet." Later while in Florida I drove at normal speed past his pleasant house in the region north of Miami. Within a mile there were hundreds of houses that were more grandiose.

For some, I am sure, a reason for wishing to avoid public notice was concern about attracting the interest of state and federal tax collectors.

About a third of the people I approached either declined or were evasive. Another third seemed agreeable but we had difficulties setting a date. Super-rich people are mostly super-active travelers and many have jam-packed schedules. Dates were postponed and postponed again. In general I tried to catch them when I was in their region of the country. One reason my group of interviewees ended up a little heavy with Texans is that I made one trip specifically to see Texans, then two months later while on a trip to Arizona I caught two late acceptors in Texas whom I had particularly wanted to see. Altogether I went off on fourteen trips and traveled about 21,000 miles.

Thirty people are not enough to be labeled as a "sample" of the extremely rich, but at least they constitute an interesting slice. In Thorstein Veblen's day at the turn of the century, any slice would have contained a number of "idle rich." Idleness then was a way of conspicuously displaying one's affluence. My impression is that idleness no longer constitutes an attribute of persons of great wealth, except among some older females. Today's big rich mostly want to be doing *something,* if it is only buying ball clubs, running a few horse-breeding ranches, owning and driving professional racing cars, or being prime movers for charity balls. Heiresses often seem to want to prove they can build their own career and have some money they can call their "own." In any case, truly idle people did not turn up in my visits.

Nearly all the people I visited have been on the *Forbes* 400 list of richest Americans at some point and a large majority still are. In a number of cases I had in hand published estimates of wealth that were higher than those of the

Forbes list. In the chapters that follow the figures I cite are approximately the estimates set by *Forbes* unless I indicate otherwise. By 1987 the cutoff point for getting on the *Forbes* list had risen by $132 million in five years; a few of the people you encounter here are no longer on the list simply because of this radical rise in the cut-off point.

It is even possible that one or two, since I saw them, have dropped below being centimillionaires because of temporary hard times in their industry or area after I saw them. On the other hand *Forbes* has jumped the assets of a dozen of the people I saw by more than $100 million — and two by more than a billion dollars. The average of the net worth of the people I visited turned out to be quite close to the *Forbes* average at the time.

Fortunately, almost every person I visited offered some particular insight into one or more of the larger questions on my mind about the ultra rich — the questions that I listed earlier in this chapter. One problem in terms of organizing a report on my visits was that many of the people in fact offered insights on two or more of the questions I have cited on the role of the ultra rich in today's society.

Nonetheless I have tried to keep each person's story intact. Only in two cases — involving Leslie Wexner and Ewing Kauffman — did I return to them in a major way. And the reader is put on notice that I will do so.

Hence readers will note some casualness about how I take up my people — primarily by how they think about money or how they use it — and some arbitrariness about where I take up each person's story. Some might have fitted in two or more chapters. I hope readers will hang loose and just take the people as they come, and watch for answers to the larger questions. So let's get to the visits.

HOW THEY VIEW

—AND COPE WITH—

THEIR WEALTH

A

Ways of Viewing Wealth

CHAPTER 4

WEALTH
AS AN EXTENSION
OF SELF

"I just love this goddamned country and
it's been awful good to me."

— JACK R. SIMPLOT, Boise, Idaho

The main impression I got
from several people I visited was that they were individuals
of notably strong egos and great intensity who saw their
business empires as a part of themselves. We will visit here
with three individuals who were particularly conspicuous in
this regard.

As readers will see, they are also noteworthy in a number of respects directly related to the questions raised in the
previous chapter:

- Only one of the three indicated much interest in social responsibility (and one declared himself flat-out self-centered).
- Only one of the three could conceivably fit into the public image of an elitist business giant.
- Two had been charged with abusing their financial power.
- And in two of the three cases, their life-styles were preposterously unrelated to their great wealth.

The Paul Bunyan
of the Northwest

When a limousine with the license plate "MR. SPUD" comes down the road in Idaho, just about anyone in the state knows the occupant is Jack Simplot. In using that license plate he is not bragging, just making a statement of fact. He is the potato king of North America, and a lot more.

His very private family empire usually does at least a billion dollars' worth of business a year. When I talked with him, he was rated as the richest man in the entire northwestern United States. Later the drop in farm commodity prices for a while caused some to downgrade his wealth, but by 1987 *Fortune,* at least, was listing him as a billionaire.

My interest in him was first touched off by a report that he had built his immense fortune by developing a patent for freezing french fries. The national surge in demand for french fried potatoes at fast food restaurants had done the rest. It sounded like a nicely ironic story. He did indeed figure out how to freeze french fries. But that was only a particularly decisive development in the innovative career of a modern Paul Bunyan who adores his mountains and who can be very rough when he wants to get his way.

Boise, the state capital, lies in a valley. From the airport on higher ground on one side of the valley you can see clear across the city to an American flag many miles away, flying on a small peak in the mountain foothills. It's Jack Simplot's flag, and quite a flag.

As you search for it by car going up Bogus Basin Road, you see a number of brownish peaks. Then suddenly at a turn the whole horizon is filled with a neatly mowed green peak. A large two-story red-roofed chalet sits atop the peak. Beside the house is a flagpole at least fifteen stories high and a flag fifty feet by thirty feet is waving from it. For years it has been floodlit at night. Of the flag Mr. Simplot said:

"Oh, hell. It's unique, anyway, and I like it."

He is still not fully satisfied with the shape of his peak. "I'll have that thing just perfect when I get through. It's tough to get big machinery up on that steep hill."

The flag got mixed reviews from some neighbors after it was installed in 1980. One said that at times it was really noisy. "It sounds like a giant whip cracking and popping and there is also the clanging and banging from the lines hitting the pole." Others complained that the floodlights cast a weird glow on their own houses.[1]

Mr. Simplot is a powerfully built man even in his late seventies, with a strong, ringing voice. One observer said it had the cutting power of a laser beam. He still loves to ride his Tennessee walking horses and to ski the Idaho mountains although it has cost him numerous broken bones. The famous radio commentator of a few decades ago, Lowell Thomas, often skied with him and in a broadcast once said: "As he goes banging down the Sawtooth Mountains on skis you can hear him singing and laughing half a mile away."

To clear riding trails Mr. Simplot swung a powerful ax and used to start his day, frequently, by attacking rocks on his trails. "A man's gotta do a little pickin' every morning to keep himself hard and tough."[2]

Of Lowell Thomas he recalled: "I went through China with him and Russia with him and he wanted to take me to the Poles and Mount Everest but I was always too damn busy."

He has indeed been a busy man.

Although his dad had a pretty good farm in Burling, Idaho, young Simplot quit school before he had finished the eighth grade. He just didn't like it.

"I left home and I never went back and I beat it all the

way up. Nobody ever put a penny with me — not one red cent."

In the first year of his career he worked as a potato sorter and rock blaster. With his savings he went into business at the age of fifteen. He rented forty acres of potato land from his father and bought a bunch of hogs. His career for the next forty years was pretty much devoted to trying to squeeze more money out of a bushel of potatoes.[3]

He began feeding his pigs a mash made of discarded or cull potatoes plus barley. In his mountain riding he noted herds of wild horses and began roping them to get some meat in the mash.

As his operations grew, he got into processing his potatoes. Potatoes are about 80 percent water. He figured out a way to dehydrate potatoes without ruining the taste. World War II had just broken out and there was a great demand for his dried potatoes for C ration fare. Luck again.

His first processing plant, at Caldwell, which grew to be a mile long, began throwing off rivers of muck, a waste containing not only culls but peelings, eyes, sprouts, and potato juice. To get rid of this slop, he went into the ranching business. Gradually he increased the amount of muck his cattle were fed until it got to be 65 percent of their feed. This gave him a big edge — 25 percent — over other ranchers in the cost of raising a pound of beef.

He got mad because the cost of fertilizer was soaring and it was in short supply during the war. He scouted around, and heard there was some phosphate rock lying right on an Indian reservation north of Pocatello. He went up with a scraper and later commented: "Damned if I didn't latch onto the biggest phosphate deposit west of Florida."[4]

The demand for french fries rose as more people began eating away from home; the problem was keeping them fresh. If you tried to freeze them they would ooze water when defrosted. Simplot set up a little lab at his Caldwell plant to work on the problem. After a couple of years they were getting good results from a process that involved scalding the potatoes to adjust their texture before freezing them. French fries became a major national food. It was not

Mr. Simplot's fault that tasty french fries tend to be high in fat and salt, which are seen by many nutritionists as primary troublemakers in the diet of Americans.

During the 1950s the McDonald's fast food chain was exploding. Mr. Simplot, a major supplier, became a member of the board of directors. And the explosion in demand for his product has continued. Annual per capita french fry consumption has soared from two pounds in 1960 to fourteen pounds in 1984, according to the Center for Science in the Public Interest.

Was it true he had a patent on freezing french fries?

"Yes, I did. To start with I filed a patent. But back in those days I was struggling and I never tried to protect it. I should have. We were first on the market with frozen french fries."

In the fifties and sixties he was spreading out into Oregon, the Dakotas, and Maine to gain access to potatoes for his processing plants. He got into processing all sorts of vegetables. And he added ranches in other western states. But primarily he was the world's foremost potato processor.

His freewheeling ways plus use of muscle got him into a mess of trouble during the mid-seventies.

He had a compelling interest in keeping low the price he had to pay for the potatoes he bought for processing. Also he was a major speculator in potatoes. And in May 1976 he and an associate created a scandal on the New York Mercantile Exchange by failing to deliver fifty million pounds of Maine potatoes worth about $4 million.[5]

That year the price of potatoes had been particularly volatile because of long-range weather forecasts. Prices on contracts for May 1976 potatoes had swung between $6 and $19. The people like Simplot holding "short" positions were betting the price of potatoes would go down before delivery date; the "long" position people were betting prices would go up from the price at which they had bought their contracts. Simplot contended that the "long" people, sure they had him in a bind, refused to sell him potatoes. Further, he charged they offered to top any offers Maine farmers received from Simplot. And he charged they maneuvered to tie up freight cars. Mr. Simplot was deeply annoyed. He

contended the longs wanted cash, not potatoes, and he refused to oblige them, since that would run up the price of
potatoes. So he let a default on delivery occur, and was
charged with attempting to manipulate prices.

The *Wall Street Journal* cited a source in Idaho as stating
that Mr. Simplot, as the deadline approached, sent out one
or more "roller cars" of potatoes to the East. These are car-
loads of unsold potatoes that are sent from market to market
and offered for immediate cash sale. The aim, the report
said, often was to create rumors that cheap potatoes are
available and hence to depress prices.[6] Mr. Simplot, when
asked at the time about "roller cars," responded: "Hell,
there's no law against rolling potatoes. Maybe we did. I don't
know. I run a big potato rig."

The *Journal* quoted an Idaho potato farmer as saying:
"Simplot has always controlled the market and it doesn't
matter if he's right or wrong about prices. He is so big he
can make himself right."

Mr. Simplot professed to take a relaxed view about the
uproar over default. "I'm not bragging but I think you might
say an old country boy got the best of the professionals. . . .
I'm happy with my position. I sleep like a baby at night. . . .
They thought I didn't have enough potatoes to wad a shot-
gun. I know potatoes, son, and I know how many potatoes
there are in Maine, just about down to the last sack."[7]

The commodities industry took a dimmer view of Mr.
Simplot's default. It was apparently the largest default in potato trading in more than a century.[8] Seven years later, in
1983, the *Journal* stated that the potato-futures market
never fully recovered "and the default tarnished the reputation of the New York Mercantile Exchange for years." It
reported that a federal court jury in New York awarded a
Detroit businessman $460,000 damages in finding that Sim-
plot and his associate had conspired to manipulate the price
of potatoes in 1976 and that the award would be tripled under federal antitrust law. And the Detroit man was just one
of more than a dozen traders who had filed suit.[9] Earlier, on
March 8, 1978, the *Journal* had reported that the Commodity
Futures Trading Commission had fined Mr. Simplot $50,000

and suspended him from trading on any futures exchange for six years.

Meanwhile, in 1977, Mr. Simplot had had to appear in a U.S. district court to cope with charges of income tax violations.[10]

It was in 1980, after the bothersome seventies, that Mr. Simplot built his magnificent flagpole. A spokesman for his company, in responding to compliments about the flag, said: "Jack cherishes and deeply believes in America, and it doesn't surprise me that a guy who has the wherewithal and the right property would order up the biggest flag he can to show his patriotism."[11]

I tried to get an idea from Mr. Simplot of the dimensions of his current operations. Was he still the world's number one processor of dried and frozen potatoes?

"Yeah, yeah. I think that is still true."

French fries? "Sure. We sell most of them."

Cattle ranches? "Yeah, we got fifteen, more than fifteen ranches. We run somewhere in the neighborhood of 13,000 mother cows and we run about 125,000 head in our feedlots. It takes about 125,000 head of cattle to eat my potato peels."

Fertilizer? "We're by far, I imagine, the biggest in America west of the Mississippi. The plant I got in Pocatello is over a mile long."

Frozen fruits and vegetables? "We got twenty-three processing plants. Fruits and vegetables. Berries, strawberries. We're branching out into Europe and Asia."

Lately he has moved into areas with no connection to food processing. Gold and silver mines. And he had, of all things, bought a microchip company. Why? "To make money. . . . It bothers me that I don't know more about it, but we have people that do."

In addition to his house on the peak he has one on a lake, "then I got a hunting club and I got a fishing club and I've got a couple other houses. All in Idaho." I mentioned the many fine-looking horses grazing around the bottom of his peak. "My gal [the second Mrs. Simplot] trains horses and rides. She works at it eight hours a day."

His four grown children, three sons and a daughter, were

all born to his first wife, whom he divorced in the sixties. His three sons and his son-in-law are all high officials of his "rig," a conglomerate that constitutes one of the nation's largest private enterprises. He explained:

"They're vice-presidents and they are active. One of them [the son-in-law] kinda looks after the food business, one looks after the fertilizer division, and one looks after the land and livestock division. And my young son, he's executive vice-president of the company."

The stock is divided up among family members. But for years he held on to all voting rights. Did he still?

"Well, I did have it all but then I had to give it away, you know." (I assume taxes were a factor.) "And with my grandkids [sixteen of them] we own it all, all the stock in the company."

Had he ever thought of going public? He answered that in an interview quite a few years ago.[12]

"It's easier to get a loan when you are a corporation than when you are a loner. I just never liked to work for the other guy. What I own, I built. It's mine . . . I make the decisions and believe me, I enjoy making 'em."

Since his current assets were reported in the hundreds of millions of dollars, I asked him if, given his current lifestyle, he could live on a million dollars a year.

"Oh, Christ! I don't spend any million dollars a year. No. How would you spend a million dollars a year? Christ! No way."

I reminded him that back in 1968 — before all the hassle with potato futures and taxes — *Fortune* magazine had put his net worth at close to $200 million and that he was clearly the richest industrialist in his state. In view of his great enjoyment of hunting, fishing, riding, and travel, and the fact that he was approaching sixty then, why hadn't he cashed in, put his money in bonds and other sound securities? He would still be the richest man in Idaho. So why had he kept charging?

"The sport's all in the chase, yeah, the sport's all in the chase. What the hell. I don't want to quit. I almost did, several times, sell out but I just couldn't and I didn't. And that's the only smart thing I've done — hang on. . . . I run my own business and we're doing all right."

Since he had apparently already shifted legal title of a great deal of his wealth to children and grandchildren it was not clear whether he had even a hundred million that he could dispose of freely to such things as philanthropy. His comments on this topic tended to be perfunctory, without the usual exclamations. He mentioned a couple of little colleges in the state he was helping, and some hospitals. And he had built an entertainment center.

Any foundations?

"Yeah, I got a foundation but they've cut those to where they're not much good anymore either." (If he still had a foundation it is not in the latest *Directory of Foundations,* which includes all having assets of $1 million.)

What did he mean, not much good?

"Well you got to get rid of 6 percent of your assets every year, [so] it only lasts fifteen years at best."

Here his facts were a little off. A certain percent does have to be spent. This law was enacted to reduce the exploitation of foundations by the rich as havens for their money. But meanwhile the assets, if prudently invested, are earning at least six percent. Many major foundations created a half century ago are still going strong.

Possibly Mr. Simplot had simply concluded that a foundation was not something that would add a glow to his family name well into the future. At any rate he said: "Yeah, there's no way that you're going to take it with you or keep it for perpetuity after you're gone. But I've done a pretty good job with my estate, I think, and I am happy with it. My kids, my grandkids ought to be awful happy with it."

Jeno's Race for Riches and Recognition

Jeno Paulucci is noteworthy in several ways of interest to us. He professes to feel uncomfortable with rich people and has lived for decades by choice in a lower-middle-class neighborhood of a quite ordinary small Florida town. Yet much of his recent fortune-building has been in the sale of homes to aspiring rich people in an immense ultra posh, snobbish, fenced-in development of enormous proportions a few miles away. He has always run a one-man show and he has always been in an enormous hurry, and is to some extent guilt driven.

My first description of Paulucci came to me during a chat with a Washington columnist who was ticking off some of the super-rich he had encountered in the nation's capital. He referred to Paulucci as a stubby, brash man seeking respectability by having his picture taken with U.S. presidents. It is true Mr. Paulucci has been pictured with five — Johnson, Nixon, Ford, Carter, and Reagan — some in his role as chairman of the National Italian-American Foundation. And he has been well acquainted with two presidential nominees: Hubert Humphrey and Walter Mondale of Minnesota.

Of the thirty super-rich people I visited, he has the most truly rags-to-riches story. He began life in a $5-a-month miners' flat in the frigid iron range country of northern Minnesota, son of two Italian immigrants. With a red cart he scrounged for lumps of coal that fell off coal cars to heat the family stove. Once, and he still hates the thought of it, he had to stand in a slow-moving line to get family food at a relief center. For some reason, presumably available calories, his mother gave him Fernet Branca, a bitter Italian aperitif, with his breakfast. A few years ago he said: "My teacher always wondered why the little Dago kid came to school half smashed."

When I visited him in 1985, *Forbes* put his net worth at $350 million. By 1987 it had increased its estimate to $500 million. He himself mentioned in a 1985 memo he gave me that his family was worth more than half a billion.

His fortune was built largely by being in the right place to tie into two trendy situations. First there was the growing interest in convenience foods with an ethnic flavor. (He helped make pizza a national dish.) Second, he launched his development on 6,000 acres of prime land in what has become probably the fastest-growing metropolitan area in America, Orlando, Florida. In 1984 a couple of Texas cities were ahead of Orlando, but they have since been hit by a slowed economy.

Jeno Paulucci spent some time at a junior college in Hibbing, Minnesota, but he was already on the road selling vegetables on commission. He became intrigued by the mung bean sprout grown in tanks by Orientals. And by twenty-two, with a $2,500 loan, he and a friend were into the Chinese food business. He has said he didn't even like Chinese food. But even from northern Minnesota his venture grew, mainly because of his manic drive.

He sought to go national with his product Chun King, a hopped-up chow mein, but couldn't find an advertising agency that satisfied him. Finally he took a wild chance on an adman who was also a comedian producing zany commercials, Stan Freberg. One of history's best-known TV ads — it has become an advertising classic — made the claim that nine out of ten doctors recommend Chun King. A doubter protests the claim as ridiculous. The camera then pans down the row of ten white-robed doctors. Nine clearly are Chinese. Wherever used, sales zoomed.

Soon Paulucci was setting up companies to produce a product closer to his interest, frozen pizza, along with pizza snacks. Again sales zoomed. He had bought into a highly efficient way to make and cut pizza crusts and recycle trimmings. (In this he joined battle with giant Pillsbury over the technology.)

Meanwhile as his food companies grew, trucking costs for national distribution from his plants in far northern Duluth were hurting his enterprise. He was by now said to be Duluth's biggest employer, with 1,500 employees. Sorrowfully he moved his food operations to Ohio — and he has been trying to make it up to Duluth ever since.

When I saw him he was phasing out of the food business, except for foreign operations, and was far advanced in creating his billion-dollar real estate development outside Orlando.

His Florida headquarters were in a small old brick building on the main street of Sanford, Florida, between Orlando and Daytona Beach. It was a war surplus building he had bought for $25,000 and fixed up. His offices occupying the second floor were indeed fixed up, looking like something out of *Architectural Digest.* It was 9 A.M. on a Saturday. His secretaries still had not shown up. He had been there two and a half hours and was in shirtsleeves fixing up the flowers in the reception area when I arrived. No one else was around. His kidney-shaped desk filled much of his nearby office.

Mostly his world headquarters of the moment shifts back and forth between Sanford and Duluth, he explained, depending on where his wife is. He had been quite a hellion with women in his early days, was engaged seven times, but since he won Lois Trepanier, a lovely, vivacious woman about his height from the right side of the tracks of Duluth, he has given every evidence of being involved in a lifelong love affair.

How did he happen to get interested in Florida when his operations initially had all been in Duluth? He explained that it related to his need for celery for his Chinese foods. Celery in Florida was packed in various-sized crates. He noticed that employees were stripping off a lot of beautiful branches of celery and throwing them away for animal food so that the celery stalks would fit the crates.

When he got back to Duluth he bought a big flatbed truck, equipped it with celery chopping and washing machines, and put a canvas frame around the truck. He had his sister and brother-in-law drive it down to Florida. Jeno flew in and took the truck out to the main celery producer in Sanford and proposed a deal: He would give the grower $15 a ton for the celery he was throwing away. A deal was struck and Jeno began getting celery for two cents a pound instead of the ten cents a pound his competitors were paying.

Jeno recalled that in the early days of Chun King he built his office area himself for $25 using reject plywood boards.

"I would always keep my hat on so that when anybody came in I'd say, 'Oh, I was just leaving.' [laugh] So that way

I wouldn't have to have a long meeting because I don't like long meetings." (He hastened to add he was not about to rush me out.) That very morning at 6 A.M. when he was making coffee for Lois, which he does every morning, he had explained to her, "I'm sorry, honey, but I've got to rush." She said, "Why?" He said, "I'm late." She said "Late? Do you have to punch a time clock?" He said, "No, I'm just late in my mind."

Like him, his mind is always whizzing ahead. "I hope I die running with a briefcase in my hand. One of my pet phobias is a red light, when nobody is using the green. Sometimes early in the morning, like in Duluth, if nobody is using the green, I'll go. I'll count the seconds sometimes. Time is so precious."

When the first of their three children, Mick, was conceived three decades ago, Lois came to his office beaming with the good news she had gotten from the doctor. It was about 11:30 A.M. She said, "Don't you think this calls for lunch?" He recalled he said, "'Honey what kind of a sandwich would you like?' And that's how we celebrated. It's just my nature that I want to keep working."

He travels about 6,000 miles a week, mostly on his Falcon 20 (worth about $6 million), though he has four other planes, three that land on water mainly used to hop up to their place in Canada, where both he and Lois like to fish.

Here's an example of our man-in-a-hurry when he travels. "The other day I left here at six-thirty in the morning, went into Washington and had a meeting with the Bureau of Indian Affairs (about a volunteer project to help Oglala Indians sell moccasins), then I went to our advertising office. Had a meeting there. Ten o'clock I had a meeting with our attorneys about the litigation we have against Pillsbury [over pizza-making machinery — some months later Pillsbury bought out his Jeno frozen pizza business]. Then I went to Ohio and visited our two pizza plants there. Left to have a meeting with the governor [of Minnesota] at his house in St. Paul. And I landed in Duluth about ten o'clock. I try to cram in as much as I can into each trip."

Right that day, he said, one of his vexing problems was

that Lois wanted the two of them to join their daughter Gina and a friend on a vacation at St. Martin down in the Caribbean.

"I look at the folder. It said snorkling, which I don't do; swimming, which I don't care about; sunbathing — a little bit is enough; dining, okay I have to eat at night; dancing, I don't mind if it's a little bit. So my dilemma is trying to convince Lois to let Gina and her friend go by themselves and we go instead to Genoa." In Genoa he could attend a meeting of the National Italian-American Foundation (which he headed). And then he and Lois could take a cruise ship along the Riviera "a little bit." The real advantage in his mind, I gathered, of cruising on the Riviera over sitting on St. Martin was that worldwide telephone service would be better from the boat.

Since he had long been in the food business, what about his own eating habits? What, for example, did he have for breakfast?

"I don't have any breakfast or lunch. I have tea all day [there was a cup of it beside him] and then I eat dinner and whatever my wife ends up with I eat. Steak I like."

What powered his enormous energy? Hardly tea.

"For energy during the day I take one Theragran in the morning and one in the afternoon. That's it." About every other evening he has a glass of Fernet Branca, the bitter alcoholic drink his mother fed him as a boy.

A few days ago Lois talked him into having lunch with some old friends at a local country club. "They were nice people but it was agony sitting there an hour and a half to eat. How long does it take me to eat? One minute."

The conversation turned to his taking his food businesses from Duluth to Ohio, since he had been one of Duluth's biggest employers. "My greatest sadness in my business career was when I had to close the plant in Duluth. My family [of 1,300 employees] there was totally unionized because I've always wanted unions, which dates back to the iron range days when my dad had to work thirteen hours a day and got blacklisted if he talked union. Fifty-three percent of my employees were disadvantaged: either people I had taken out of prison, alcoholics, drug addicts, one eye, one arm, one leg, mentally retarded, whatever. Most of them we succeeded with." He found them extra-conscientious about doing a good job. They did not goof off and, perhaps most important to Mr. Paulucci, they arrived on time. Most, though, could not make the move to Ohio.

The result is that for years Jeno Paulucci has been crusading with some success to help build back Duluth's economic health. He has offered several million dollars' worth of inducements to get new businesses into the city and has fought to get a civic center in Duluth. In 1986 he said, "I've got a debt and I want to repay it."[14]

Jeno Paulucci has also thrown himself into helping Eskimos up in Bethel, Alaska, Indians around Nut Lake in Minnesota, and most recently the Oglala Sioux Indians in Pine Ridge (Wounded Knee), South Dakota. He found they had been taken advantage of and were nearly $2 million in debt with their moccasin factory. He worked with their creditors and congressmen to get their debt reduced, persuaded the Oglalas to get rid of low-selling models. He said: "And I will go selling with them. I'll make calls on Sears, Penney, and the others. Then I'll feel I've accomplished something." He even declined the headdress they sought to give him.

Wouldn't it have satisfied him simply to give them a check?

"No, what are they going to do with it? I've got to show them how to make money."

In short his idea of philanthropy is hands-on-by-Jeno activism. He gave the impression that he is not strong on making simple bequests from his fortune (although he does have a small foundation). In fact he said as much: "I don't give very much money. No. Unless it is because a church needs a building or something to help people survive while they are trying to find a new job. . . . I'm for finding out what is your problem. I've got a convict up in Walla Walla, Washington, that keeps writing me to take him out. So I said give me your whole history. . . . I've told my secretary next time

I'm out west someplace, remind me. I'll run up there and see him eyeball to eyeball, and see whether or not I want to take the chance on him."

Several years ago he wrote, "I'd like to make peace with my entire life, including this 'terrible problem' of being very wealthy." And more recently he added, "Money alone makes an empty life, believe me."[15]

There is another side to Mr. Paulucci's use of money to achieve his goals in public matters. In his own promotional literature he boasts of his "political clout" in arranging for public funds for projects. Some are do-good projects but some plainly do him good in particular.

The *Wall Street Journal* noted that he had managed to get Congress to include in a highway bill $14 million for a highway interchange near his new Heathrow development.[16] And in mid-1987 the *Orlando Sentinel* did a long, critical report charging him with using his political clout — due at least in part to tens of thousands of dollars in political contributions which it listed — in order to prevail in selling Seminole County 2,800 acres of mostly swampland, at a profit of $4 million, in a deal that will also assure him enough sewage service to develop thousands of acres he owns in the area. It charged, "Paulucci wields his political clout with the same brashness he used to build his business empire."[17]

Much of the title to his wealth has already gone to his children. For example, he gave them the frozen pizza company long before it was sold and put son Mick in charge of it. They all have houses or lots in the family's big new development, Heathrow. And he has bought a couple of town houses there for personal use or investment.

Given his net worth of, say, $500 million, could he live comfortably on one of those million a year?

"I could comfortably live — and my wife would adjust herself to, $50,000 a year." Simple, just go back to their honeymoon house at 6 Minneapolis Avenue in Duluth, which they still own. Sell off the other stuff. But his thoughts rushed on and he didn't try to cope with sorting out the business versus private use of his several planes and four pilots, his two housing compounds in Sanford and on Pike Lake near Duluth, his apartments in New York and Washington, the house in Jackson, Ohio, near the food factories, a fishing camp in Canada, a house bought partly for sentimental reasons in Italy that he never goes to, et cetera.

He boasted of the beautiful needlepoint that his wife Lois does. She did one for the entrance of the executive offices in Duluth that reads:

IN CASE OF DEATH

SEND FLOWERS

KEEP WORKING

Mr. Paulucci was naturally too busy to waste time showing me his house and the Heathrow development. But he had made arrangements. Mrs. Paulucci would show me the house. And an executive at Heathrow would show me the development. He called his wife to have her lead me to their house. Within a few minutes she was in the office and was indeed lovely and gracious. They kissed in a way they apparently do every time they have been away from each other for more than an hour.

Mrs. Paulucci in her Oldsmobile led me to a street in an oak grove a few minutes away. No stately houses. Jeno Paulucci had told me that one of the houses right next to his had sold for less than $50,000. Across the street was an ordinary house where the pilots stayed. Their housekeeper lives on the same street. "We're not with the affluent and we like it that way," he said. Mrs. Paulucci had insisted the three children go to the local public school. As for the house she said: "I've always been a firm believer in rearing children in average income neighborhoods."

The house which the Pauluccis built and had been living in for twenty-seven years was a pleasant one-story house, partially cinderblock. There was no evidence whatever of security precautions. She showed me proudly through the house and grounds. It had a large living room. The main thing that made it different from others on the street was that it had a screened-off swimming pool.

Mrs. Paulucci said, "It's hard to get him to swim. But his

chair is over there. See the telephone." We laughed. She held up her hands which were red in spots and said, "I'm into quilting now." The whole place seemed geared to kids. (They have four grandchildren.) By the outdoor barbecue there was a sign: "Jeno and Lois Restaurant." Another sign read: "Required To Hang Guns Here."

Mrs. Paulucci said there was no one in the house after three o'clock. No live-in help.

To the rear of the main house was an ordinary-looking guest house. Their daughter Cindy's family was currently staying there. Mrs. Paulucci went to the door and called Cindy, who as a girl had won prizes in horsemanship. She sauntered down, a handsome young woman in blouse, shorts, and moccasins. All looked as if they had been bought at the local five-and-ten-cent store. She was about to go to pick up her little girl, who had been at a slumber party, and would lead me to the parkway that goes past the Heathrow development.

Mrs. Paulucci explained that arrangements had been made to receive me at the gate and explained: "You have to go through security."

Security indeed!

As Cindy led me to the highway that goes past Heathrow, I reflected on Mr. Paulucci's account of how his family had gotten into real estate development. Mrs. Paulucci had promoted the idea. Three decades ago she and her brother had bought a couple hundred acres of nice rolling (for Florida) land at $500 an acre. Jeno Paulucci recalls: "I thought they were crazy at the time." But the land grew in value as Orlando expanded toward it. When a decade later he sold Chun King for about $60 million, "my wife said why don't you take some of our money and put it in land across the road? Little by little I did what my wife told me. We bought piece by piece like a jigsaw."

A few years ago he began pouring tens of millions into building the "infrastructure" for a development based on "excellence." He cleaned up the lake, built a "championship" golf course, laid out miles of roads, et cetera. And then he began selling his lots. "I don't know anything about building. We just sell land, let them [mainly builders] build the houses" (under tight control). He added: "It's not just a place for millionaires. It is a place for people that want to work as hard as millionaires."

When he put the first eighty lots up for sale at $100,000 per acre, they went within twenty-four hours, and Jeno Paulucci decided he was not charging enough. When I was there it took between $150,000 and $400,000 to buy an acre. The higher prices were mostly for office buildings and so forth.

The entrance to Heathrow exudes grandeur and elegance: a perfect circle reflecting pool with several high-spraying fountains . . . wide entrance and exit roads made with 300,000 hand-laid bricks, with beige bricks creating a center line for traffic. The entrance sign is of polished brass set on Norwegian emerald pearl granite. My host proudly took me into the English-style guardhouse with slate roof with a security gate through which everyone must pass. In the guardhouse he showed me $500,000 worth of high-tech communications equipment. Many posh southern developments have guard gates — partly to connote exclusivity, partly for "security" — but this facility for TV monitoring every house was something else. If a burglary was in progress, the machines would bring up in color graphics a floorplan of the house for guards or police. Company literature compares the security of Heathrow with that of the Pentagon. Every house must be electronically monitored.

My host drove me over much of the nine miles of roads of Heathrow. The houses, mostly English style, were then selling in the $500,000 to $4 million range. As I left, those TV cameras that could aim at every house lingered in my mind. What if a gentleman whose wife was away wanted to call on a lady whose husband was away? Would he be on camera? Probably no, possibly yes.

But it was intriguing that the son of an Italian immigrant then living in a partly cinderblock house on an unguarded, barely middle-class street a few miles away would create such a snooty, mostly English-gentry-style development featuring high security. Presumably he just had a good feel for the Florida market.

Arthur Jones's
Wild Kingdom

Mr. Jones became known as Mr. Exercise Machine. His Nautilus Sports Medical Industries, Inc. sold hundreds of thousands of exercise machines of unique design during the past decade, when Americans were undergoing a surge of interest in physical fitness, and when the building of athletes was becoming more and more a science. The exercise machine, though, was just the centerpiece of a highly personal fiefdom that confused, among others, people from the Internal Revenue Service. In 1983 *Forbes* put his net worth at $125 million; thenceforth it gave up because it has trouble obtaining reliable figures. Mr. Jones ran an extremely private operation.

Getting to see him required more persistence than it did for any other very wealthy person I visited. When I first got through by phone to his secretary in Lake Helen, Florida, she said he was out of town. Would he be back soon? She said: "Mostly Mr. Jones sets his own appointments and he is not likely to know where he may be two days ahead."

She did finally acknowledge that he was that day staying at a specific motor inn in Panama City, Florida.

Mr. Jones was gruff when I got him on the phone, said he had never seen my letter and more or less dismissed me. About fifteen minutes later he called me back and was much more congenial. He had found my letter in a box of correspondence and noted with interest a fact I had carefully mentioned, that the first book I ever wrote was on animal intelligence. I knew he had been a wild animal hunter for circuses and a zookeeper in Louisiana, and understood he still had a considerable interest in wild animals.

If my following account of the discussions we had on the

phone and at his home seems a bit jumpy, it may be because Mr. Jones has a very busy mind and makes quick leaps to topics as they occur to him.

We got to talking about animals on the phone. In the course of this long talk he dropped some words of wisdom about attaining happiness. For example: "A man is as young as the woman he feels." That day in Panama City he was with his twenty-two-year-old wife, Terri, a glorious-looking former model who was there completing training to fly transcontinental jet planes. He was in his mid-sixties and is a pilot. Each of his five wives was under twenty when he married her.

Meanwhile I was trying to pin him down on when I could see him during a trip I planned to make to Florida in a couple of weeks. Finally he gave me his unlisted number in Ocala. If he was around, he would try to see me.

When I arrived in central Florida I called the number he gave me in Ocala, his second headquarters. No answer. So I called his office at Lake Helen. Terri got on the phone. Pleasantly she told me she didn't know where he was but that they were flying over to Ocala that night for the weekend. She suggested I call Ocala the next day.

I did. I called at least fifteen times with no answer. Then in mid-afternoon Mr. Jones's barking voice came on the phone. I reminded him of his promise to see me. He complained that the reason he delayed coming to Ocala was that he felt sick, flu or something. He didn't want me to catch it. I said I would take a chance. The upshot was an appointment at 2 o'clock the next afternoon, a Sunday. He gave me directions. They were complex, with many turns. He didn't know the names of some of the roads but said if I passed an embankment I had gone too far.

En route I reviewed what little I knew about him. He had put up with school a year longer than Jack Simplot. He quit at ninth grade (even though both parents were physicians), ran away from home, rode the rails, joined the navy, and afterward got deeply involved in capturing wild animals. Between hunts he did a TV series called *Wild Cargo*.

Meanwhile he worked for years on an idea for a new type of exercise machine that varied the amount of strength required depending on whether weak or strong muscles were involved at any given point. He studied anatomy books and cadavers. One of his three children of his third marriage, Eva, who became a doctor, recalled: "We always had an arm or something in the freezer."[18]

His solution for varying the weight load on muscles was to use a cam, a rotating device shaped vaguely like a nautilus shell. In addition to his machine he produced videotapes on exercise at a studio reportedly costing more than $50 million, published a couple magazines on exercise, developed a big exercise apparel line, sold a vast number of franchises based on use of the word Nautilus at fitness centers, and ran an astonishing promotional program for educating and entertaining people in charge of exercise programs. And he was still involved with live animals.

Although his organization was farflung, an official had recently explained that basically everything flowed from Mr. Jones. His personal philosophy, he had been quoted as saying, was somewhat to the right of Attila the Hun.

After a few wrong turns I did see an embankment, but it was not exactly a heap of earth. It was an earth and masonry structure about fifteen feet high. And above it I could see the tail of an enormous airplane. The embankment obviously was a blast fence. I backed up to a security gate. Mr. Jones, in shirtsleeves and baggy pants, strode out to meet me. Past the gate I could see planes of various sizes and a very broad runway that stretched out on the horizon. Mr. Jones directed me to follow him in his Buick across the runway to a parking area near a mansion then directed me to get in his car.

Silently he drove directly to an area full of wild animals, stopped, and strode over to a fenced-in pool containing an enormous crocodile.

"This is by far the largest saltwater crocodile in captivity and it's within less than two inches of being the absolute all-time world record. A museum in London has the skull of the one supposed to be the longest, found in 1820. But I have a skull found in New Guinea precisely the same size as the one at the London museum." He proceeded to spend several minutes explaining the formula for projecting the length of a crocodile within half an inch just by skull measurements. This specimen was just one of hundreds of crocodiles his enterprise owned.

I sought to divert him from his crocodiles. "What kind of a plane is that?"

"Which one?"

"The big one."

"That is a Boeing Intercontinental 707-323c." And turning, he said, "This is an adult male rhinoceros. We have a newborn baby eleven weeks old. Rhino milk has got to be the most potent substance on earth, because that baby rhino has gone from sixty pounds to three hundred pounds in eleven weeks." I nodded toward a herd of elephants. "We brought sixty-three of these in by plane on one trip from Africa."

"How long is your runway there?"

"One point four three miles, exactly. It may well be the largest nonmilitary runway in the world, not the longest but the widest." Its width makes it easy to take off or land using varying approaches. The 707 is a convertible, so human seats can be taken out when hauling animals.

"What is the main function of the big jets, in addition to hauling animals?"

"We haul people in them. People for our continuing medical education program."

People flew in from all over America to take part in indoctrination programs on making the most of exercise programs, specifically those using Nautilus machines. From the Orlando airport (about sixty miles away) they were whisked here by plane, to be registered, told what was about to happen, wined and dined, and given a chance to look at the animals for about an hour or so.

Then they were put in the 707 and flown a few hundred miles to Merida, Mexico, among the Mayan ruins of the Yucatan peninsula. The plane is rigged up to be very spacious.

Although Mr. Jones does not drink, there were two bar lounges on the plane. In Merida the guests would get three days of education on exercise along with sightseeing.

He got back to his animals.

"We're not animal dealers in the normal sense. But we're doing various types of research. I hate to even use the word because it connotes cutting up things. The type of research we do does not involve hurting anything. We do growth studies. We're studying some of the medical problems that occur in both animals and humans. Elephants, for example, have got very similar problems with arthritis as those in people. We donated three million dollars about three years ago to the University of Florida's School of Medicine for a study in bone changes of the kind that cause elderly women to have broken hips."

We drove next toward what used to be one of the lesser Vanderbilt mansions. A long portico led to a reception auditorium that can seat 1,000 people. The house, I gathered, was used in part for entertaining.

Mr. Jones led me through the mansion's front door. It was not really a personal abode since it also served various company functions. He waved toward a couple of large plush living rooms, one sunken, then led me to the kitchen, where, I gather, he spends much of his time, using the table as his second office. When seated, I mentioned I was curious to know how he saw himself.

"I couldn't tell you that in ten days." Shortly he got on to religion. "Did it ever occur to you that you were part of a totally insane race of animals that believes in things like miracles, and God, and angels and heaven and hell and virgin birth?" If we professed such beliefs, he explained, we were either fools or frauds.

I remarked that during our phone conversation when he was in Panama City he had made some rather sensuous statements about young women. He had no idea what I was talking about and asked if I wanted some cream with my coffee. I pointed to a luscious picture of a pin-up girl in briefest bikini tacked to a kitchen cabinet and inquired about it.

"That little gal just happens to be my wife!"

I quickly said I had had a nice talk with her on the phone. He went on to say that in a few weeks she would be twenty-three and be old enough to qualify for an airline transport pilot's license. "I've been teaching her to fly for five years." She was a writer for *Nautilus* magazine and was being groomed to be host of a talk show he was developing.

He noted a man was approaching the house. "That's Dan Baldwin, the president of the company and a minority stockholder. I am chairman of the board. He had to go to Ocala to pick up some stuff at a motel and I asked him to pick me up some lunch at Burger King."

President Baldwin seemed an earnest, serious man. While Mr. Jones was taking out the burger, malted, and french fries, they chatted for a while about business matters.

After Mr. Baldwin departed I sought to confirm how many children Mr. Jones had. I had read he had three, all by his third wife. His response: "Who counts?" I mentioned hearing of three.

"Three? I've got at least five kids that I know about."

"Did you really say that you weren't going to give them a nickel when they grew up?"

"That's right. Are you going to give anything to yours?"

"I don't have much to give."

"If you did would you be dumb enough to leave it to your kids?"

Mr. Jones had been quoted as saying that leaving money to people destroys them. And his daughter, the New York doctor, didn't seem to hold it against him; she called him a "gentle giant." When she comes down to visit she usually rides horseback with Terri, her substantially younger stepmother.[19] And Mr. Jones in his car has chased after them to bring them ice cream.

We got to talking about the future of interest in physical fitness. He said that things looked good there but added: "The trend of the world today, Vance, is not good. And if you can't see that you're utterly fucking stupid." That got him into drug traffickers. He contended that the only logical way for society to handle them was to "just kill them. That's all."

I mentioned I had read somewhere that he usually packed a .45 gun but I couldn't see it on him.

"I don't always carry it on the property, but usually do. Anytime I go off the property I certainly do. When you need it, you need it badly and quickly."

I observed that I did not see any butlers or other people who might take care of the mansion and asked if he had a professional staff that came in.

"My wife's grandmother comes over here and cleans up the house and my wife normally does it or I do it. Why should I have servants? Who the hell needs them?"

Who cooks the meals?

"Well I either eat in a restaurant or I fix it myself or my wife fixes it." What was he going to have for supper? He said he had just had it with the burger, et cetera. Both lunch and supper. He might have a few cups of coffee.

"I eat very little, don't particularly enjoy it. Some people live to eat. I eat to live. To me eating is a burden."

He fretted some about the hazards of business. I asked him why he didn't go public, gradually cash in his money and be very rich the rest of his life. He said he had thought about going public but hadn't yet, first because he was growing so fast and then because going public "generally involves baring your soul to the world, handing your competitors a club to beat you with. . . . [They learn] whether or not some line was profitable . . . what doesn't work." He added that they had recently gotten into athletic products for home use and he was thinking of spinning that division off as a public company.

But in general he liked the idea that only he (and his president) knew his sales figures. Why should he tell anyone when he wouldn't even tell the government? In 1981 the Internal Revenue Service got after him for failing to file a personal income tax return in the 1974–1976 period. He was acquitted of all charges after his lawyer explained: "Mr. Jones was laboring under a misconception of the tax laws. He thought that since he personally was not making a profit he did not have to pay taxes. He was incorrect, so he immediately settled his liability with the IRS."[20]

I inquired if he had considered going into the health food market, since he was getting into home equipment and athletic apparel.

"I'm not a bullshit artist, and under no circumstances am I going to get involved in the so-called health food market, which is one vast con game."

Did he have a way to relax, ever take a vacation, lie in the sun at Palm Beach?

"What would I do at Palm Beach!" he virtually snarled, and seemed affronted.

What did he give Terri his wife for Christmas? "Nothing. What do you give to someone who has everything? Oh, maybe a box of candy."

Which of his wives had he been married to the longest? He didn't remember.

Did he get involved in public affairs?

"As little as possible."

I said I had the impression he had at times been benevolent.

"No, not in the sense you probably mean. Everything you do in life is done for self-seeking reasons."

I reminded him of his gift of three or four million to the University of Florida.

"Yes, but I hope to get something in return." (Presumably research contracts or research findings. Later he gave more millions specifically for research on lower back pain, an ailment that interested Mr. Jones for business reasons.)

He had been reported, two years earlier, as being a centimillionaire. I asked if he could live on $1 million a year.

"I could live on $10,000 to $15,000 a year. What are you talking about! I don't spend anything personal. I eat very little, maybe $30 a week on food. I don't have an extensive wardrobe. I don't have any fucking hobbies. Occasionally I do go to the movies. I read a lot but often I buy pocketbook editions or borrow from someone and change them around with my employees. Any parties are strictly business."

He added that about the only television he watched was *Hill Street Blues.* "We have a 100-inch TV screen in there but it doesn't work. I haven't bothered to get it fixed. Everything I got with very few exceptions is part of the business."

He obviously enjoys much of his work with wild animals but insists it is not a hobby. However, he said the business aspect was too complicated to explain while he was feeling lousy with the flu or whatever it was that was bothering him.

I sensed that as a hint. He escorted me out the front door of this mansion that has an entryway dominated by four huge columns. Off to the right a few hundred feet, apparently off his property, were some mobile homes on cement blocks. Inside the circular drive to his mansion were two neatly trimmed hedges that formed the letters *T* and *A*. Ah, I said, Terri and Arthur.

Also tits and ass, he responded.

As I was about to drive my car back across the wide runway he hollered to me to move over by the gorilla pen. I obeyed, and within a few seconds a medium-size jet whooshed past me, taking off for somewhere.

A year after my visit Mr. Jones became weary of manufacturing exercise equipment, now that the field was getting crowded. With his usual secrecy he sold off most of his stake in the exercise business to a Texas company. He stayed in Ocala with his multitude of wild animals and began marketing to doctors and corporations a machine for diagnostic use on patients with lower back and joint pains. His new company is called MedX. He claims his machine can isolate specific muscles for testing, can greatly strengthen specific muscles, and can detect fraud in injury claims.[21] Medical people have been showing substantial interest.

CHAPTER 5

WEALTH

AS A PROBLEM

TO BE ESCAPED

"Sometimes I wish I didn't have all this f—— money."

— FITZ EUGENE DIXON, JR.,
heir to streetcar fortune[1]

Mr. Dixon made the above statement to *Forbes* in 1983 when it listed his fortune at $150 million. He said the happiest sixteen years of his life as an heir had been while he was serving as a schoolteacher at his old prep school, Episcopal Academy. Since he made that statement he has been very active in philanthropy and yet his fortune had grown to $450 million by 1987.

Like Mr. Dixon, many people of extraordinary wealth do not consider themselves blessed. Some make a considerable effort to escape from the roles expected of the very rich.

John Dorrance III of the Campbell soup fortune has spent years as a working rancher in Wyoming.

Here we will drop in on two people who have actively sought to escape the roles expected of them as very wealthy people. Because of their escapist tendencies, both requested some vagueness in descriptions of where they lived, and the Rockefeller heiress asked if it was possible, as a courtesy to her husband, that I omit her married name. I have done so.

Christopher Bancroft's
Hideaway

Mr. Bancroft is a tall, rugged, friendly man in his mid-thirties who is trying to make a go of it as an entrepreneur in a southwestern community where he retreated and which he likes. He has operated two ice-cream parlors; he was in the process of opening a restaurant; and he has gotten his feet wet remodeling a few houses. Mr. Bancroft has no business school education and he admits he has made mistakes. But when I saw him he was enormously pleased that he finally was getting close to being in the black on his projects.

He has a couple of fine kids, lives in a Cape Cod–style house outside town that cost $250,000. Mr. Bancroft loves to cook, and cooks many of his meals. His office is in one of the houses he remodeled, a pleasant old blue house with ten-foot ceilings. He shares it with a few other small entrepreneurs.

Christopher Bancroft was damned annoyed, however, when a few years ago *Forbes* listed him as one of America's 400 richest individuals, with a net worth up in the hundreds of millions of dollars. Townspeople who heard about it began looking at him in a new light.

"I wanted people to deal with me as an individual for things that I was doing and not for what I was labeled as or what I had by luck fallen into."

That was why he had tried to escape into this typical

American town after going through a lot of mental turmoil which was at least partly due to his discovering, in his early twenties, that he had come into a ton of money. He recalls:

"I knew there was something coming but frankly ... when I got the money suddenly I felt myself on guard. I felt, my God, what am I going to do with this? What is this? I didn't even have a concept of the size of it. I didn't know what it was, how to manage it."

He said it was like winning an elephant in a raffle. "I won this elephant. What do you do, you know? I had the choice of running out and going crazy and flying all over the world and spending money. But I was taught that people who flaunt their money ... are really insecure. I was certainly insecure about this windfall. I didn't know what the hell to do with it."

Regarding his reference to "luck," his was even more exceptional (and surprising) than that of most heirs. He has no direct blood line to a fortune-founder. Technically he is the great-grandson of Clarence Barron, who founded the Dow Jones Company, which publishes the *Wall Street Journal* and *Barrons*. But his fortune came down through an adopted daughter. She married Hugh Bancroft. They had three offspring: Hugh Bancroft, Jr., Jessie Cox, and Jane Bancroft Cook, who in turn all had offspring.

Jane Cook, Christopher's aunt, is the only one of the three still alive. She lives in pleasantly but not outstandingly large houses in Cohasset, Massachusetts, and Sarasota, Florida. A close acquaintance told me: "She is a tremendous, warm person. I feel so sorry for her because she is hounded by people trying to get her to contribute money." (In mid-1987 she had about $900 million worth of Dow Jones stock.)

Hugh Jr., Christopher's father, weary of the active socialite life deemed appropriate to his great wealth, moved his family to a small ranching town in New Mexico. Christopher never really knew him because he died when Christopher was age two. Christopher's mother, who had encouraged the move and was not enchanted with money, eventually married a local doctor. They raised Christopher, his brother, and two sisters, with what Christopher calls the "upper-middle-class" values of that small town "in the middle of nowhere." He gradually gathered that there was money in the family. But he had no idea he and his siblings were inevitably going to become vastly rich. "My mother obviously didn't know much about it [the trusts] or didn't really want to deal with it. It was something uncomfortable for her.

"I received an allowance for household chores. I took summer jobs in roofing, construction, working on my mother's ranch . . . a good-sized ranch for that community, but it wasn't huge. We had to earn our spending money. And that is probably one of the reasons I'm doing what I'm doing today. Somehow I picked up a work ethic instead of a play ethic."

And so it was that in his early twenties he was suddenly notified that through inheritance he had a great fortune, "an elephant," on his hands. When I saw him he owned approximately $150 million of Dow Jones Company stock.

He had hit college (the University of Denver) at about the peak of the wildest phase of the counterculture and had got in with a crowd that was deep into drugs. He dropped out of college after about a semester. Although he never got into "hard" drugs, marijuana did crazy things to him. He had become good enough at skiing that in between drug trips he was able to earn money as a professional skier. Meanwhile, he was going through what he referred to as "an identity crisis when I got my inheritance. I had thought that wealthy people were to be scorned. And suddenly I was a wealthy person."

He ended up spending a couple of years in a clinic to help him straighten out his drug and identity problems. Finally he got back into college in a small city in the Southwest where virtually nobody knew of his financial situation. He learned to like the town and its people and after graduation he embarked on his entrepreneurial career there.

He took some lumps in learning to be an entrepreneur. For example, he built one of his ice-cream parlors by a park where a large group of young people hung out. He got an unpleasant surprise when he opened for business. "We opened and there weren't any kids there. Where were the kids that were hanging out at the park [just] the summer before and two years before when we did our demographics? We didn't realize that the park had now become a gay hangout, and all the straight kids stopped coming."

In some of his early ventures he took on partners. A couple proved to be disappointing and in at least one case he feels he was "taken." He said he had "learned maybe to identify people better." Now he operates primarily on his own.

When we talked he was in the process of completing a seafood restaurant complete with a fine jazz band on a hill outside the city. In fact when I arrived he was on the phone interviewing a possible chef and showed considerable expertise in his questioning.

The food business fascinates him because "I've been cooking since I was a little boy. My mother and father gave me a little camp set, and I started cooking in our garage.

"I'm having a ball trying to figure out how to do business and how to get in the mainstream here. This is a real exciting time for me. . . . I'd like to be successful as a business-person but I don't know if that success is going to be the part that is the best. I think that the most fun for me is the pursuit right now. . . . I don't have to work. It's something that I enjoy doing. If I don't work I find myself getting quite nervous and feeling pretty low about not producing something." He said he was too busy to have many friends. And for a while after news of his windfall came out he found himself being mistrustful that prospective friends might just see "the label that is stuck over my head." Those friendships that he has now developed are mostly with professors, architects, lawyers, and so forth. He just wants to be known as "a nice person who is involved in things." And, he added, he was trying to develop "a more community side to my personality . . . and get more involved in more groups in the community."

Like many in his age group, he was, after eight years of marriage, going through a divorce. He stressed it was not hostile and he had custody of the kids half the time. He said he was intensely interested in the growth of his son and daughter and that "they share a lot of my time." He had cooked supper for them the night before.

Would they be ending up with the same amount of wealth that he had?

"Well, there is nothing I can do to stop it. . . . My parents' trust will go to them. That I have nothing to say about. See, I have no say over those things. I don't know exactly what it is. [By "it" he meant the trust situation.] I know that I will benefit from those trusts and that they will benefit from them regardless. . . . See, I have no control of the assets that I am the beneficiary of. Those are already tagged . . . and those trusts expire upon the death of my children or their thirtieth birthday. . . . So I must now think in terms of how I want to train my children to deal with what they are going to be paid. I don't want them to be brought up to believe that their life should be spent pooping around the countryside . . . imagining themselves as wonderful people who never put anything back."

Mr. Bancroft said he used to worry about justifying his windfall but now he thought of it primarily as Fate. "Things happen that we have no control over."

He spoke briefly of philanthropic interests and said that maybe sometime he would set up a foundation with his money. "I have an obligation I feel to this country and to this community to produce something, to put something back." But first, he said, he was trying to figure a way "to keep myself afloat" as an entrepreneur.

The elephant, in short, was only secondarily on his mind.

Laura and
Her Rockefeller "Cousins"

Laurance Rockefeller's daughter Laura is a good example of how several members of the fourth generation of the Rockefeller clan have reacted to their immense wealth. Although by her account she suffered from "moderate depression" for the first half of her life, she is today a woman of great warmth and energy and a hardworking psychiatric social worker.

A tall, slender person of sunny disposition, she is married to a professional man highly respected in his field. They live in the Greater Boston area and have a large but sparsely furnished old summer house on the New England coast.

Although she was raised on perhaps the greatest estate in American history (Pocantico Hills, New York), she felt a need to apologize for the "extravagant" purchase of that big old summer house and land. They bought the property primarily to save fifty acres of beachfront which was about to be chopped up into little lots by a developer.

Laura already has a great deal of inherited money. And in 1986 *Forbes* estimated that her father and his immediate family held close to a billion dollars in net worth. She told me flatly that there was no way she could justify all the money she has. When I told her the *New York Times* that day had announced her father was giving $36 million to the Memorial Sloan-Kettering Cancer Center for research — one of the largest individual health-care gifts ever made — she said: "Wow! I knew he was going to give something, I didn't know it was that much. Wow!" She clearly was elated.

At the summer place, where I visited her, she takes long jogs about the countryside, often walks the beach barefoot. When she wears a dress it is likely to be one purchased from a mail-order catalogue. Her husband and she knocked out some walls of a Victorian parlor in the house and converted the area into a kitchen-eating-lounging area. She invited me to remain for a small supper they were having, and she cooked the supper while joining in the conversation. (Their only servant there is a part-time cleaning woman.) She apologized for the fact that she had forgotten to get vodka and vermouth.

Laura's great-grandfather, John D. Rockefeller, founder of Standard Oil, was in his time by far the richest man in America, and probably the world. He stated: "The good Lord gave me my money." On advice of a public relations counsel he improved his harsh image by giving away dimes to everyone he was in contact with (and plunged heavily into philanthropy). John D. had only one childbearing offspring, John D. Rockefeller, Jr. But John D. Jr. had six childbearing offspring, five of them sons (John D. III, Nelson, Laurance, Winthrop, David, and Abby). He sought to see that they be a credit to the Rockefeller name, and set up an elaborate family headquarters charged with making arrangements so that the Rockefeller dynasty would extend into reasonable perpetuity.

This headquarters, known variously as Room 5600 or just "The Office," has long occupied two floors of Rockefeller Center and is staffed by a variety of experts on money management, taxes, trusts, philanthropy, and so forth. Staff members offer family members firm guidance but more important they see to the functioning of a web of trusts that tend to lock up the money, although in certain circumstances some "invasion" of principal is permitted.

The twenty-two offspring, including Laura, who comprise the fourth generation, call themselves the Cousins. They receive income directly from a set of trusts involving a few hundred million set up in 1952. And they may get direct gifts from parents. The dynasty plan seemed to work quite well for the above-cited third generation, known as the Brothers even though there was one sister. At this writing two [Laurance and David] are still very much alive. The really big trust money rolls in from blockbuster trusts established in 1934 for them. These six trusts have a current value of about $2.3 billion according to *Fortune*.[2]

"Brothers" get the income of their trusts while they live, then the income passes to their offspring. Gross inequity soon was apparent in the fourth generation. Nelson had seven offspring (six still alive) whereas Winthrop had only one. Hence in 1986 *Forbes* listed Winthrop, Jr., something of a loner living out in Arkansas, as being worth $750 million. Nelson's offspring are lucky if they have $150 million each.

Most of the twenty-two Cousins have a reunion every

year at the old Pocantico Hills estate for fun, planning, and comparison of experiences with The Office, and learning of new developments in the various family organizations. They compare complaints about being "infantilized" by their financial caretakers at The Office, or viewed as "trust fund babies." One success they have scored on The Office is getting about $20 million placed in their own little "Family" foundation whose agenda is more reflective of their priorities, concentrating on more of today's major problems, such as nuclear arms control, conservation, women's rights, etcetera, than the Brothers Fund, almost ten times larger.[3]

The Cousins are a curious mix. Some lead the kind of proper lives that befit subdued splendor and may arrive at the reunion through the great gate in high-line Mercedes. Others arrive in jeeps or long-used station wagons. Several are sick and tired of the dynasty idea and just want to be free to fulfill themselves as they choose. (The dynasty idea has also been somewhat undercut by the fact that only nine of the twenty-two cousins are male and the fact that nine have had at least two spouses. Of their fifty-two offspring in the fifth generation, only twenty bear the name Rockefeller. And as of 1986, not one of the seven youngsters so far born into the sixth generation bore the name Rockefeller.)

As for the fourth-generation Cousins, consider three of John D. Rockefeller III's children. One daughter, Hope, won awards as a newspaper reporter. Another daughter, Sandra, not only renounced the Rockefeller name but tried to give away all her money. She was thwarted by terms of ongoing trusts. John D. Rockefeller IV, or "Jay," was an antipoverty worker, became Democratic senator from West Virginia, one of the nation's poorest states, and has acquired a $6 million home in Washington.[4] Steven Rockefeller, son of Nelson, married a Norwegian maid in their house, went through psychoanalysis, became a professor of religion then dean of the highly respected Middlebury College in Vermont. Currently he has chosen to return to teaching as head of the department of religion. Laura's brother, Larry, has devoted several years to trying to conserve a beautiful area in the Catskills and is a conservation lawyer. One of her two sisters, Lucy, is a doctor; the other, Marion, is a professional painter.

What's it like to grow up on a fenced-in, manicured 3,600-acre estate with several palatial houses and servants galore? I refer again to the famed Pocantico Hills, or in Laura's words, "Tarrytown." Laura's folks lived in one of the great houses; the Nelson Rockefellers lived in one of the others. Grandfather was still in the main mansion.

Laura recalls "living inside the gate" as like being in a "verdant cage," beautiful to the senses but in many ways oppressive. She delighted in running around playing Indian with her sister and cousins and living in the treehouse building. She particularly liked being around Cousin Steven, now the college dean. She says they were like twins and that even today "I am closer to him than to anybody in my generation."

But there was relatively little close contact with her parents. Wealthy parents in that era were expected to travel a lot. In the sprawling mansion, parents slept far away from the children. There were often more servants than family members. At various times Laura had as her nurse a person who was German, Swiss, Scottish, or French, which probably was broadening. Her nurses tended to be strict and did not permit her to make choices.

"I longed to wear white socks to school like everyone else. The nurse in charge at the time insisted on sickly tan or navy blue." She was not permitted to try to learn any basic household skills such as cooking because that would be interfering with those being paid to do that job.

When her favorite "primary caretaker" left, it was as traumatic as losing a parent. And there was always "the severe conflict of loyalties between some of the professional caretakers whom I knew better and felt closer to than my parents. I had a need to hide my loyalties from my parents."

Then there was the fear of kidnapping of the wealthy in the decade after the famous Lindbergh kidnapping. At Pocantico there were not only guard gates, but armed guards, alarms, growling watchdogs. She and her cousin Michael in play got too close to one of the dogs and Michael's cheek was slashed open. Neither of the two chauffeurs was at the estate and none of the servants knew how to drive. It took five phone calls to find a driver to get Michael to a hospital.

Of course she didn't live all the time at Pocantico Hills. She followed her parents when they went off to their places owned or rented in New York City, Washington, Fishers Island, New York, Jupiter Island, Florida, Jackson Hole, Wyoming, or Saranac Lake in the Adirondacks. The relocating tended to be upsetting and break up friendship patterns. She had been so protected that she got her first glimpse of poverty one morning on an overnight train trip from New York to Jupiter Island, and saw mile after mile of shacks along the railroad, which left her puzzled and troubled.

Laura feels that private school and college (Bryn Mawr) helped her develop "independence and spontaneity that offset the zombie-like compliant and withdrawn person I became at home."

She was of course warned that men might court her for her fortune. So it was easy for her to fall in love with a young man, the son of a college president, who was unimpressed by wealth and aspired to be an educator (and in fact started his career as a high school teacher). She fell in love and married at the early age of nineteen. In retrospect she has also wondered if it was a way to get rid of the name Rockefeller.

For her the name had always been a burden. "The more I cared about the person I was speaking to, the more I was tempted to look away when I spoke my name because I could not bear to see myself disappear in their eyes" and become a stereotype of someone spoiled, elitist, reactionary.

She continued going to college after marriage and was graduated magna cum laude. And at one point she was caught up in the radical activities of Students for a Democratic Society.

For much of her early life, she recalls, "the deepest conflict has been between a desire to disappear, become anonymous, invisible, to run away, and a wish to be known, recognized, appreciated."

She continued taking college courses for many years after graduation, mostly in government and later social work, while raising three children. At the same time she was trying to work out her conflicts through psychotherapy. After fourteen years of marriage there was a divorce and she married a man of congenial interests who brought to the marriage three of his own children, who were of parallel ages to her own.

And in her late thirties she plunged into building a career in social work. This meant enrolling full time in the Simmons School of Social Work. She learned that she had developed outstanding skills of "heartfulness" that enabled her to relate easily to all sorts of people. Her casework training took her into homes and child-guidance clinics in some of the roughest areas of Boston.

Today she is a licensed psychiatric social worker with her own office. Mainly she deals with people suffering from depression, marital problems, and problems in sustaining intimate relationships.

She has become a recognized authority on using role playing (or psychodrama) as a swift way to help people work out their problems. She contends it is frequently more efficient than conventional therapy involving analysis and talk. Now she is being invited to stage demonstrations at clinics, which are attended by psychologists, social workers, and occasionally psychiatrists. She has in short become respected on her own merits! In her spare time she is writing a book on psychodrama techniques. Very few of the people who are her patients or attend her demonstrations know that she is a Rockefeller heiress.

Meanwhile she has been giving away a substantial amount of her income to projects involved in helping people. Two are her favorites. The first is Spelman College in Atlanta, a college for black women, where she is a trustee. (Spelman is her middle name; the wife of John D. Rockefeller, founder of the dynasty, was named Laura Spelman and her family ran an underground railroad in Ohio for escaping slaves, which pleases today's Laura.)

Her second favorite is the Children's Defense Fund, a national organization that fights for children with some sort of problem. "It's a lobby for kids, mostly poor, mostly black, mostly minority. It's got the families, the kids, the central policy, the teenage pregnancy center, minorities — they're all my interests." Laura is a long-time friend of its president, the noted Marian Wright Edelman.

"My relationship to the money I have earned is very different from the money I have inherited. I keep the latter in a separate account. I feel that earned money is 'mine' and experience a freedom in relation to it that is different. What I mostly choose to do with it is to give it away anonymously — on my terms — without having to account for it to anyone, including the IRS, because I do not want to get tax or other 'credit' for it. In contrast, to this day, I cannot keep in mind the figures about how much unearned money I have. I always have to look it up.

"People who make a lot of money and don't give it away ... just enrage me. To not return to the system which allowed you to receive this bounty some portion, not even what you get a tax write-off for ... makes me very, very angry.

"I feel by my values that I should not be in a position of having so much unearned wealth [but] I just stopped needing to justify it. It became a fact of just simply accepting it and just using it effectively. ... My having so much inherited money and my children's having it in time is not a circumstance I would have chosen for myself or for them. It violates my sense of what is fair. I also feel increasingly that it's just as unhealthy for the wealthy ones as extreme poverty is for the poor. It takes exceptional genes and/or luck to rise above the undertow of surrounding circumstances that tend to pull one into the sea of dulled sensitivities and partially realized individual gifts.

"My financial inheritance is one of the realities I have with difficulty developed the serenity to accept. I have struggled to transform my guilty energy into the courage to discover and try to change the things that I can change, if only a little."

When her father appeared before a congressional committee to refute the allegations that the Rockefellers were running an "empire," he read a note Laura had prepared for him:

"The vision of 'empire' . . . can only seem ironic to someone who happens to be a Rockefeller. . . . There *are* ties that bind the family together. However, these ties have little to do with the exercise of business power and almost everything to do with having a shared set of common experiences. . . . An inventory of the vocations of members of this family indicates that most have succeeded in finding a way to do his or her 'own thing' rather than a 'family thing.'"[5]

Laura also showed me a statement by the cousin she admires so much, Steven Rockefeller, who puts it even more strongly: "I feel there are just too many of us for the family members to go parading around talking about our special identity. . . . My feeling is that the family as an institution was the creation of a certain culture and a certain time in the history of this nation. It has had its day. Once the original generating energy goes out of an institution, it just dies. That's the way it is and ought to be. The dynasty stuff — that's all finished."[6]

Except, of course, for the river of money arranged by The Office.

CHAPTER 6

WEALTH

AS AN

EGO PROP

"I don't want to give you a headache, but
listen, I'm a multifaceted guy."

— SAMUEL LEFRAK of New York City

When Adnan Khashoggi, the
Arab middleman once called the richest man in the world,
held a birthday party for himself at his estate in the hills
back of Marbella, Spain, it was an interesting display of
splendor.[1] A five-foot-four man weighing about 200 pounds,
he brought in a good assortment of European and Hollywood royalty. The theme was Renaissance and guests entered an archway made of crossed swords held up by fifty
costumed pages. When the guests finally got to dining they
found an easel at each setting displaying Khashoggi's face

beaming from the cover of *Leaders* magazine, which purportedly only goes to heads of state and chiefs of major world corporations. And after dessert an actor dressed as Henry VIII read a proclamation hailing Khashoggi as "the world's greatest." With a flourish the fifty pages released 2,500 balloons, each with the words "world's greatest" on it.

That of course was Arabian ego. In America we have an image of masters of wealth accumulation as taciturn, reserved, poised, formidable, and exhibiting the serenity of ultimate accomplishment. Of the thirty people I visited, only one actually fit that personality pattern: Sigfried Weis, a supermarket monarch of central Pennsylvania. Three or four others partially met the description, but most were clearly humans with warts. And a few still had clear ego needs, needs for admiration — despite their fabulous financial success.

With Samuel LeFrak, it was sometimes difficult to distinguish display of ego needs from exuberant accounts of accomplishment aimed at proving he is more than just an extremely rich man. And he insisted — despite his occasional arm-waving and shouting — that he was a "low-key guy."

A Tycoon Still Eager
for Applause

Mr. LeFrak is the largest landlord in America, probably in the world, owning about 87,000 apartment units, plus a lot of other buildings. "We own more bathtubs than American Standard," he quipped. And he is involved in a project to create a twenty-first-century–type city on the New Jersey side of the Hudson River, which he describes as a bigger deal than building the Pyramids.

His net worth rose about $100 million a year for four consecutive years. When I saw him he was in his late sixties and his net worth was $800 million. Satisfied? Hardly. By mid-1987 he was still charging and had a net worth of $1.2 billion (or $350 million more than the highly publicized New York

realtor Donald Trump). And by mid-1988 *Forbes* had Mr.
LeFrak's net worth up to $1.5 billion.

To get to see this folksy, amiable, chunky man with sil-
ver-rimmed glasses, I had to rise early. He is up every morning at 5:30 and once he leaves his Fifth Avenue apartment
on Central Park he is on a whirl. So I got up at dawn in Connecticut to have breakfast with him.

New York City has at least 150 people worth more than
$100 million. Most live in buildings that can be seen in an
easy stroll. They live in heaviest concentration in a half-mile
stretch of high-rise, austerely trimmed red brick buildings
on Fifth Avenue between 60th Street and 70th Street. (It
houses or has housed people with names such as Rockefeller, Ford, Getty, Bass.) Another cluster is in similar buildings
two blocks over in the lower 70s of Park Avenue. And some
live in individual houses in the short stretches between Fifth
and Park. The immensely rich do tend to run into each other
at social events, but most live in a setting of anonymity,
largely unaffected by this physical proximity to others of
equal wealth. For example, a publisher worth $200 million
lived just up the street about a block from the building
where Mr. LeFrak lived and expressed surprise when I told
him that he and Mr. LeFrak were neighbors. (The LeFraks
have a second home well out on Long Island and an apartment in a London hotel. They used to have a house in Palm
Beach but got rid of it for lack of use.)

Mr. LeFrak once owned the apartment building in which
he lived but he had condoed it so that now he just owned
one floor. "We have eleven rooms. You see, I'm a very modest guy." His son Richard, the president of his company, was
on the floor below him. Mr. LeFrak's floor had cost about
$90,000 to build and was now worth $3 million. "Not a bad
deal," he said. Security seemed to dictate the lobby and elevator arrangement. The lobby was small, with attendants,
and you had to step into a small niche, after being announced, to get to the very small elevators. Clearly dwellers
were protected from jostling with strangers on the elevator.

The LeFrak apartment was pleasant but certainly not

spectacular despite its $3 million price tag. The ceiling was of ordinary height. There was a maid but no butler. The walls, however, were thickly laden with paintings by such artists as Renoir and Picasso. There was an excellent view of Central Park. Mr. LeFrak pointed to a couple of brown skyscrapers jutting up behind Central Park South and said he had built them.

Mrs. LeFrak stopped by briefly. She was slim with long brown hair, was formally polite and seemed young for having been married to Mr. LeFrak for forty-four years. Son Richard dropped by to have a word about business before departing. He was serious, handsome, tall, lean, and looked much more like our image of a successful executive than his father.

Mr. LeFrak, cordial and affable, was in shirt and bright tie, with a blue jacket draped nearby. He was breakfasting on juice, muffins, and jam. For lunch he is apt to have a tuna fish roll with tomato and a Tab.

This morning he was still preoccupied with a wedding — "a whole production" — he had arranged for his middle daughter, Francine, at the Metropolitan Club. It ran for nine hours ending at 4 A.M., having included four fairly distinct events. About 100 people were invited for the ceremony, about 300 were invited for the reception, about 300 were invited for a dinner party, and about 700 were invited for a late-night "celebration." (He rarely drinks himself.) "*W*" magazine, which focuses on society, stated in 1987 that the cost of having just a wedding reception for 300 in Manhattan can run into the hundreds of thousands of dollars.

Mr. LeFrak, despite his colorful mannerisms, is greatly respected in the world of real estate. He is a tough negotiator, and he is conservative financially, prudent, and he scorns high-flying deals. Further, he is one of the few major builders in New York City who has openly denounced the pervasive role of the Mafia in the city's construction industry. He comes from three generations of builders with roots in France and Jerusalem. His father was a successful builder in Brooklyn. And Sam, in gradually taking over his father's company, built a lot of plain six-story apartment buildings in fast-growing Queens that were called "money machines." He first got public attention by building a huge development called Lefrak City in Queens. Since his son, already successful, brings in the fifth generation of LeFrak builders, Sam scorns the common wisdom about wealth being temporary. "When they say shirtsleeves to shirtsleeves in three generations, don't believe it."

Over the phone he had recited to me a poem he had composed many years ago:

> In the struggle for power
> O the scramble for pelf
> Let this be your motto
> Rely on yourself.

At breakfast he said: "I don't want to impress you. . . . But you know I am basically a teacher. That's why I do all the lecturing."

In *Who's Who in America* he lists six universities where he has given speeches. He also lists twenty-three decorations and awards he has received, including Citizen of the Year award of the Brooklyn Philharmonic Orchestra, where he had previously served as a patron.

He told me: "I've been knighted by the pope . . . I've been knighted by the king of Sweden . . . I've been knighted by the president of Finland." (It may or may not be relevant that the Finnish consulate in New York was in a building he once owned and that he ordered a great deal of Finnish design materials for one of his major projects. But that is nit-picking.)

The biography his office gave me starts: "Dr. Samuel J. LeFrak is a distinguished business leader, scientist, developer, builder, urban expert, yachtsman, patron of the arts, philanthropist and humanitarian . . . an experienced statesman."

Whenever LeFrak's secretary called me she stated: "Dr. LeFrak would like to speak with you."

The doctorate is strictly an honorary one from a college where he has been a trustee.

I was supplied not only with a text of the speech he gave to Oxford University in 1984 but with a videotape of it. The man at Oxford introducing him on the videotape addressed him as "Doctor." And Dr. LeFrak proceeded to introduce his talk by running a film giving the big picture on super-projects of creative construction that had occupied his attention. He spoke as a camera on a flying machine came in from the ocean over Ellis Island to provide a kind of moon-shot look at the greater New York metropolitan area. Off to the right, Dr. LeFrak indicated was Lefrak City for 25,000 people which he had created from a wasteland. (True.) ... Here down at the tip of Manhattan was where "we" created Battery Park City by filling in 100 acres of the Hudson River, using fill excavated in creating the World Trade Center. And almost directly across the river in New Jersey, he indicated, was the beginning of Newport City, being created on a desolate area crying for renewal. All indeed were immense, some even gargantuan, projects.

The film, made a couple of years earlier, did not include a towering project much on his mind as we had breakfast. "One of the things that I'm quite involved with is building the tallest building in the world ... near the Coliseum." He had drawings. It would be 135 stories high, 1,625 feet.

Was there some sound reason why he needed to go 1,625 feet?

"Yeah, we want the tallest building in the world. You know, pride. The tallest building today is in Chicago." He explained he was bidding against some other guys and it was a local government project, so pride was a factor. (Months later I read that the project went to some other guy — and not as the world's tallest building.)

Sam LeFrak did indeed play a major early role in Battery Park City though not quite the role implied in his *Who's Who* entry: "Creator, sponsor, builder, Battery Park City." It was a state project. He had as a codeveloper in much of his part of the project the Fisher Brothers. LeFrak was deeply involved in creating the seawall, a complex undertaking. He told me: "I created the beachhead and developed the first section and made it all viable. At that point the politics got in and they really screwed us because they took it and gave it" to another outfit.

"I told them to buzz off and went across the river" to involve himself in creating Newport City.

It undoubtedly galled him when in 1986 *Time* had a piece describing how the Reichmann brothers of Toronto had moved in on the U.S. skyscraper business. It wrote of "The glittering centerpiece: their new $1.5 billion Battery Park City project . . . with its elegant copper-and-granite towers."[2]

With Newport City, again in his accounts he occasionally becomes notably self-appreciative in relating what "I" and "we" have done. He pointed out to me that the famed Holland Tunnel "goes directly into my city. . . . I own the land under the Holland Tunnel. The Port Authority only has an easement" because it had never been used for a railroad.

How long had it taken him to acquire this?

"A long time. We had to wait for three railroads to go bankrupt. I bought it from the trustee of bankruptcy."

So Newport City had been on his mind a long time?

"Well actually I myself was not in it that long. . . . A man by the name of Glimcher had access to the trustee in bankruptcy, and a guy by the name of Simon who builds shopping centers, his name is Mel Simon . . . went to Glimcher and said he would go in there and develop the thing. He didn't know what the hell to do. He is not a builder." (This is something, as we'll see, that would surprise Mr. Simon.) "I'm a builder. There aren't too many guys who know how to build cities."

Anyhow, by LeFrak's account Simon went to various major New York banks for funding and all suggested he needed someone like Sam LeFrak as a partner. LeFrak observed: "All roads lead not to Rome but to me. Mel came to me . . ." and so a relationship began on a mammoth futuristic project that may ultimately cost $10 billion.

Subsequently the *New Yorker,* in a "Talk of the Town"

item, added a further accounting of how Mr. LeFrak saw his role in Newport City.[3] In Mr. LeFrak's presence an aide had explained, "The Simons [Melvin and Herbert] had the land but the redevelopment people said there had to be more than a shopping center on it." (Things such as apartment towers, office buildings et cetera.) At this point Mr. LeFrak took over the briefing:

"I told them, 'An orchestra has one leader. You can put your name next to mine, but don't get in my way.' . . . I told them, 'You're giving me chaos. I'll make order out of it.'" LeFrak told a visitor that for the "signature" building he had planned to build a structure with "a hundred and thirty-five stories — the tallest in the world," presumably the same super-skyscraper he had failed to sell to New York authorities. But the idea was dropped. "I didn't want to intimidate the Statue of Liberty."

Newport City will have many amenities such as band shell, repertory theater, aquarium, marina, and a museum. *Forbes* (1986) said of LeFrak that the museum would in substantial part be "for his French Impressionist collection" and quoted him as saying, "Jersey's a little light on museums."

A few months after my session with Mr. LeFrak I happened to be seeing Melvin Simon, a tall, good-humored man, on another matter (see chapter 7). I mentioned some uncertainty about the beginnings of Newport City. He explained he had brought the project to LeFrak and that they were partners. Then, when I indicated uncertainty as to who had done what, he grinned and said, "He likes me to be low key. . . . I love Sam. I just spent the afternoon with him."

In March 1986, the *New York Times* carried a map showing big new projects going up on the Jersey side of the Hudson. Newport City was labeled: "Glimcher/Simon/Lefrak."

As great buildings started rising on the hundreds of acres of once dilapidated riverfront, Mr. LeFrak found that Jersey City was not a paradise for building either. He was in a battle with city officials who charged that the bulldozing at Newport City had sent vast legions of rats into settled parts of the city.

By 1988, as he reached age seventy, Mr. LeFrak made peace with New York City in a big way. He made front-page headlines by agreeing to build 1,200 middle-income units on land owned by the city in the Lower East Side on a limited-profit basis. Still not at a loss for words he announced that the proposed project would "provide me with an opportunity to present a civic gesture to the City of New York."

Erecting monumental realty projects is just Mr. LeFrak's major business interest. He has had big investments in oil and gas, and has a successful entertainment company very much involved in motion picture production, music publishing, TV, and the theater. His two older daughters, Denise and Francine, through the company, have been involved in several successful projects. And Mr. LeFrak, through the company, has been very much involved in helping Barbra Streisand become, as indicated earlier, probably the wealthiest performer in the entertainment world. Barbra as a girl lived in a Lefrak apartment in Brooklyn. He saw her in her first booking ($50 and car fare), decided she was a winner. His operation has not only played a part in managing her but has reportedly cut her in on some sweet deals.

At our breakfast we got to talking about what he was going to do with all the wealth he had accumulated. He indicated he had already given to many projects and didn't seem eager to talk.

"Everybody wants a piece of me. . . . You know, I am an explorer. The *Titanic* was my expedition with Jack Redmond. Did you know that I also have an expedition in northeast Ethiopia now looking for the Missing Link. . . . We found Lucy, the 3½-million-year woman." (A landmark find.)

"You found that!"

"Sure, with the archaeologist of course. Who do you think has been funding these things? . . . But I have to do everything quietly. . . . Right now I am thinking I want to find the cure to cancer and the common cold. And I'm going to be leaving a lot of money for that." He said he wanted to "fund a cure for AIDS. . . . I'm going to help the physically handicapped and the impoverished." He had helped a lot of displaced persons.

What was his biggest philanthropy?

He said he didn't know but it was nothing in the tens of millions for a specific case.

Could he live on a million dollars a year? He indicated that would be a "sentence" even though he had gotten rid of the Palm Beach house. He loves his ninety-foot boat loaded with teak and enjoys taking people like the ambassadors of Australia, Argentina, Egypt, and India for a cruise around the New York harbor.

Were there any limits to his goals or did he just want to keep on going? "You know Picasso painted to the very, very end, ninety-five, ninety-six years." He said he had thought of phasing out of construction and letting his son carry on. "I want to make movies, I want to shoot some television, I want to write some things." But his son, Richard, had dissuaded him.

"You could put me in a rocking chair and put a cat on my lap and I would be like Whistler's Mother. No, what the hell. God gave me life. He said, live, live, enjoy. I'm in the dessert of my life, now. . . . That's the sweetness. I had my appetizer, my entree, my salad. Now I got the dessert. I do what I want to do. . . . And by the way there are no skeletons in my closet."

As we headed for the elevator I wondered how he would get transport to his office in Queens, where he was headed, since he had made no calls. From the lobby I could see no limousines. He nodded to the doorman and said, "Tell George I am ready." Within thirty seconds a medium-size, light-colored Mercedes equipped with telephone pulled up at the curb.

Walking to my car some blocks away I reflected on one of his final comments: "You will probably leave and say, Jeez, what kind of a lunatic did I talk to? You know, the lunatic that built more housing than anybody else in the world. . . ."

CHAPTER 7

WEALTH

AS A WAY

TO KEEP SCORE

"I need to be busy. If I wasn't busy I'd drink too much."

— CLAYTON WILLIAMS, JR., whose net worth a few years ago was put at $200 million

Some years ago I made a study of traits crucial to executive success.[1] Seven abilities seemed to count greatly. And the trait that leaped out above all others was the ability to maintain a high level of thrust.

The thrust that drives people to attain great success as self-made entrepreneurs does not automatically switch off when they achieve that success. They keep on charging even after they accumulate fortunes so vast that the wealth attained is hard to grasp in individual terms.

Of the hugely successful self-made entrepreneurs I

visited in this study, a clear majority were people with a high level of thrust. One of them, Jeno Paulucci, as we saw, had so much restless energy he could hardly sit still. And a large majority of them said they wanted to keep on testing their ability to make money. Dollars were just the way to keep score.

They did not want the game to stop. In large numbers they rejected the idea of cashing in their chips and enjoying themselves. They *were* enjoying themselves, even in cases where they had encountered setbacks and were finding the going rough.

Clayton Williams's
Climb to High Places

Mr. Williams of Midland, Texas, is a happy warrior and a one-man conglomerate who has been running a billion-dollar-a-year empire. At one point he was the biggest independent oil and gas man in Texas. He also acquired a lot of ranches. And he took on the "old family" bankers of Midland and set up his own ClayDesta National Bank. He built a great ClayDesta Plaza containing a million square feet of office space at the north end of Midland. The word ClayDesta combines parts of his first name and that of his wife, Modesta. He confided to me: "The women like that."

In the early eighties, as he sensed that oil and cattle prices would dip, he did quite a bit of liquidating and put about $60 million into building what he saw as a serious need, a regional digital microwave communications system. He said that while his oil business currently was "fibrillating," his communications system was doing extremely well.

With all this volatile activity his asset base, after taking a plunge, had been swinging by tens of millions of dollars a year as he was fighting to rebuild it so that he could move on. Since he sees himself primarily as playing games with money, swings just make the game more challenging. He said to me, by way of explanation: "I think you probably are finding that with an awful lot of people of affluence the money really doesn't make that much difference. They drive to achieve because [a goal] is there. Why do the mountain climbers climb the mountain? Because it's there." It's the process of achieving that counts.

Nine-tenths of the gratification, he said, comes from anticipation and only one-tenth from realization. And he added: "The money is how you keep score."

We were supposed to meet at his five-bedroom house with pool on twenty acres outside Midland but that appointment had to be canceled and he suggested we meet at a Manhattan hotel where he and his wife would be staying. So I showed up at the elegant, gleaming Carlyle Hotel on the Upper East Side at the appointed hour. Most of the attendants there wore white gloves. I called his room several times but got no answer. Perhaps he had forgotten. I sat down near the elevator. After about twenty minutes he swept in with his aides.

I stood up and he came directly to me. He was wearing a cowboy hat and boots. His jacket did not match his pants. He was of medium height and seemed a bit bow-legged, but that may have been from a sore knee. His ruggedly handsome face bore a grin. He apologized for being late and explained: "You can't walk out on bankers."

In the elevator he said, "I live such a crazy life. Once I owed half a billion dollars. Now we've got it down to $250 million." (Maintaining a sizable debt, as we'll see, can be a good strategy for keeping one's taxes down because it means you have tax-deductible interest payments — if you can keep the debt well below assets.)

The hotel has suites but he and his wife were staying in a standard room, smaller than an ordinary Holiday Inn room. He stripped off his coat and tie and said he wanted to give me "a little fun and get us warmed up a little" by viewing some commercials he had just made for his thriving communications network. A projector was set up in a nearby room where his aides were staying. When we were going down the hall I inquired if he had brought the room key.

"Goddamnit, no, I didn't. I have to go get another. I'm in

too many businesses." So we went down through the posh lobby, he in his shirtsleeves, which didn't seem to bother him, and got another key.

The commercials were indeed excellent. There was a beautiful shot of a cowboy on a horse galloping full speed down a ridge, across a creek and whirling to an expert stop in front of the camera. The cowboy was Mr. Williams, who grinned and went into his drawling commercial for his high-speed digital phone company.

Shortly after we got back to his room and were seated in the only two chairs, Mrs. Williams, a handsome brunette and obviously an outdoor type, came in from shopping. She propped herself comfortably on the double bed and occasionally joined in the conversation.

Mr. Williams got directly into explaining who he was — and how he regarded money — by starting with his grandfather, a surveyor and Harvard law graduate who had tuberculosis and went to the arid far west Texas village of Fort Stockton for health reasons. He managed to survey such west Texas towns as Lubbock despite buffalo stampedes. And he wrote a history of the early West. Clayton Williams's father was an engineer and small rancher who also spent the last thirty years of his life as a historian.

Clayton Williams, Sr., being busy, put young Clayton in charge of the farm-ranch from the age of twelve, and when Clayton Jr. reached college age he went to Texas A&M to study agriculture. Times were tough.

"I waited tables at night, me and eleven other black guys. I was the only white boy there. Which was good training. You really observe people, how they treat you as an inferior since you're a waiter. You can tell real good people from the horses' asses when you're subservient to people."

After college the farm-ranch had been sold, so he began selling life insurance, which he called good training for anyone since you're selling not only a product but yourself. He drifted into selling oil and gas leases on commissions. As business improved in oil-rich west Texas, he began persuading other people to finance his own drilling.

Gradually he got into processing, piping, and marketing the gas he drilled, and, as they say, profited greatly. He claims he did it with brains, not any really big strikes.

Meanwhile he had gotten deeply into his real love, ranching. In our talk he said: "I have too damn many ranches. I got fourteen ranches and I need to own about eight. I have about 220,000 acres and probably should have about 100,000 [for prime profitability because of farm price trends]. One year I had nearly 80,000 head of yearlings." He said that people who have fancy ranches as playthings don't understand how he makes money ranching. He had made a lot of money at it because he knows farming and is personally involved.

"One reason I make money in the cattle business is that when we work I'm there working in the pens with my cowboys. When I go to the ranch and we're working cattle, I like to sleep in a bedroll at the cow camp by the chuck wagon. That's fun. Get up in the morning with the cowboys and get your breakfast and coffee."

From boyhood he has known Spanish and two of his best friends are Mexicans, managers on his ranches. He said they are social friends and "they'll be pallbearers at my funeral. The Mexicans, if you get to know them, are fine people."

Mr. Williams was a man of numerous interesting facets. During the spring semester each year at Texas A&M, he said, he has been flying to his alma mater every week to teach a three-hour-credit course to seniors and graduate students in entrepreneurship. His pay: $1,200 a month. He said he was telling the kids the mistakes he had made, how to be careful, how to motivate people, what the business world is really like.

In jest he had said to the students: "Kids, we're going to call this course Bullshit 201." After the course had proceeded a few weeks a student raised his hand and said: "Mr. Williams, we want to change the name of your course. Your bullshit is so advanced we'd like to call it Bullshit 438."

Each year he and Mrs. Williams take a novel month-long

vacation. They don't have a vacation house at Palm Beach or anywhere else. Their only boats are rowboats. Their vacation consists of disappearing from civilization. They go somewhere in the world where they will be above the timberline. In thin air they hunt for wild sheep.

Mrs. Williams, from the bed: "It certainly gets you away from the telephones and the doorbells."

Mr. Williams: "We spend a few weeks every year living in a tent, and I love it. It brings me back to earth. You don't have an inside toilet and those kind of things. Such living brings you back to where the real world is.

"We hunt mountain sheep at high altitudes and the terrain is difficult. It's a very miserable type of hunting because you're cold, hungry, tired, physically exhausted. I have to exercise a little all year to keep in shape for it.

"I've hunted in Alaska seven times, Canada ten, Mexico three, western U.S. many times, Afghanistan for the Marco Polo sheep, China for the elk, Nepal for the blue sheep. Mrs. Williams goes along almost every time. She's tougher than I am."

Why sheep and not mountain goats?

"Goats are just not as smart. It's the opposite of the domestic. Domestic goats are smarter than domestic sheep. But the wild sheep is keenly intelligent and has great eyesight. The Rocky Mountain goat is one of the dumbest game animals of all."

The Williamses have five children, all covered by a trust. The two oldest are daughters of a previous marriage. When Clayton and Modesta Williams married about twenty-three years ago, they didn't have any luck conceiving children. He recalls: "She and I adopted two boys and then we learned how to have our own and we had our own — a darling little girl."

Mr. Williams was concerned about how they would grow up. He said he hates pretentious people — rich people going around acting like rich people — and he has been concerned that his children not act like that. "I've got one boy that would tend to be but the other four are down to earth, which is what will serve them best."

He continued: "My children will never be able to be as motivated as I was because they have things. I teach my children to work. I had the boys building fences, doing ranch work since they were very young. But I can never instill in them the drive that I had because I was without. They're not without. We fly to the ranch whereas I would have had to go by bicycle. So that's the difficult thing of [being] someone of wealth. You raise your kids in an unreal world and they can't have the drive or the satisfaction that I have had in building."

Mr. Williams said their family runs on a budget of about a half a million a year, counting the hunts. And this man of great wealth said, "That's a lot of money."

He considered that he has been something of a philanthropist since he has given the equivalent of six or seven million to Texas A&M and had helped put a lot of poor kids through school. But he acknowledged he had not been much involved in civic affairs. "I have great difficulty with a committee sitting around a room spending two hours bullshitting."

Texas Business a few years ago had a picture of Mr. Williams on its cover and suggested he might be "The Next Billionaire." That was before all the problems with oil and farm prices. Mr. Williams recalls: "I was a hell of a long ways from being a billionaire and I'm a good ways from being there now. But I'm still working and maybe some day I might be a billionaire. Probably not. The oil business has really been kicked around." Still, a billion obviously sounded like a nice score to achieve for someone still in his mid-fifties.

Some months after our talk *Forbes* had an article, "Hard Times in Texas," that focused on Midland as being particularly hard hit.[2] But it cited Clayton Williams, Jr., as one who was making an impressive comeback. His office complex was 90 percent occupied. Thanks to cautious lending, his bank had $110 million in assets and an 18 percent return on equity. And his microwave long-distance phone system was growing more than 100 percent a year. Mr. Williams was quoted as expressing regret that he was not currently on the magazine's list of 400 richest Americans. (Cut-off for admission had risen to $180 million.) But he added:

"Watch out."

Melvin Simon's
Playful Pursuits

Mr. Simon of Indianapolis has made himself the richest man in Indiana by building the new fantasy-type town squares of the 1980s which encourage people to spend their money with abandon. These are better known as shopping malls. He has built hundreds of them, some enormous, and in the process had gotten his money score up to around $250 million when I saw him. Less than two years later *Forbes* had him up to $500 million. Now past sixty, he is still driving with ever-bigger projects and claims he gets his kicks from tackling such projects at full speed. It doesn't take great personal wealth for such a person in real estate to get on a fast growth curve. As we'll see, banks usually are eager to supply the money in the mall business once you establish credibility as a good operator.

Even more than Mr. Williams, Mr. Simon has a playful approach to life, apparently always has had. He has an owlish face partly covered by large glasses. Some have suggested he resembles Groucho Marx without the mustache. He is apt to show up at his office in a black shirt or at the golf club with orange socks. In his Beverly Hills mansion he has had a life-size dummy of singer Bette Midler sitting on the piano. Even *Shopping Center World* referred to him as "comic." It also called him frank, open, unpretentious, and highly effective.

Also, still more than Mr. Williams, Melvin Simon has a high level of thrust. Tall and lean, he goes through his days somewhat like a whirling dervish. He prizes energy. To that end he fights to keep lean.

"Your weight," he told me, "very directly has a lot to do with your energy." He has sought to lick his problem of excess pounds by going to a Pritikin program, going to the glamorous sweat shop at La Costa, California, and "to a number of other places," and currently was pleased with a new program called "Fit For Life." "It stresses ways to combine foods," he explained.

The way he handles eating is that he has only fruit for breakfast and usually just a salad of some sort for lunch. At dinner he permits himself only one "concentrated food." For example, if he has meat he won't touch potatoes. "If I want any dessert or something sweet I'll wait three hours after my meal." This was a man worth a quarter billion dollars talking about food, a major source of pleasure to most people. He spoke of food primarily as a fodder. And as he talked he was sipping from a can of diet cola.

At each of his four houses — in Fort Lauderdale, Indianapolis, Beverly Hills, and Aspen — he has a treadmill on which he spends close to an hour each morning getting warmed up for a fast day. (He still doesn't have treadmills in his New York and Chicago apartments.)

After I saw him I learned he had picked up a Vanderbilt mansion in south Florida for $6 million. At the time of our visit he was living mainly out of his Fort Lauderdale, Florida, house, where his second wife, Brenda, prefers to spend the cold months and runs her own successful career as an interior designer. Their young son, Joshua, much younger than Mr. Simon's four other offspring, was going to school. Typically, Mr. Simon got there weekends, and then enjoyed using their "small" thirty-seven foot boat. Their Indianapolis-area house is in Carmel, a suburb. It's a large white clapboard house with columns, on twenty acres, and has a tree-lined driveway. They have no live-in help at any of their houses.

Our visit, starting at seven P.M., took place at the family's Manhattan apartment. It's in the new, elegant, high-security Olympic Tower. For central location it's unsurpassed in New York, at the corner of Fifth Avenue facing Rockefeller Center and St. Patrick's Cathedral. He had been traveling around the New York–New Jersey area in his stretch limousine during that day. The block in front of his tower is perhaps the hardest spot in Manhattan to find a parking space. His stretch limo was parked almost directly in front of the tower entrance. What kind of clout, I wondered, was required for such a happy coincidence? After our talk he was going to be driven to a meeting about a mile away and then to a company plane that would whisk him to his Chicago apartment for the night.

The most prominent feature of the apartment's main room, built on two levels, was a great black granite slab for a table. There was a lot of foliage and near the door a computer panel with flashing lights. His daughter Debbie, a plump, quiet TV producer, was there. During our talk his wife called from Fort Lauderdale worried about an approaching hurricane. Also during our talk his daughter-in-law, wife of son David, slipped in and then left with Debbie. David was working at First Boston on mergers and acquisitions.

Mr. Simon explained he had been running ever since he was a hard-driving basketball player at City College in New York, where he had an academic scholarship. He took most of his courses at night so that he could work daytime as an investigator for an accounting firm. His father was a sewing-machine operator.

Of all the self-made centimillionaires I interviewed, Mr. Simon was the only one who made a major effort to get a Master of Business Administration degree, and he almost succeeded. Then he was drafted into the army and was assigned to an army finance center in Indianapolis, which accounts for that city becoming the center of his empire. Since he had a kind of eight-to-four job, he worked late afternoons and into the night selling first encyclopedias and then pots and pans. Upon discharge he planned to go into the cookware business, but his new wife said, "Your education is too good."

So he went to work for a company trying to start a brand-new industry in that area, developing a shopping center. His job was to coax merchants to move their stores to, or set up stores in, the center. He was a good coaxer, and after about five years he began developing his own shopping sites, with the help of his brother. At first he developed filling station sites, then shopping strips, then shopping centers, then finally shopping malls, first open and finally enclosed.

By the time he got into the mall business it was exploding and the best sites near big cities seemed to be taken. So he and his brother (since retired) built their first malls in small cities, first Bloomington, Indiana, and later in Anderson and Muncie, Indiana, and Fort Collins, Colorado.

This gave the brothers their first requirement for being mall builders, "credibility" with bankers, based on their "track record." He said they delivered on promises even when it caused them losses. The second requirement is to find a prime location in terms of "demographic needs," one surrounded by the right kind of prospective customers. The third requirement in building a mall is to persuade some well-established department store to make a commitment to serve as an "anchor." Building shopping malls, he explained, is quite different from building office buildings. The mall can have a kind of monopoly for that area because the big, popular department store is not going to weaken itself by building another store anywhere in that area.

Once you have "credibility," an "anchor," and a good site demographically, Mr. Simon explained, obtaining money from banks is usually remarkably easy. When the banks appraise plans for income-producing real estate they are estimating "not only the bricks and mortar but the actual value you create. So if I have a deal that would cost me $1 million and when I'm finished building it it's worth $2 million, they would lend me 75 percent of the $2 million [1.5 million]. So we were able to borrow more than needed and that's what we used in order to fund our next project."

The projects went on and on, and got bigger and bigger. Malls started in downtown St. Louis and Indianapolis were enormous. By 1985 Melvin Simon & Associates was the nation's number-two mall-builder (second only to Edward DeBartolo of Youngstown, who had had a big head start).

Simon's company had built 120 shopping facilities in twenty-five states and still owned and operated ninety of them.

And by the early 1980s he was into one of the most monumental projects in American history, to create a city within an urban area with largely private funding. This is, of course, Newport City, New Jersey, on the bank of the Hudson facing lower Manhattan. (Readers will recall we discussed this project in reporting on Mr. Sam LeFrak.) At the time I made the appointments to see the nation's biggest apartment landlord (Mr. LeFrak of New York) and to see one of the nation's two biggest mall-builders (Mr. Simon of Indiana), I had no idea they had a project in common. And Mr. LeFrak, when I saw him, had, as related, indicated he was the guiding genius in their common project. Mr. Simon, speaking affectionately of Mr. LeFrak, said:

"I originally had the deal with somebody in Columbus [the Glimcher Company] and I brought Sam into it because Sam has a great expertise in apartments, which I don't have any expertise in at all. . . . He's doing the work on the apartments. We're doing the work on the retailing. And we're doing the office building together and the hotels together. . . . What he says is a little different, but we're partners. . . . It's going to be one of the great projects of this century."

Mr. Simon's great thrust of energy has not been confined just to building a real estate empire. For about six years, starting in the mid-seventies, he was spending a week out of each month seeking to become a movie producer.

He said, "My daughter laughs at me. I thought I could bring some real estate principles to the motion picture industry." The problem was that movie-making was more fantasy than science. He found himself often dealing with flaky people with no regard for budgets. And he had neglected to buy an "anchor" to assure distribution. He stuck to low-budget pictures and a long series of them were bombs. Out of eighteen released, three were successes. The biggest was *Porky's*, a deliberately vulgar comedy about high school boys braving a whorehouse. It was a real box-office hit.

Wearying of reading bad financial reports from Hollywood, he phased out of movies and shifted his excess energies to buying, with his brother, the Indianapolis Pacers basketball team, and the area arena. During their first years of ownership the Pacers were a distinctly unremarkable team. But in basketball-crazy Indiana they still drew good crowds. Simon said they took on the Pacers primarily as a good thing to do for the city. After some losses the ownership was becoming "a wash." But the team did bring a lot of people into downtown stores, including those he was building. He said: "Today a sports team is not an economic deal — I don't care what anybody tells you."

The Simon philanthropies seem to be pretty much confined to local things such as the symphonies in both Fort Lauderdale and Indianapolis and to religious groups. As for a foundation he said, "I think we're putting one together now." All his children seem to be well taken care for by trusts. He said: "They all have their own trusts, you know, which I like to borrow from all the time."

As for their cost of living, which obviously was pretty high but hardly putting a dent in $250 million, all he said was "I'm pretty tight. I don't give anything away. I fight with my wife, I fight with my kids. I fight with all of them not to spend money."

And as for any problem of grasping the size of his fortune, he said, "I never think about it." And he added: "I never make a deal — or look at a deal — as a way to make money. I look at a deal as a challenge."

CHAPTER 8

WEALTH AS A CHALLENGE FOR TRUE-BLUE CAPITALISTS

"I believe the deity has looked with favor on my lifestyle and what I've done and has afforded me opportunities and guidance."

— HARVEY "BUM" BRIGHT of Dallas, Texas

A Dallas columnist told me that Bum Bright was the epitome of the Dallas spirit. Regarding money, long a particularly important status symbol in Texas, Mr. Bright once said a few years ago, "I haven't got enough of that."[1] This was stated at a point when *Texas Business* credited him with being worth $500 million or, as they say in Texas, five units. Such enormous wealth would seem to represent a progress in prosperity that should please anyone, especially since only two years before *Forbes* had put his worth at less than $125 million. Mr. Bright claims, however, that he has always been driven by a fear of going broke.

For a long time he had not gotten much credit in Texas for a man with really heavy money. He was not known as the "king of" or "baron of" anything, even though King Arthur was his hero and a King Arthur scene has long been featured in a tapestry behind his desk.

It was hard for outsiders to get a line on Bum Bright because he usually owned everything he got involved with 100 percent, and he usually had a lot of things going. In short, he is a very private operator, with more than 120 companies in such fields as real estate, mortgages, oil, trucking, insurance, waste incinerators, equipment, manufacturing, and savings and loan. Publications listing just his major involvements would usually end up with "etc."

Being an et cetera man in Texas is not good for the ego but it fit Bum Bright's formula for excelling, with minimum sleepless nights, at capitalism, which he takes very seriously.

And in the mid-eighties Bum Bright suddenly emerged into the limelight as a really big man to reckon with in the Southwest. He was the primary buyer of the Dallas Cowboys in perhaps the biggest deal for a sports team in history. The team plus stadium lease came to more than $80 million.[2] The Bright name started appearing in the skyline over his "bancs" (savings and loan institutions) in Texas. Observers noticed that he was getting a mighty big position in savings and loan. And despite the hard times that Texas had for a while, his net worth by mid-1987, according to *Forbes,* had jumped to $600 million.

The *Wall Street Journal* did a front-page profile on him after the Cowboy deal, and labeled him "The Thrift Tycoon." And the *Dallas Times-Herald,* in a profile by society columnist Nancy Smith, devoted almost a page to a full-color photo of "Bum and Peggy Bright at home." He stood with his military erectness, his iron gray crew cut, horn-rimmed glasses, benign smile; she (his one-time secretary) looked a poised, pleasant, handsome brunette.

Mr. Bright speaks with a really gravelly drawl. And with

me he spoke flat out about how true-blue capitalistic thought dominates his political philosophy: "I am very far out to the right. I'm a rock-ribbed, unrepentant, right-winger." He recalls that when he was checking out Peggy, who had been recommended as a possible secretary, "I went in and told her, 'Little lady, I got to tell you, I don't want any wild-eyed liberal women in here and I want to know what your political philosophy is.' And she said, 'Well, I'll go door to door for Mr. Goldwater and I have been soliciting for him.' And I said, 'That suits me just fine.'" Mr. Goldwater, an ultra conservative, was then running for the U.S. presidency. (Mr. Bright married her after the mother of his four children died.)

Although the Brights aren't particularly social, they live in Highland Park, which socialites consider to be the choicest area in greater Dallas. It is a village inside the city, a village inspired by Beverly Hills, California. The main street in fact is called Beverly Drive.

Fourteen-year-olds too young to drive have stretch limousine parties for friends at night, cruise the city. Many high school girls carry Gucci bags. The high school stadium has box seats.

Highland Park has an occasional grand manor such as that of Ed Cox (net worth $200 million in 1986) sitting back in the woods. Houses run mostly in the $2 million to $8 million range. And the best street in town is Lakeside Drive facing the park and water. It would be hard to get a place there for less than $3 million, and Bum Bright seemed to have the biggest house on this super-elite drive. It's a vast corner house of Tudor design that has seen a few decades and reportedly cost about $5 million. His next-door neighbor in a smaller house is Nelson Bunker Hunt, who in 1986 still had $400 million despite a failure to corner the world's silver market and annoying bankruptcies in a couple of his family operations. Bunker's house was puzzling architecturally, with a cluster of columns toward the right side. Bum Bright said he sees a lot of Bunker.

Inside, the Bright house has a huge living room with a

ten-foot Moroccan-style marble fireplace with columns. Mrs. Bright, politely pleasant, showed me two large libraries while looking for a book we were discussing.

Although they have four servants, Mrs. Bright gets up promptly at 5 A.M. with her husband to prepare his breakfast. He had disciplined himself to operate on a pretty fixed schedule: newspapers 6 to 6:30, and so on.

He wasn't always disciplined. His father nicknamed him Bum because he was unruly, got in trouble for throwing eggs at vehicles, things like that. Dad, a salesman, thought a military school might help straighten his son out; and Mr. Bright has stated that it did help him immeasurably in life. He told me he also had been lucky in his timing. World War II did not disrupt his life as it did for so many others. Pearl Harbor occurred when he was a junior in college so he was in a "hurry-up class" for officer training, and got married before being rushed off to Europe. He became a captain and so was sending good money home to his wife. Since she was living with her folks, the money went straight into the bank.

"When the war was over I had $6,500 in the bank. I had my sit-in money to be able to buy a stack of chips and get a hand in the game."

The game he soon chose was buying and selling oil leases, and he said he was lucky to be in a dynamic environment for such an enterprise. The game was to buy a lease on a few thousand acres for $1 an acre and sell it for $3 an acre.

Old acquaintances have said he has always been a "stroker and leaner." He softened people up by stroking, then leaned and leaned till he got what he wanted. In one case he persuaded the wife of a west Texas farmer not to let her husband in the bedroom until the husband relented and sold Mr. Bright a lease on 5,000 acres. Later, when he got into buying up trucking lines, he showed the same heavy leaning tactics. He chased the part owner of a California trucking firm into the bathroom of a country club to get him to sign an agreement to sell. Then he found that the other part owner, who had been agreeable, had suffered a stroke.

So at the hospital he strapped a pen to that man's hand with a rubber band to enable him to scratch his signature. The man survived.[2]

His empire grew. In the 1970s, when inflation became bothersome, he sought to get some funds into the money-changing business because then, whatever the price of money, you can "just maintain a spread.

"Every time you handle money, well, you take a little cut off of it." Because the movement of money was soaring in response to both inflation and technology, he saw an obvious opportunity to grow. The question was whether to be a banker or go into savings and loans. He found being a banker in Texas involved all sorts of bothersome regulations if you wanted to add new banks. Under Texas law, to add a new bank, you had to have a separate set of offices, separate set of directors, and so forth.

"Whereas in the savings and loan you can branch. . . . All it takes is a storefront, a desk, and a girl and you got a branch." Gradually he exploded into savings and loans. But he still liked the sound of the word *bank*. His son-in-law, who ran the savings and loan operations, sought with the help of a consultant and other officers to come up with a nice ringing name for his major savings and loan company. Mr. Bright said an officer proposed an idea that pleased everybody including him very much: Bright Banc. Mr. Bright explained to me:

"He said everything about it is uplifting. The synonyms: brilliant, shining, shimmering . . . and it rhymes good: bright and right. . . ."

And so it was adopted, and large Bright Banc signs began appearing on many buildings in Texas. Of the sign he said: "It's a savings and loan. If you look it says 'Bright Banc' and in little bitty letters it says savings association."

Regarding the extraordinary diversity of his operations, was it true he deliberately sought, for reasons of safety, to have a lot of pockets in his corporate pants so they never all would be out of funds?

"That's true. We own 100 percent of everything we privately own. Myself and trust for my children. No public shareholders [in the private companies]. And you know with that you can cross-reinforce without conflict of interest. We have identical ownership to everything.

"We file about 120 different tax returns from my floor [in his Dallas office building], and this doesn't count others like Bright Banc or the freight line or the leasing company or the mortgage company. They're on different floors."

This situation led to his novel search for names for his companies.

"If you're going to have a company in Georgia, what would you name it? You've got to come up with a name and if the name is taken you've got to go back with another application. So I started a whole series of companies I just named for rocks or minerals. Antimony Corporation, Azurite, Beryl, Barite, Calcite, Pyrite. They're real estate companies, equipment companies. The name has nothing to do with what they do. . . . Chalcopyrite is an Arkansas real estate company. Wolframite is a California real estate company.

"We ran out of good rocks and we got another series of companies we call the South Seas. That was Sulu, Java, Timor, Celebes, Seran." And then there are the spaghetti companies — Manicotti, Fettucini, Lasagna, and all of those dishes."

Security analysts have suggested that one of the appeals of savings and loan associations to Mr. Bright was that they could supply his other operations with cheap funding.[3]

Mr. Bright's ideas about propriety around his office hark back to an earlier era of capitalistic enterprise. And maybe to King Arthur and his gallant knights. "I do not allow my women to wear britches. They come in a dress and I expect them to look like ladies, act like ladies, talk like ladies, and they are treated like ladies. I don't allow any swearing in the office."

Did he have any lady executives?

"Not on my floor. But we do in the companies. That takes a broader-minded person than I am."

He said a lot of people in the company had been after him to get a company airplane, in vain. "I'm in a position now where they all come to see me. [laugh.] They cannot demonstrate to me the economy of an airplane."

And he can be stern in his private life about unreasonable spending. A few years ago he and Mrs. Bright found themselves in a Honolulu hotel and as usual got up at 5 A.M. to start the day with coffee. They found the hotel café would be closed until 7 A.M. and so went out on the street and finally found a snack bar. It wanted eighty-five cents for a cup of coffee. Outrageous. Mrs. Bright broke down and ordered a cup but Mr. Bright, despite his $500 million, refused the coffee on principle.[4]

The Brights have a 2,400-acre place "with a lot of pine trees" over in Smith County, east Texas, that he gets to about once a year. They also enjoy a "little house" on a fishing lake they share with seventeen other families near Athens, Texas. He said he had an eighty-six-foot boat with a crew of three at Fort Lauderdale, Florida. But he hadn't been on it in seven years. The kids used it and some of his companies use it for entertainment. "It's a good entertainment vehicle." As for himself, he says, "I'm not one that does a lot of going out. I've got a small circle of very close friends. We see each other twice a week (often for poker) and that's about it." He wouldn't dream of going to any of the top night spots around town with their "idiot music."

Mr. Bright's one passion for relaxing seems to be his workshop at the back of the house. He makes all kinds of lead soldiers from molds for his grandchildren. "My wife paints them. As we get close to Christmas, I build dollhouses and doll furniture for the kids."

Mr. Bright is clearly dynasty oriented as well as family oriented. His two daughters and two sons are all married, with a total of twelve grandchildren, and all live within four blocks of him. One son-in-law, as indicated, runs his savings and loan operation; another son-in-law runs his trucking operations. One of the two sons runs field operations in the oil business. But the second son has been a vexing problem. He is not in the family business.

"He does not like to work in the family business because he says, 'When you're down there you have to do everything just like Daddy says to do it.' I said, 'Son, you broke the code. That's the rule down here. I am the boss and we will follow my policies.' And so he has now elected to go back to school and try to become a lawyer."

In any case all the sons and daughters and in-laws and grandchildren along with a mother-in-law — a total of twenty-one people — gather at the Brights' spacious home every Sunday night.

"They get here at six o'clock. We feed them and the kids all play together.... We do this every Sunday. A rigorous thing. The families mix."

Mr. Bright has served on an appropriate number of civic boards and was currently chairman of Children's Medical Center. That center and Texas A&M, his alma mater, have been recipients of his main philanthropies. His term as head of the board of regents at Texas A&M was marked by some interesting controversies. He fought to keep women out of the all-male marching band. And he followed sound capitalist logic on how to make the college thrive: Get more money from alumni. To do that, get a winning football team, which he felt meant getting a hot coach. So he pushed through a deal to lure a hot coach with a six-year contract for $1.6 million. That divided out to $267,000 a year, which hurt some feelings. It happened to be vastly more than the president, the deans, or any of the most eminent professors made.

We got to talking about money. Would Mr. Bright keep on working on his 7 A.M. to 6 P.M. schedule if he wasn't making money at it? He guessed he would and alluded to his fondness for poker. Money was a way of keeping score.

I inquired why, since he had always been worried about going broke, he didn't in effect cash in his chips now, put his hundreds of millions in Treasuries and enjoy life. My suggestion was particularly plausible because within a couple of years the ailing Texas economy put considerable pressure on him to try to ease out of the Cowboy ownership and make other major adjustments. The idea of selling out, however, bothered him. He indicated two objections. First, this long-held fear of going broke emerged. He mentioned that his next-door neighbor, Nelson Bunker Hunt, had a couple of companies in bankruptcy. (But Bunker hadn't put his money in Treasuries! He had in fact been a relentless big-time plunger.) Second, the work he did was fun and gave him a sense of achievement. If skiing was more fun he'd move to Colorado.

He alluded to painters and sculptors who kept right on creating until they dropped. Others among my thirty interviewees also made the comparison between themselves and famous painters who refused to quit and usually mentioned Picasso or Braque, who were still going strong in their eighties or nineties. Mr. Bright said, "I guess Van Gogh painted until he died."

Technically he was correct. Van Gogh whipped out more than a hundred paintings, including some of his best, during his last year of life. But he had cut off an ear and for a while stayed in an insane asylum. He shot himself at the age of thirty-seven.

At any rate Mr. Bright has resolved to try not ever to be a burden on society. Despite his $500 million in net worth at the time, he was keeping his family strictly on a $200,000-a-year budget.[5]

Whatever his fears of going broke, if he had just put his half billion in a safe with orders that the money go toward a Bright family budget of $200,000 a year, it would take 2,500 years before the family would be down to its last $200,000.

CHAPTER 9

WEALTH

AS AN INCIDENTAL

ASPECT OF LIFE

"I was always a full-time hospital staff person never interested in private practice. I was not interested in money making."

— DR. LASZLO TAUBER,
Potomac, Maryland

Dr. Tauber proved to be a slight, formal, good-humored, very soft-voiced man past seventy. He was in full operating garb including mask and cloth sacks over his shoes when we met in his office. A few minutes earlier he had just finished an operation and there was a chance he might soon go into another involving an eight-year-old child. The child was bleeding in the liver and he was waiting for the results of two tests before deciding whether to operate. One report came in as we talked.

Surgery has been the passion of his life, and he insisted

he has never let any other interest significantly interfere with that. He said he has virtually no social life. He did, however, have an interesting sideline.

That was building buildings, especially enormous buildings. Some he had never bothered to look at after they were completed. He got into building largely to obtain money to fulfill a dream of having his own hospital. That way he could escape the handicaps he faced for years as an immigrant doctor. In the process he became, among other things, the largest landlord of the U.S. government. And he had found himself an absorbing hobby.

His awesome success in building in the Washington suburbs was clearly aided by a trend. The federal government had elected to try to ease the congestion of downtown Washington by renting office space in the suburbs.[1]

Dr. Tauber came to America with $700 in 1947. Earlier, during World War II, he had escaped from a Nazi concentration camp in Hungary. When I saw him, *Forbes* put his net worth at $300 million. Dr. Tauber thought that was probably a little low. By 1987 the publication's richest 400 list had him up to $450 million.

Tauber was raised in a primarily Jewish neighborhood in Budapest by his mother and an uncle. The famous Gabor sisters were raised nearby and he knew them well. Laszlo Tauber became a nationally famous gymnast. And he managed to get acceptance into a medical school despite a quota on Jews. During the Nazi occupation Tauber did not at first have to wear the yellow Star of David because (1) his father had died fighting in World War I, (2) he was a national athletic hero, and (3) there was an acute shortage of doctors. By 1944, however, all exceptions were wiped out and he was swept up in the Holocaust. He was doing forced labor in a camp where mass murder was occurring. As the Russians approached, the Nazis began moving the camp and in the confusion Tauber escaped and went to serve in a vast ghetto hospital. At the age of twenty-nine he was chief resident of surgery at a hospital that served most of the 250,000 Jews still locked in Budapest.

After the war he studied neurosurgery in Sweden and got

a traveling fellowship that eventually brought him to the U.S.A. At about that time tens of thousands of U.S. military doctors were resettling into civilian life, and foreign doctors without U.S. certification were scarcely welcomed. Neither his Hungarian certification as a general surgeon nor his medical degree was recognized. In order to establish some sort of medical connection, he finagled a teaching fellowship by borrowing $1,600 from the Jewish Social Service and donating it to George Washington University. The university then paid him that amount of money minus taxes. "So I got $116 a month. That was my salary." He said it was a "very sad situation" that in the early days he got more help from gentile colleagues than from Jewish colleagues.

The reason he ended up in the District of Columbia was that "this was the only place in the United States of America [except Indiana] where a foreign graduate could take the license of examination without having first papers for citizenship." He readily passed the exams despite his heavily accented English. He said some of the people at George Washington University began seeing him as competition and told him goodbye. In pleading with the chief, he cited his hero Abraham Lincoln. That was not helpful because the administrator, a Virginian, disliked Lincoln.

"I tried to get a job and I could not get a job at all. So I opened a general practice on Good Hope Road in the District of Columbia and worked day and night. In nine months I had one of the largest practices in Washington as a general practitioner." And one hospital let him do surgery on his own general practice patients.

"For twelve years I did not even take a day off, not a day off. Average sixty, eighty patients a day." That included, almost every day, some surgery. Eventually one hospital, then others, accepted him as being somehow a staff member. And eventually some even recognized him as a surgeon.

Meanwhile he was putting his money into real estate and gradually set a goal, among others, to build his own hospital.

Grateful patients gave him tips on investment. He started in the early 1950s by building a small apartment building in a blue-collar neighborhood, largely with bank loans. His

Hungarian mother was shocked. Mixing business with doctoring was a shameful thing in the old country. Soon he found another cheap piece of land and built a shopping center–residential complex in Bethesda, and it quickly was surrounded by elite homes. In expanding the complex by adding a big office building, he landed his first federal tenant and signed the government to a ten-year lease.[2]

Tauber learned to love having the U.S. government as a tenant. Its credit-rating was A-plus. It had to accept the lowest bid. It usually wanted plain, uncomplicated buildings. For a while it was willing to take buildings erected on cheap land zoned for industrial use costing him, say, $1 a square foot instead of on "commercial" land that would cost $4 or $5 a foot. The competition screamed foul, but he knew the regulations. There was nothing in them that prevented Tauber from doing this.

He would borrow the full appraised value, say, $50 million, and by keeping his staff and other overhead low come in with a building that cost $35 million. That gave him $15 million to use to start on his next project. And so he constructed several vast buildings to house federal office workers. The largest, in Rockville, Maryland, housing 7,000 Health and Human Service people, was for a time one of the largest privately owned office buildings on the East Coast and in 1984 was estimated to be worth $150 million.[3]

Tauber explained: "If I had rented to private tenants I could have made much more money, but I could lose more money. I'm satisfied with long-term government leases." He said you can forget them and added, "You cannot do surgery and worry about tenants."

As he prospered at real estate while working full-time as a doctor, he took action to become a full-time surgeon and rid himself of general practice. He built his own sparkling 120-bed hospital in Alexandria, Virginia. At first he managed it personally. "When I was in charge, no patient was turned down." If a patient didn't have money, he said come in anyhow. "I cannot see empty beds. So when I was in charge there was 90 percent occupancy or higher. I never made a penny." But handling management details interfered with his surgery, so he leased the management to a company and just collected rent. "Now these people are running it and they have 60 percent of the beds [in use] and they make $2 million a year profit." He remained medical director and chief of surgery.

A former real estate associate recalls that he often got Dr. Tauber on the phone at the hospital when he was not operating and asked for instructions. "We'd say we need so many million tons of concrete, so many hundred thousand linear feet of sheetrock. He would think a second and say, 'No, that's too much.' Then he'd give you the right number."[4]

Originally he had a good friend from childhood running his real estate company. During that long period it really was true "that 5 percent of my work was in business and 95 percent here. Now unfortunately, because my friend died, I have to pay more attention. . . . I have a tremendous amount of work, usually after I go home.

"Officially I have an office but I never go there. We have in one of our buildings a large office with about twenty-five people . . . but I am [there] just through the telephone line. I don't think I spend five hours a year there, physically.

"Everything that we built, I planned it." He said that in some cases he never saw the inside of the buildings after they were finished. "I am not kidding with you. I did not even go in. I was not interested." During the days when he was still in general practice, his builder would ride in the car while Dr. Tauber made house calls. "We talked when we were driving." And he insisted, "Nobody can interrupt me when I am doing surgery."

In the late 1970s, with interest rates soaring, Tauber switched from building buildings to buying and managing them. These were not only in the Washington area but in Pennsylvania and New York City. While in New York one day, he was curious to see a great penthouse in a building at Park Avenue and 57th Street that he had owned for nine years but had never entered. The penthouse was being leased by a major Texas millionaire. Tauber, the landlord, was told that special permission was required from the Texan's office, so he said forget it.

Dr. Tauber has a large white French provencal house he and his wife designed on forty-two acres in so-called horse country, twenty-five minutes from his office. It has a stable because his second wife, a former nurse, is into breeding horses, dressage horses.

He calls the house "very nice but not obnoxious. Over 10,000 square feet." In essence he got the house free because he bought 136 acres, got his money back by selling nearly 100 acres, and used the money to build his own house.[5] He says of his household: "[My wife] has two girls working in the barn and one gardener and two ladies with the housecleaning and cooking. They are living in, all."

As for himself, he watches his dollars. Not counting housing, he said his total living costs don't amount to $10,000 a year. He was outraged to have to pay $120 a night for a hotel room in New York, so he bought a small cooperative there that he gets to maybe three times a year. Also he has a two-bedroom condominium at Key Biscayne, Florida, and in Jerusalem he has a condominium that he has never seen. His children wanted it. Mostly he drives to work himself in an old Cadillac and has never had a bodyguard. "If somebody wants to get me," no number of bodyguards would help.

He has a grown son and daughter whom he talks with almost every day. The son, a scientist in Boston, is a world authority on one part of the white blood cells. Dr. Tauber has an agreement regarding money with his son. "If he stays in academic medicine, as I always wanted to, then I give him twice his salary as a bonus. And if he goes into private practice I give him nothing." The son is married with four children. Tauber's unmarried daughter is a doctor in clinical psychology in San Francisco. He says if one day goes by and he does not call her, she calls and asks: "You remember you have a daughter?"

Dr. Tauber gives quite a bit of thought to philanthropy. In the last few years he has given about $8 million to hospitals that have been important in his life and to Holocaust studies. More interesting, he has searched out and found about fifty persons he was involved with in his early European days, both gentile and Jew, and has put them on his payroll.

His major philanthropy is still to come and it will be a whopper. Upon his death 20 percent of his fortune goes directly into a Tauber Foundation. If we are dealing with, say, a $400 million fortune, that would mean about $80 million would go directly into the foundation, and the remaining $320 million would go into trusts for the two grown children and thence to the grandchildren. But he makes a fascinating stipulation. The children and grandchildren can never touch the capital. And each can draw from interest earned each year no more than the salary of the president of the United States, currently $250,000. "The rest stays in trust. I don't feel sorry for anybody that they have to live on the salary of the president."

At a modest investment growth of say 7 percent a year, the children's trusts, right off the bat, would be earning about 100 times the president's salary. By the time the grandchildren die, the trusts should be growing by hundreds of millions — perhaps a billion — dollars every year.

Upon the death of the grandchildren all the money is to go in to the Tauber Foundation to make it perhaps the biggest foundation of all time.

And then what is supposed to happen? One quarter of those billions is to go to the governments of Israel and the Netherlands. And three-quarters — the great bulk — is to go as a donation to the government of the land that has been so good to him, the U.S.A.

June Hunt's Quest
for Nonfinancial Riches

Miss Hunt of Dallas is technically a great heiress but has never bothered to act like one. She has what she feels are much more important matters on her mind. In 1986 her net worth was somewhere between $200 and $400 million.

To put her in perspective we need to look first at the families, real and alleged, of H. L. Hunt. What he wrought in the way of family complications and in-fighting makes the TV *Dallas* carryings-on seem tepid. The complications illuminate the problems of trying to create an ongoing family dynasty in the real world of today.

H. L. Hunt of course was the legendary oil wild-catter and professional gambler who for several years was known as the richest man in the world. He is said to have won his first oil well in a poker game. Politically he was farther to the right than a monarch. He published a slim book proposing a novel constitutional amendment that would recognize that persons of wealth should be given considerably more say in how the government was run than ordinary citizens. Individuals of great substance should be allowed many more votes in an election than people of modest substance. At the polling box the number of votes a person could cast would be based on how many dollars in taxes he or she paid.

Mr. Hunt lived to be eighty-five. He carried his lunch to work in a brown paper bag and insisted that his family eat apricots in some form at virtually every meal — apricot cobblers, apricot whips, apricot cake — so that he could get (and ingest) the meat from the seeds, which he believed to be extraordinarily health-giving.

A biographer of the Hunt dynasty, Harry Hurt III, says: "H. L. Hunt thought he carried a genius gene. He believed that by fathering children he was doing the world a favor."[6] Just how many children he created or how many women he married has been a matter of argument. He had two wives officially, and a third woman living in Tampa, Florida, claimed she had been married to him and bore four of his children. She said she knew him as "Major Franklin Hunt."[7] There is always the possibility, of course, that her claim to a married relationship began when she learned that H. L. Hunt was a man of enormous wealth. But there seems to be some record of at least the claim of a childbearing relationship. A breakdown of what the Hunt "family" owned, published in the *New York Times*, lists as part of the "family" the "Children of H. L. Hunt and Franie Tye."[8] Their assets were described as unknown. At any rate, her claim to being a wife was energetically contested both before and after Mr. Hunt's death. Hurt states that payments in the millions were made. If the marital claim had gotten legal affirmation, Mr. Hunt would have been guilty of bigamy for several years, which might well have created acute problems regarding inheritance.

So when people talk of the Hunt family of Dallas they are really talking of two (or three) families with little love lost between them, money especially being a source of contention. The alleged "family" headed by the alleged Major Franklin Hunt is often referred to as the third family. At one point in the early 1980s the money of families created by H. L. Hunt amounted to $6 or $7 billion.

The family usually referred to as the "first family" — and the most celebrated — consisted of the six offspring of H. L. and Lyda Hunt: Nelson Bunker, Lamar, Herbert, Hassie, Margaret, and Caroline. The three first-mentioned "boys" — bulky Bunker (who seems to cultivate an unkempt look), Lamar, and Herbert — have pretty much carried on in their father's pattern of grand-scale wheeling and dealing, but with some spectacular failures. The fourth son, Hassie, has long had a severe medical ailment. His stake of about $400 million has usually been watched over by sister Margaret, the oldest of the offspring and reportedly the one who takes charge at first family business meetings. Caroline, the one who is often called the richest woman in the world, is a folksy person who lives in a fairly modest house (one-story) by Highland Park standards, and had owned a chain of super-luxurious hotels such as the Mansion in Dallas and the Bel Air in the Los Angeles area. Since she is crazy about pumpkins she has usually insisted that her ultra-chic restaurants carry desserts involving this ingredient.

In 1982, when *Forbes* could find only fourteen billionaires in America, five of the fourteen were first family Hunts.

The three active "boys" then fell onto hard times. First (and
even before the *Forbes* listing) they were caught up in a
spectacular, suspenseful, and finally futile move in 1980, led
by Bunker, to corner the world's silver market. Then oil
prices fell. And they were caught in some unfortunate commodity plays. The three of them suffered the biggest dollar
loss within a family in American history, mainly because of
their problems with their Placid Oil Co. In 1986 when they
sought protection from creditors to reorganize under Chapter 11, they were estimated by *Time* to have between them
barely a billion in remaining assets that would be hard for
creditors to get at. Meanwhile Margaret and Caroline, who
kept clear of most of their brothers' speculations, were still
billionaires or near billionaires.

Which brings us to H. L. Hunt's extremely interesting
"second family." Author Harry Hurt III has provided in some
detail his version of how it came about.[9] The essential facts
are these. A beautiful, cheerful, intelligent, and spiritually
inclined woman named Mrs. Raymond Wright or Mrs. Ruth
Ray Wright lived in a brick bungalow within a few blocks of
H. L. Hunt's place, a copy of George Washington's Mt. Vernon residence. She had once worked as a secretary for Mr.
Hunt's oil company and she had four handsome children:
Ray, June, Helen, and Swanee. They were in or approaching
their teens when they came to public prominence. Two
years after Mr. Hunt's first wife died he married Ruth Ray
Wright.

Some years ago *Time*, in mentioning young June's career, called her a stepdaughter of H. L. Hunt. For three years
Forbes, in describing this second family, said H. L. Hunt
"legitimized" it by marrying Ruth Ray Wright, and added
that H. L. "long kept [the two] families secret from each
other." In 1986 it dropped the reference to "legitimized"
children and simply stated he adopted the kids at the time
of marriage, but it retained the reference to his having "long
kept [the two] families secret from each other."

At any rate, H. L. demonstrated considerable fondness
for the children. When he had guests he often asked June,

who had a lovely voice, to sing during dinner. And H. L. Hunt created a considerable commotion in his first family by naming Ray of the second family as the sole executor of his will.

Relations between the two families were strained at best. One of the only times they came together and joined forces was to try to head off the attack on the will by the third family.

The second family offspring were a notably different breed from those in the first family. Swanee, for example, married a minister and studied for a doctorate in pastoral care. In 1985 she explained: "Instead of trying to change what I was born — a Hunt — I'm trying to change what the name 'Hunt' stands for."[10] Helen taught at a predominantly black high school before marrying a commodities man.[11] While the brothers of the first family were sinking into trouble, Ray greatly expanded the quite large inherited fortune of the second family by success in oil and Texas real estate. He built the dramatic Reunion Tower which dominates a part of downtown Dallas, and he has won much admiration by being very active in civic affairs.

The leaders of Dallas have had a hard time figuring out how to treat the principal Hunt families. *The Dallas Social Directory* in 1985 included no members of the second family but included four of the first family (Caroline, Margaret, Bunker, and Herbert). On the other hand, the most exclusive men's club in Dallas, the Idlewild Club, which is the closest thing to an Old Guard, has Ray as a member but none of his half-brothers.[12]

Ray is caretaker of the second family's assets, which *Forbes* put at "more than a billion" in 1986. The magazine made the assumption that the mother and her four offspring were each worth at least $200 million. Some months later a *New York Times* article put the second family's total assets at $2 billion.[13] Well, whatever. If so, June might be worth close to $400 million. In any case she has big money.

So let's get to our focus on June Hunt of the second family. June was second born and grew up with the nickname

Peaches. She recalls that her mother always kept a plaque in the kitchen: "Bloom where you are planted."

June bloomed both before and after being transplanted into the Mt. Vernon home of the world's richest man at the time. She has claimed she knew nothing about the Hunt wealth until a classmate mentioned it. Her references to father Hunt are invariably fond, even when she tells about the apricots or of having to memorize his charts on how much electricity is wasted if various-sized light bulbs are left on.

At Southern Methodist University near her home she majored in music, was in the student senate, and won an award for outstanding contribution. She had become deeply committed to religion and after college she was director first of the Junior High Division and later the College and Career Division of the vast First Baptist Church of Dallas with its tens of thousands of members. This role led naturally to invitations to speak on such subjects as "The Bible Can Be Fun." And she found she could speak better if she combined it with singing and strumming her guitar.

Soon she was devoting almost full time to her personal evangelical ministry, talking and singing in her warm, strong voice, whether to people in nursing homes, to college audiences, or to embassy personnel in North Yemen. The noted evangelist Billy Graham, a kindred soul in regard to religion, wrote a nice foreword to her book *Above All Else*, mainly a collection of her talks on religious themes. He described her as "an affluent young lady" who had chosen "to describe materialism in terms of the Christian faith." She dedicated the book to "my father." In a chapter on "Humility — Just Plain Folks," she wrote: "Because of Dad's industries, Mom has often had the responsibility for entertaining visiting royalty, important diplomats and well-known celebrities ... however, she has never been too busy for her children. Many nights Mom and I sit propped up on her bed talking. ... Her sense of humor is beautiful and we laugh a lot."

June Hunt is busy enough to need two offices. When I saw her she was unmarried and in her early forties, with well-rounded cheeks and golden hair.

She was living on a circle in what might be called a lower-upper-class part of greater Dallas. Her pleasant one-story, two-bedroom house was surrounded by larger two-story houses. There were cow horns by the entrance and a sign on the door saying "Welcome." Directly inside the door was a sweeping area combining living and dining rooms.

Despite the sign and a pleasant greeting, we got off to a rather rocky start because a family lawyer was there with a 600-word agreement I was supposed to sign before talking to Miss Hunt. It provided protections against uses of material from our talk I had never dreamed of. Despite having traveled hundreds of miles specifically to see her, I prepared to depart. The lawyer started suggesting deletions. We deleted for about half an hour until we got it down to a simple agreement to let her see a transcript of our talk and correct any errors (which I would have been glad to do anyhow). Once the lawyer departed, Miss Hunt and I got along fine. She took me through a kind of playroom, which had an ancient telephone on the wall, to the back porch, where there were redwood swing chairs.

In back, there was a deep, shaded lawn with a hammock near the rear. Her Oldsmobile was parked by the porch. She mentioned that after our talk she could drive me back to my hotel but that turned out not to be necessary.

In the course of our extended talk, luncheon (to my surprise) was served for the two of us at a long table. It consisted of a nice little corn soup, salad, small vegetable-based delicacies, and a sherbert. Before we dined she said a two-minute grace that ended with her putting in a good word to the Lord for me.

She explained that the three-year-old house was "just country" so that people coming in, for example, to her Bible classes could feel "real comfortable" there. The living room–dining room was designed to create an openness, to permit the gathering of good-sized groups. She said: "Okay, what we do is tomorrow night we will have this place transformed. It will be full of chairs. We'll have maybe sixty people here and microphones and overhead projector. There's a screen there that I pull down and I use that for words to music. You start out and you have about thirty minutes of music where we just sing what I call Heart Christian music. Then for the next hour and a half we have a group discussion over the homework that's been done. I teach a course where people have done about five hours of homework a week. Right now we are in Genesis.

"We finished a year-long study of the Book of John last year. Before that we had done a course on the Sermon on the Mount, a four-month course. Another four-month course we did was the Book of Judges.

"My bottom line," she said, "is to change lives. . . . I feel that Jesus Christ in the life makes a difference." And the change does not always just involve teaching groups. Recently a young woman in one of her classes confided she was in a mess of trouble with divorce from a drinking husband. June Hunt said she assured the woman, "We'll walk with you through this."

When she travels — which is much of the time — to do her talks and singing, she usually takes a guitar with her. Some of her songs are not conducive to the guitar. In that case she will use background tapes for music.

She has no set fee. Usually organizations will pay expenses. "I never ask for anything more. They usually give an honorarium, but I don't even know what it is. I feel that God has been more than gracious to me."

Did she have her own plane for her travels?

"The same one that you do. Any one that will take me. I love it when I fly. There is a type of work that I get to do on airplanes that is so much harder for me to do when I'm in my own office because on the plane I have uninterrupted time . . . no telephones. Or if I am in an airport it never bothers me if I have to wait. I'm always carrying plenty of things to work on or to read. . . . Most always I fly coach." She usually manages to get an aisle seat with a vacant seat beside her. And when possible she gets a seat up next to the first-class partition "so that people don't lay down in your lap."

When she travels, she said, she is usually by herself. And sometimes she does get a little uptight about things going wrong. For example:

"I was not very smart and took a tour during the month of December in Montana. I flew to Denver and the plane out of Denver was eight hours delayed. I was supposed to get into Butte around ten in the evening. I got in around four in the morning. And we were kept waiting and waiting and waiting for the luggage." One man who was waiting began losing control of himself, became almost violent. Miss Hunt recalled: "I felt sorry for him because . . . he just apparently did not know how to accept the sovereign things that you cannot change."

Finally an airline attendant explained that they couldn't get the plane's baggage compartment door open because it was iced over. They had even tried a blow torch. The passengers were advised that the plane was leaving and that the airline would send the baggage back from the next stop.

"I thought, oh my goodness." Not only her clothing but her sound equipment and her guitar and everything were departing and she had a talk-sing program at noon. After a brief nap she rented a guitar at Pete's Guitar Shop and the show went on.

Her personal possessions, she said, consist almost entirely of what I saw on my visit: her one house and her Oldsmobile. She has no boat. She used to jog but says, "It never was a joy." Her great joys have been racquetball and skiing. As for hobbies, she says she is too busy for them.

About a decade ago she evaluated what she was doing. She had let herself get on the boards of a number of things. "I got off of as many things as I could and only would take those things which would enable me better to reach the target."

How did she address the fact that she was one of the richest people in the country?

"I just don't think about it. I really don't."

She lives on, at most, a few hundred thousand dollars a year.

One of her pleasures is giving money to organizations that are seriously in the business of changing people's lives. The example she mentioned was an organization that supports churches for the deaf.

"Many people," she said, "do not realize that having a name that is readily identifiable with money can be a tremendous disadvantage." She has had people come up to her after presentations and apologize and ask forgiveness because they came there ready to shoot her down.

Miss Hunt said she was in the process of starting something called The Cornerstone Foundation, but hadn't figured it all out yet. On her tape *Who Is June Hunt?*, she says, "Money can't buy happiness. Not the deep inner peace that faith in Jesus gives." Her richness comes, she says, from sharing her faith with others.

B.

Ways of Using Wealth

CHAPTER 10

SEEKING TO

LIVE IT UP

"Wealth unused might as well not exist."
— AESOP

There is a widespread assumption among Americans that the richer you are the more magnificent your place or places of abode. People of great wealth are supposed to live in grand manors with vast, carefully tended grounds. And they are supposed to be absorbed with the highest levels of high society. This notion that centimillionaires and billionaires develop life-styles appropriate to their incredible net worth is — I discovered — largely fantasy. Given the size of great modern-day fortunes, it simply takes too much bother and grand-scale imagining for most extremely wealthy people even to try to live in a style befitting their wealth.

Malcolm Forbes, the wealthy publisher of *Forbes*, is one who finds it fun to try. He has maintained grand mansions in several parts of the world, and entertains on one of the world's most expensive private boats. He is prone to throwing private or company parties that run into the hundreds of thousands, or millions, of dollars. In 1987 he had a fleet of thirty-three helicopters and a fleet of 300 limousines bring notables to a party on his estate in Far Hills, New Jersey, where they were greeted by 100 bagpipers. Yet he remains on his magazine's list of the 400 richest Americans.

We'll meet, shortly, a few others who make a gesture at trying to live in a manner appropriate to their wealth, but even most of these do not do it for the sake of conspicuous display. Robert Guccione lives in a dazzling mansion but it is used partly for business purposes. Leslie Wexner has some exceptionally splendid houses, but he is a very private man and rarely stages even medium-size parties. Terry Allen Kramer, in contrast, is one who seems to love conspicuous display. She really works at acquiring palatial homes. Also, she runs with the jet-setters and throws grand-scale parties. The more conspicuous thing about her though, to me, is that she is an heiress seriously seeking to build a career of her own. (See chapter 12.)

In general there is not only the sense of futility that many feel in even trying to live in a style appropriate to their wealth, but apprehension that doing so would make one conspicuous to criminals. This too forestalls display. Also, today's enormously rich people may find that their status with comparably rich peers, especially old-money peers, is enhanced if they strive for a genteel life-style (however that is defined). A number of centimillionaires I saw have suffered snubs from people with far less money. People today who are rich enough to buy anything they want do not necessarily constitute any kind of social elite.

Opulent life-styles today are largely confined to the people of substantial wealth in the $10 to $40 million range. It is easier for them to make the effort, and they may be more prone to status-striving.

Private ballrooms in particular — which used to be a must for people seeking recognition for achieving wealth — have become a rarity in the houses of the rich during the past quarter century. They require the type of mansions that have gone out of date. The major balls almost all take place in decorated hotel ballrooms where the guests feel good about dancing for some disease. Status is largely assigned on the basis of who gets invited to whose place for the pre-ball parties.

If you want to display your status by having a really *big* place, you are caught up in competing with people such as little Joe Hrudka, former drag racer from Cleveland who made a modest-size fortune selling auto parts. Mr. Hrudka is fascinated with grand houses. He bought Roundwood, a forty-three-room estate in Hunting Valley, the elite Cleveland suburb. It took a couple million dollars to fix it up. He also bought the great mansion once owned by F. Woolworth Donahue right on the ocean on the Gold Coast of Palm Beach, Florida. He picked up a third mansion in Palm Springs, California. At last report he was building a really big place (the size of twenty-five average houses) in snooty Scottsdale, Arizona. Harry Reasoner of CBS asked an old-time socialite in Palm Beach if Mr. Hrudka was being welcomed into the community. The man would only say, "You really can't buy your way into Palm Beach." A lot would depend on whether Mr. Hrudka sought to be "low key" or would seek "high exposure."[1]

Finally, if uniqueness is sought, taking the grand-manor approach is likely to be an enormous bother. The biggest private residence in America is Biltmore House, in the mountains near Ashville, North Carolina. It was built by George Washington Vanderbilt, who already had a big place in Newport, Rhode Island. It has 250 rooms and more employees, including forty gardeners. It is still in the family but no one tries to live in it in style. The manor turns a profit because a steady line of paying tourists goes through it.[2]

At South Salem, New York, one of the manor houses built by J. P. Morgan on thirty-two acres is now the site of a large, elite restaurant. And not far away in Garrison, New York, Dick's Castle, overlooking the Hudson River, soars eighty-six feet high and is on a ninety-three-acre site. As planned at the turn of the century, it was to contain fifty-two rooms but was not fully completed. In 1986 it could be bought for a mere $2.5 million.

In Greenwich, Connecticut, where there were once many great estates, most of the larger ones now are either being torn down, turned into schools or clubs, or used as centerpieces for subdivisions. Elsewhere it is the same, estates becoming corporate retreats or nonprofit seminar centers, or community centers, or posh apartment buildings. Such places often show up as the grand residences of cinema.

During my travels to visit some of the richest people in the land I did not find a single host living in a thirty-or-more room manor. About a dozen of the extremely wealthy people I visited lived in fine, large — but not enormous — houses. Five or six were living on a grand enough scale to warrant a Wow! Here we will visit with three who have experienced grand-scale living — and will introduce two others who are living well and whom we'll come back to later in connection with their interesting philosophies.

The Mansion That Porn Built

Robert Guccione himself did much of the design for the one really palatial homestead I encountered in my travels. I say palatial because he built a place that would tickle any prince. It has been called the largest private residence in Manhattan. What he did was merge two grand six-story townhouses and totally redo them onto nine levels. This creation sits on a street in the 60s between Fifth Avenue and Park Avenue. In short, it is in the heart of New York's zillionaire territory. Dozens of centimillionaires or billionaires live within a half mile of him. He doesn't socialize much except for business and some of his ultra-rich neighbors might be nervous about throwing a welcoming party for him anyhow.

The 1987 *Forbes* put his worth at about $350 million, up from $220 million when I visited him. He is a publisher and movie and cassette maker, best known for his primary product, *Penthouse* magazine. Riding the trend of high sexuality, he produced the first major magazine to present frontal views of handsome naked females tiddling with their sexual organs. As he explained it to me: "The so-called pubic war between *Penthouse* and *Playboy* really began when *Penthouse* published the first unretouched full frontal nudes showing pubic hair. It took *Playboy* a long time to follow us." (The rival may have been nervous about losing advertisers.)

The residence he created cost $20 million, according to *Forbes,* and the art masterpieces in it, Mr. Guccione advised me, had a value of another $20 million. He has said it costs him $3 million a year just to maintain the house. Presumably he passes off some of this to his company because he also uses the house as office, studio, and for entertaining advertisers.

To get into the residence you must pass guards. Mr. Guccione mentioned that he has a bodyguard everywhere he goes, but guards presumably were also needed to protect the art. There is a grand staircase that leads up to a ballroom foyer. The ballroom itself, with side salons, stretches for seventy feet. On one side, set into the floor, Mr. Guccione designed a twelve-foot-long mosaic that would please a Roman emperor.

The dining room table is a fifteen-foot slab of marble. On another floor there is the regal swimming pool under a great chandelier. Attached to silver-laced mosaic tiles on the walls are bronze lighting sconces in the form of women touching their breasts. Anyone swimming in the pool, however, must wear a bathing suit. I saw no nude playgirls running around his pool or elsewhere.

Mr. Guccione, after two divorces, has been living for many years with his "life partner," Kathy Keeton, who pretty much handles the staff supervision of the magazines. (In 1987 they were finally talking publicly of marrying.) She came in from work in leather pants, gave Mr. Guccione a peck on the cheek, nodded to me, and headed for her quarters. Ms. Keeton is rather solemn with straight hair and an almond-shaped face. She was a dancer earlier in her career. The bath Mr. Guccione designed for her has marble Corinthian columns and a gold-leaf toilet seat. the toilet and bidet were carved from solid blocks of marble, while the 24-karat gold water taps are shaped like swans. The bathroom is further decorated by a Picasso and a Dali.

Photos I had seen of Mr. Guccione suggested he perpetually wore a jaded, aristocratic frown. He greeted me with a loose shirt open to the breastbone and gold chains hanging from his neck and wrist. He occasionally smiled, and explained the frown by saying he hated to be photographed. In a deep voice he tended occasionally to produce lofty platitudes, but in general he was forthright.

Carrying a can of Pepsi in his hand, he proudly showed me some of his finer works of art. He believes he has the best private collection of Impressionist and Expressionist art in the country. In the ballroom foyer, for example, there were a Van Gogh, a Renoir, a Matisse, and a Pissaro. In the ballroom there were two Rouaults, two paintings by Degas, a Chagall, and a recent acquisition that particularly pleased him, a Modigliani called "Young Man with Red Hair." He had to pay $1,750,000 for it. Another recent acquisition that pleased him was the Botticelli of a woman freeing herself from a chastity belt. In a nearby Georgian room there were a Vlaminck, a Léger, a Holbein, a Gauguin. A description of his art work fills six typewritten pages.

Mr. Guccione also has his own small movie theater, where he mostly watches scientific documentaries. He is a science enthusiast, publishes a handsomely crafted science magazine called *OMNI*, has invested in a nuclear fusion device, and has produced a series of TV documentaries that have appeared in sixty countries, including China.

He admitted that power fascinates him. The subtitle he put on *OMNI* was "The Science of Power." His favorite spectator sport is boxing. One reason he had produced the movie *Caligula* and was producing one on Catherine the Great was that they were persons of total power. (Also they had interesting sex lives.) He said he hopes to create America's largest private corporation, and without partners or major loans.

The son of a New Jersey accountant, he skipped college to try being an artist in Italy and later in France and England. As he accumulated a family, he took odd jobs as a cook, a movie extra, a detective, a cartoonist. In England he looked in the Help Wanted section under "Management and Executive." He explained, "Having had no managerial or executive experience in my life I assumed, bathed in my own self-esteem, that if I was going to work (seriously) I should work as a manager or as an executive." He landed a job as general manager of England's oldest dry-cleaning firm and says he started the first 24-hour pickup and delivery service in England. "So that's my claim to fame." By some reports he was fired. At any rate, he was soon general manager of a weekly newspaper, the *London-American.* It was while in this position he got the idea of establishing a British equivalent to *Playboy,* and in a few years had a lusty *Penthouse* successful enough to think of exporting it to the U.S.A. And now he is putting out on TV "electronic magazines" such as *The Girls of Penthouse.*

One of the oddities of the issue of *Penthouse* I inspected was that in the editorial matter there were no men in sight: just photo series on individual girls in a kind of strip-tease format, or two girls fiddling with each other. Mr. Guccione said that occasionally they introduce a male but the decision to stick pretty much to females was "made purely on psychological grounds. If he [the reader] relates to the girl [or girls] in the photograph, which is the whole purpose of the exercise, he doesn't want to see another guy getting in there before him. . . . He can accept two girls because in the theater of his mind they are performing for him."

The Penthouse organization is very much a family operation. Mr. Guccione thinks that is as it should be — "a very Italian attitude, the importance of family, importance of blood." He pointed out that his father was secretary-treasurer, his sister a vice-president, and of his five children four were already in managerial roles and the youngest was getting training for such a role.

As to having personal assets in the hundreds of millions of dollars, he said he had thought a lot about it. He seemed annoyed that Americans seem to value "old money" more than "new money," such as his. "New money is really represented by the entrepreneurs who create it. So I am very proud to represent new money.... I feel it's a great mistake ... that those who follow me, my children and their children, will be given somehow more credibility because they will represent old money. I think that's a mistake because they will have lost all of the excitement of the game, excitement of the sport ... the wonderful memories ... I had in getting there in the first place." When he is looking at himself in the mirror while shaving he says what a lucky guy he is. "Lucky because ... I couldn't find a partner. I couldn't find anyone who was willing to risk ten cents on me. And to this day ... I thank God that I couldn't and I thank God I had to do it alone."

Mr. Guccione doesn't travel much except for business, and scorns any playboy image. He claims he does not smoke, drink, gamble, go to nightclubs, use drugs, or chase after women. But he had become interested in getting a summer place, a second house. He had offered $5.5 million for a big place in Westchester County but refused to go along when they jumped the price a couple of million. What he wanted was "a rather grand affair, big, with a lot of property. It will be something eventually for my children to have, and one of the uses that we will have for it is the breeding of Rhodesian ridgebacks [lion-hunting dogs]. You can see we're very fond of ridgebacks and we want to breed them." I had indeed noticed the huge animals, rare in America and known for their aggressiveness, stalking the precious premises.

His dream of marching into the future exercising total power at the head of a total family dynasty received a setback in late 1987. His son Robert Jr. had been running *Spin*, a pop-music monthly, as his own project under the Penthouse umbrella. Father was insisting that he, father, have 100 percent control of everything associated with Penthouse International, including trademarks. Robert Jr. resisted. He decided *Spin* would go its separate way; and father and son had not spoken to each other for two months.[3]

Swinging Along with Harold Farb

Mr. Farb had an intense experience with high living, thanks to some creative ideas of a second wife. It sometimes left him feeling worn out. He was known as the apartment king of Texas, with a net worth in the early 1980s of around $150 million. When I saw him he was single again and cherishing the simple life while preparing to remarry.

His father had owned two small movie houses in Houston and Harold was running one of them at the age of ten, even booking pictures. When he came out of military service, he gave up on college and joined his father, who had decided that TV would knock out movie houses and was now into real estate. Oil was already starting to cause a boom in Houston. The Farbs, as partners, couldn't afford to buy downtown property but began buying and selling corners of empty lots just on the edge of downtown. They figured that corner lots, facing two streets, would be more in demand.

They were in demand, and the Farbs were tripling their investment within a few years. When they had enough money, they switched to apartment complexes. And so they grew and grew with Houston and Harold's family grew with four daughters and a son. Harold's father dropped out, feeling rich enough, in 1960, and Harold went on to build a fortune up into the hundreds of millions. With his children grown, he and his wife decided to divorce.

Once he was out of his fairly conventional family cocoon he felt that with all his money he ought to be getting more fun and excitement out of life. It was at a singles party at the

Bachelors Club that he found what he thought was the answer: a shimmering blonde, Carolyn Shulman, in the midst of her second divorce. She knew a lot about the Las Vegas way of life. Her grandfather had been a professional gambler.[4]

Carolyn and Harold married and he moved his bride into a $5 million mansion in the ultra-exclusive River Oaks area. A lot of servants were hired, but she insisted in testimony six years later during her claim for a whopping settlement that she always looked after him, even to the extent of buying his favorite pineapple pies.

She thought the mansion was kind of plain and started renovating it so that she could have big charity parties that would enhance his image (and hers). What she did in creating an appropriate dressing area for herself, located off her private beauty salon, made news. It was the size of a six-room house. There was a nice big sitting area with chandelier, and various small rooms for different types of clothing: one room for gowns, one for cocktail dresses, one for suits, a special area for ninety pairs of shoes. Each pair had its own lighted glass compartment. They were on about ten shelves. Then there was an area for her sixty hats and a place for her fifty evening bags. As the marriage progressed she assembled at least $750,000 worth of apparel.[5] And then of course there were lots and lots of jewels. All this, she apparently felt, would help Harold feel good about himself.

She began throwing parties and organizing balls for all sorts of charitable causes and urged him to get into other fun things while enhancing his image. For example, largely as a fun thing he created a dazzling $5 million white marble and glass restaurant, the Carlyle, with fountain inside, standing all by itself in the elite Galleria area of Houston. In one part was a grand-style restaurant, in the other a supper club. Since Harold had always liked to sing sentimental songs from his young manhood such as "Embraceable You," Carolyn encouraged him to sing at both the supper club and elsewhere. In one case the Houston Symphony was rented for $25,000 to accompany him in a Gershwin concert and at least $100,000 went into cutting albums of him singing, with such titles as *An Evening with Harold Farb,* which he handed out as party favors.[6]

To identify the couple further with Texas high society, Harold Farb was encouraged to undertake another fun thing, a magazine designed especially for rich Texans called *Ultra.* It told readers where they could buy gold-heeled cowboy boots or $31,000 fur wraps.

After a few years, Mr. Farb was ready to quit the marriage, but it was not as easy as he had assumed. They had signed a prenuptial agreement stating that she would get $1 million if the marriage didn't last. However, it seems that although prenuptial agreements became legal in Texas they weren't legally binding at the time of their marriage. Carolyn went after him in court with lawyers and economists showing how much she had helped his career. In his sworn deposition he complained she was in a dream world and never came down to earth. "There was no satisfying Carolyn. I'd buy her a small ring or a small necklace, and she'd say it was beautiful ... and trade them in for bigger ones. . . ."[7] The final settlement was said to be worth $28 million to Carolyn in cash and assets that included the mansion, two Rolls-Royces, and a Jaguar.[8]

When I saw him a couple of years later he was single, or as he put it, "between marriages."

As I was riding in from the airport to see him, one of the first things I saw were large areas of Farb complexes. He was waiting for me at the outside entrance of his restaurant–supper club. Soft-voiced, amiable, somewhat slight, he was dressed in a study in grays. After we lunched he took me over to the apartment tower where he lived, about two blocks away. Each floor in the tower had four apartments. His apartment had been a three-bedroom affair, but he had remodeled it into a one-bedroom place to gain a library and sitting room. It was his only home. He was now living on a lot less than a million dollars a year, but recalling the past said, "I can live on a lot more. . . . I don't think money should be the criterion by which we judge a person because he can be very unhappy with money."

Was his ex-wife Carolyn still living in the River Oaks mansion?

"I'm sure she is."

He was not bitter in talking of her. It had been an interesting experience. But he spoke more fondly of his first wife.

One of his principal pleasures lately was going to neighborhood movies. "I go to a lot of movies. I see all the good movies that they come out with.

"My life is very simple right now. You would be very unimpressed with my personal life. I'm not traveling as much and I find I'm enjoying my life by doing a lot of things that I sort of missed during those years." And he had managed to take off fifteen pounds.

His idea of fun now was what he had done last night. He had dressed up in old pants, a western shirt, and with old friends had gone to a tiny Italian restaurant in an old rooming house where he used to do a lot of dining in his pre-prosperity days.

Also, at least once and usually twice a week he was going to his "favorite" restaurant in Houston, Rosnovsky's, which sells hamburgers. It is a converted little grocery store. "My father told me a long time ago to eat hotdogs once a week so you'll always have the common touch or feeling, you know, for how it feels if you don't have a lot of money and I still do that."

His son and daughters are all somehow involved in his business, the son particularly. They all have a piece of his family fortune, through trusts. The rest would probably go to worthwhile causes, but he wasn't specific beyond mentioning the medical field. He was at the moment more concerned with keeping his fortune reasonably intact. The big drop in oil prices had hit Houston hard, and rocked real estate values. The demand for oil was starting to come back, but he was diversifying into other cities outside Texas and getting into things like shopping centers. (After I saw him he unloaded the restaurant and a substantial number of his Houston apartment holdings.)

Since he was then living alone in his apartment, I wondered if he employed a cook.

"No. I just have a houseman who comes in in the morning and fixes breakfast for me. He does cook if I want him to, but I eat out most of the time. I only eat breakfast at home. Once in a while I just open up a can of something. I can't cook, but I can heat."

Seeking Happiness
with Nine Houses

Allen Paulson is a quiet, amiable, aw-shucks-type mechanic who kept thinking of better ways to use or make airplanes. Then he put together a couple of ailing airplane companies costing $77 million to create Gulfstream Aerospace Corporation. It primarily makes big corporate jets. He sold it within a few years to Chrysler for $640 million, while remaining chairman. By 1988 Gulfstream had 5,000 employees. His net worth in recent years has ranged between $225 million and $500 million.

It was Mr. Paulson's son Mike who was the victim of a kidnap attempt after news of his father's new wealth got wide publicity in 1953. Mr. Paulson recalled, when I saw him at his office, that his son had a premonition there might be trouble and got a permit to carry a small derringer. The kidnappers grabbed him in front of his Georgia house and left a note demanding $1.2 million in ransom. Mike killed one of the two kidnappers and wounded the one who fled, and got praise from the police and FBI.

Mike was now working in his father's company. Another son, Dick, was a county sheriff in California, and a third son, Jim, had his own airplane company. Mr. Paulson was twice divorced.

When swamped with wealth Mr. Paulson turned his passion for building things to building houses. During an intermission in our talk while he took a phone call, his charming executive secretary Kathy explained he had built four houses in the six years she had been working with him and had three houses going up now. I inquired if he built the houses because he enjoyed having places to go to. She replied: "I think it is to drive me crazy."

She has to keep track of many details about them even though there is a caretaker at each place.

Mr. Paulson's explanation was that he does a lot of traveling in his $11 million Gulfstream and he would rather drop in on his houses around the country than "go to some fancy hotel. That's not my bag." He started enumerating his houses:

"I have a home here in Savannah. I also have a home in Los Angeles and Palm Springs. I have a home in California in Encino. I have a penthouse in Miami, and a ranch in Claxton, Georgia. I've got a ranch in Lexington, Kentucky, and I've got a ranch in California."

He confirmed that he had recently sold his place on Hilton Head, South Carolina; and apparently he had pulled out of Pistol Creek, Idaho. Mr. Paulson also usually has a boat in the 100-foot range in Georgia or Florida. He instructed Kathy to arrange for me later to get past security to see the spectacular homestead, his ninth or tenth place, he was just finishing on an island near Savannah.

Another reason for his preference for houses over hotels is that he likes home-cooked meals. He didn't get much home-cooked food while growing up. His folks had a farm near Clinton, Iowa, but they soon split up. By the age of thirteen he was fully self-supporting from such jobs as making beds at a small hotel.

He drifted to a job milking cows in California, became fascinated with airplanes at a nearby airport, and became a plane mechanic. He took night courses and got some courses in the air force. Altogether, he said, "I didn't have probably a year of college if you wanted to add it all up." At TWA he saw the need for spare parts, bought a surplus B-29 engine, modified the parts so they performed better, and sold them to airlines. Soon he had modified a hundred engines. Later he expanded to converting surplus planes to cargo carriers, and converting piston planes to jet planes. And so he grew. Until he found himself worth hundreds of millions of dollars.

What could he do with the money? He doesn't believe in

luck but he was always something of a gambler, enjoyed poker and played the horses. So he took a big gamble by buying one-third of one of the nation's major steel companies, Wheeling-Pittsburgh. At any rate the company, perhaps the most technologically advanced major steel producer, had run up a lot of debt to achieve that advance at a time when the steel industry was hitting really hard times. As he fought to save the company, he became chairman and deeply involved. At one point he found himself on the side of the workers.

The company filed for reorganization under Chapter 11 of the Federal Bankruptcy Code. The reorganization did occur and at this writing investment advisers are stating that the company probably has a brighter future than most steel companies. Mr. Paulson put about $50 million of his own money into the company. By the time he pulled out, his shares were estimated as being worth $13 million. He in fact sold his shares to an old friend for $100,000 and took a real nice tax loss.[9] Mr. Paulson is still worth hundreds of millions of dollars, and his annual living costs are up in the low millions.

His thinking apparently had still not turned more than casually toward philanthropy. He mentioned that he "gave money to colleges." One gift for $1 million was for a stadium at Georgia Southern College. As for creating a foundation, that might be "somewhere down the road."

One of the greatest influences on the life of this mighty man was reading, years ago, *The Power of Positive Thinking,* the big best-seller by Norman Vincent Peale. He was so stirred up by it that he bought copies for all his employees and asked them to work by it.[10]

Since he had had private companies all his life, one wondered why he had finally taken Gulfstream Aerospace public while keeping 71 percent of it.

"It did a lot for me and the company. You know, you can be the richest man in the world on paper and not have a dollar, unless you go public and convert some of your interest in a business into cash. Owning 100 percent of Gulfstream before it went public, all I could take was wages."

When he made his big killing and was worth half a billion, why hadn't he cashed in, since he had plenty of enthusiasms including horses, tennis, boating, and houses? Put the money in bonds and never have to worry about a thing?

"Ah, but I'm not that kind of guy. I like building things. I'm a builder. I've built a lot of houses and farms for that reason. And I like to fix them and fix airplanes. It's just my nature to build things, and I love building airplanes."

Just for the heck of it, in 1988 Mr. Paulson, at age sixty-five, took one of his off-the-line Gulfstream IVs (nineteen seats) and, with three other pilots, took off around the world. Four stops. Average speed 638 miles per hour. They set a new around-the-world speed record of thirty-six hours and eight minutes.

Mr. Paulson also loves to build up horses that become winners. He had about 200 horses at the time, was reported later to have 300, at his ranches in Kentucky and California. Kathy had the impression that when he went home at night he spent a lot of time on the phone talking to his trainers. He confirmed it. He said: "I've really done quite well. It fills a big part of my life."

And so I went to visit his latest creation in houses, which might or might not go into his permanent collection. Anyway, it was fun to build. It was on an island quite a few miles away. He described it as "a real nice home . . . a takeoff from one of the famous homes in Mississippi. A period home. I've expanded on it."

I had to go through a security gate even to get onto the island, then there was a second gate at the approach to his place, which involved dozens of acres. There was an arched white bridge and a vast circular roadway of brick leading to a very handsome house of pink and white, long and slim. From the main house there was a covered, columned walkway to a smaller house for overflow guests and servants. Altogether on the outside there were fifty-four columns; plus ten that I noticed inside. The grand stairway of twenty-two steps led to a ballroom, a paneled library, and a master bedroom with lots of marble. It was a fine house but not a vast one with wasted rooms in the old grand-manor style:

maybe a dozen rooms plus the cottage. Outside there was a floating dock with a deep channel to handle big boats, a man-made lake, a tennis court. And there was a six-hole golf course.

Mr. Paulson had been kind of apologetic about there not being enough land for a nine-hole course. But, always the positive thinker, he pointed out that there were eighteen ways you could play the six-hole course.

Big Thinking under a Gold-Coated Ceiling

Ewing Kauffman is a bald, bouncy, amiable handsome man past seventy with an engagingly forthright way of speaking. He was explaining how nicely his company's stock had been doing. In the last three weeks, he noted, he and his wife, Muriel, had made $43 million. Muriel is the company treasurer. "Our stock is now worth $387 million." That was in late 1985. By late 1987 *Forbes* was reporting that Kauffman (or the Kauffmans) had a net worth of $1.3 billion. His company had been enormously profitable. After the Black Monday of October 1987, when his stock in Marion Laboratories had dropped a few hundred million in value, he explained, "But that's only on paper. I didn't lose anything because I didn't sell." The next day the market smiled on the Kauffmans and returned about $150 million to their net worth. He and Mrs. Kauffman were said to be still worth almost a billion dollars.

He and his wife have not been the only winners in the company's success. Eighty-three senior people at the company have had stock worth more than a million dollars. "The more we share, the more we make," he said, alluding to the company's exceptionally attractive employee stock-ownership and profit-sharing plans.

The name of his drug company, Marion Laboratories, is itself interesting. He started out as a one-man company selling pills to doctors and druggists. In making calls he couldn't very well say to them, "I'm Ewing Kauffman of the Kauffman Corporation." So he used his middle name, Marion. As for "Laboratories," that apparently just struck his fancy, because it was some time before he had a research laboratory of any consequence. In those early days one doctor complained his sales literature didn't contain a single scientific fact.[11] Only in recent years, as his company has gotten into the big league of drug firms, has it become a big spender on basic research. It has always tried to figure out innovative ways to use common knowledge and has made deals to get access to that knowledge, as for example making a joint deal with a Japanese firm.

Yet his company's stock year after year has soared in a way to make other drug companies envious. In 1987 a chart of just six recent years of its price looks almost like a 45° diagonal line. For example, a $10,000 investment in 1980 would have been worth about $250,000 in mid-1986.

Mr. Kauffman has been helped in the past few years by the growing demand for both calcium and anticalcium pills. But the major secret of his company's growth over more than two decades is that he is a super motivator of people, whether they be employees or customers considering his products. He's always been a man with super sizzle.

Ewing and Muriel Kauffman live in the biggest of all the residences I visited in my exploration of very wealthy people. In Mission Hills, an elite suburb of Kansas City, their vast twenty-eight room house of Italian Lombardy architecture, complete with tower and arches, sits back up on a hill. The approaches to it by foot are a pair of sweeping steps forming an oval around a pool where fountains, at the touch of a button, soar twenty feet high. The fountains were added because Mrs. Kauffman loves fountains. There are two large flagpoles about one hundred yards apart at each side of the house. There are two because Mrs. Kauffman is a Canadian and likes to look at the Canadian flag. She was an insurance broker in Toronto. Both she and Mr. Kauffman have been widowed. Between them they have three grown children.

Mr. Kauffman had called my hotel and instructed me to drive up to the gate, sit there, and he would arrange to let me in. Apparently on closed-circuit TV he can inspect persons arriving and if he wants to see them he can push a button and the huge iron gate will slide open. But tonight his chauffeur, Mr. B., a large middle-aged dark-skinned man, was waiting for me. Mr. B., I learned later, was also a bodyguard complete with handcuffs, blackjack, gun, and seven purple hearts. And he told me proudly, while driving me back to the hotel in one of the Kauffman's limousines, that as an "associate" of Marion Laboratories he owned $500,000 worth of the company's stock.

It was seven o'clock at night. Mr. Kauffman greeted me in pajamas and dressing robe and introduced me to Mrs. Kauffman, who was similarly attired. She was short, plump, rather plain looking but very bright, cheerful, and direct. As we talked she did not hesitate to set her husband straight. Her reputation for being very direct sometimes has unsettled staid socialites.

The Kauffmans bought the sixty-year-old mansion about two decades ago.

Mr. Kauffman: "She bought it. It looked like a mausoleum to me. But she said you buy it and I'll fix it. Now I love it." She brought over Italian craftsmen to help. Pointing to the high ceiling of the main room, she said: "That's pure gold up there." And the Florentine leather walls, now glowing, had been grimy black when they bought the place.

Mr. Kauffman: "She collected every piece of furniture here and designed these rugs. An interior decorator never set foot in here."

The house also has a vast outdoor swimming pool, a steam room, an organ, and a pistol range.

As we sat down to chat in the study, I mentioned the great iron fence around their property and the guard gate. Had the fence come with the property? No, he said, that had been Muriel's idea. Partly it was because there was a period when hippies would come and sit around and dip their feet in the fountain. That annoyed Mrs. Kauffman. Partly it was because after they had put Kansas City successfully into major league baseball (the Kansas City Royals), they had suddenly become celebrities. And baseball fans from eighty miles away would come by on weekends, knock on the door, and ask to see their suddenly famous house. And one day an escaped criminal mistook their driveway for a street and so was caught walking on their property. Mrs. K. asked for and got the iron enclosure.

The Kauffmans said they had eight people on their "personal" house staff, which didn't include Mr. B. He was Company. One day quite a few years ago Mr. Kauffman was driving to work while his mind was deeply immersed in company strategy. He explained: "I'm going down the street and — boom — I have an accident. So she [Muriel] goes to the board of directors and convinces them they should give me a chauffeur."

On the coffee table between us was an unusual looking chess board. It turned out to be computerized. Mrs. K. gave it to Mr. K. as a Christmas present in 1984, and he has spent a lot of hours with it. He tries to beat the computer, which can be set to any of ten levels of difficulty. He soon was playing at level ten and often plays the game backward to make it even more difficult.

Mr. Kauffman didn't pick up his mathematical skill and logic at Kansas City Junior College, the extent of his formal education. Apparently he got it from his father, who, though a poor farmer and later a poor insurance salesman, was a mathematical whiz. He routinely challenged his son to perform feats of arithmetic in his head.[12]

This knack came in handy when Ewing enlisted in the navy during World War II. He played a considerable amount of poker and came out with more than $50,000 in winnings. He recalls: "My nickname was Lucky because I'd win, win, win. But it isn't that at all. It's skill."

When released from the navy, he started selling pills for a small Illinois drug company, and soon had a problem because his commissions were greater than the president's salary. So he formed his own company, worked out of his basement where he did the bottling, and featured a pep pill for tired people. He read about a bone specialist who contended that broken bones healed faster if patients simply consumed a powder made from calcium-rich oyster shells.[13]

Kauffman arranged for an oyster company in Mississippi to send him shucked shells. He got a grain miller to grind them into a powder and a drug company to press the powder into pills he called Os-Cal. Today Os-Cal accounts for around $50 million of his annual sales. Oddly, his even bigger seller, licensed from Japan, is Cardizem, which inhibits angina by fighting calcium! Too much calcium apparently can constrict coronary arteries.

But, as noted, Kauffman's success is based far less on calcium than on his power to inspire. When he was still on his own as a salesman, he became known as a guy who could sell rubber crutches. And when he started dispatching salesmen he let them know they had the choice of being outstanding or just out. Nothing in between. They were ordered to see at least 20 percent more doctors and druggists a week than the competition, turn in an even better proportion of orders. He found he could get more hustle from husbands than bachelors, from salesmen raised in small towns who went to small, nonelite colleges. He would stage sales contests in which the top ten might get $500 shotguns, or vacations to Hawaii; the bottom twenty salesmen might get crying towels imprinted with a common excuse: "My territory is different."[14]

He gave awards to wives who reported their husbands were out working from eight to six. On top of all this, as a full-time motivator, he offered employees, as indicated, both stock-option plans and profit-sharing in a big way.

Mr. Kauffman has never spared himself. In fact he seems to relish a frenetic pace and tries to keep in shape for it even though past normal retirement age. He thrives on his daily swim in his heated pool even in midwinter. "I go swimming outdoors every morning even if it is zero degrees. Just go in stark naked. I've got an Olympic-size pool out here with diving boards. I used to be a diver. I have waded through sixteen inches of snow to reach the pool. But you get used to it."

He enjoys playing golf, which is why they bought a place outside Palm Springs on the golf course where the Bob Hope Classic is played. When snow covers Kansas City courses, he goes there for a few weeks and takes much of his house staff with him, although the Palm Springs place has a staff of two. It was Mrs. Kauffman's idea that he try to build a really big league baseball team in Kansas City to take his mind off his work. A kind of hobby. It became a passion, not eased until he had taken an expansion club to a World Series championship.

He is still instinctively a gambling man, believing he can beat the odds. Off and on he has raised a few dozen Thoroughbreds. And for many years he flew into Las Vegas frequently to gamble. Sometimes he stayed overnight, sometimes just for six hours. But it has lost its allure.

"Now that we've made money it's no fun. Gambling is only fun when you need the thrill of trying to get something that you can use and need. Once you have it, then gambling loses its allure."

In short, being a zillionaire can take some of the fun out of life, even if you can buy an awfully nice house.

(We will be returning to Mr. Kauffman's interesting thoughts about money later, particularly his provocative views about passing fortunes to one's children and installing them in a succession role at the company.)

A Private Man with $33 Million Worth of Residences

Leslie Wexner, a supermarketer of women's apparel, has six residences in Ohio, New York, Florida, and Colorado that were worth about $33 million when I saw him. But he is hardly feeling land poor. These splurges in splendid houses amount to just a wee bit of his net worth in 1986.

He soared to the top rank of billionaire faster than just about anyone in recent time. Look at the record:

- In 1982 he appeared at the bottom of the *Forbes* 400 richest Americans list with a net worth of $100 million.
- In 1985 his worth had increased by ten times. He now appeared at the bottom of the list's billionaires with $1

billion, counting the shares in his company held by his mother and younger sister. (He is a bachelor.)

- In the very next year, 1986, he soared past such billionaires as David Rockefeller to rank in a tie for fifth among the nation's twenty-six billionaires, with $1.4 billion.
- In 1987 *Forbes* clocked him at $2.1 billion. And his mother was on the list of the richest 400 with an additional $365 million.

The October 1987 stock market crash knocked quite a few hundred million dollars off the value of his stockholdings. But *Forbes* found he still had a billionaire rating.

His explosion of net worth in a few years illustrates the capability of successful chain operators to make big money fast in today's world of fast transportation and instant communications throughout the nation. Mr. Wexner operates specialty stores for women's garments. The company, The Limited, is now well known to almost every investor — and to millions of mall shoppers. By adding units and acquiring other chains his company was, by 1986, operating about 2,700 stores. As he explained his success, "Themes that work in Columbus work in Albuquerque. Fifty years ago you didn't have a national market."

He might also have mentioned that fifty years ago you didn't have shopping malls across the land, where people spend their money like crazy. The sweetheart stores of the malls are women's apparel shops.[15]

Our visit was on a Sunday afternoon. His Columbus-area home was in Bexley, about ten minutes from the heart of Columbus and opposite the governor's mansion. It sat back partly out of sight, a contemporary gray stone and plaster house. A butler in a plain trim suit, the only butler I ever encountered in my visits, greeted me and led me to the inner part of a stunning double room where the ceiling was about seventeen feet high, and the floor was covered with a lot of thick white carpeting. Two enormous areas of plate glass surrounded a twenty-foot-wide fireplace. Over the mantel was a giant dramatic painting in black and white.

Beyond the windows one saw a great lawn hundreds of feet deep sloping down into woodland. Along the inner walls were modern art and sculpture by such respected twentieth-century artists as Rivers and Nevelson, and there were also pre-Columbian pieces.

I could see Mr. Wexner pacing with a phone in hand in his office off the main area — a tall, slim man then forty-nine years old with deepset eyes. He was wearing corduroy pants, denim shirt, and slippers, and he paced with a natural grace. I knew what he was talking about. It had been in the papers. He was wrapping up the purchase of Bendel's, the famed high-fashion New York store. It was for him a busy day for a Sunday. Earlier he had chaired in that living room a meeting of the Columbus City Council and the Capitol Committee, a group of presidents of city companies which he headed, to talk about civic improvements.

Mr. Wexner was apologetic when he strode out. All smiles, he confirmed that the Bendel deal was 99½ percent closed. He didn't say so then, but he planned to put his special touch to the store, make items somewhat more affordable and then replicate the store, with a lot of class, in other cities.

Despite publicity about his great wealth I saw no sign of a bodyguard. He had, however, taken a class in executive security. He insisted that he has not let security concerns cramp his life-style. He's a jogger and "If I decide to go jogging at eight o'clock at night I will do so. And I like to drive." He will hop in one of his many cars and spin around Columbus or the countryside alone. All his recreations tend to be solitary.

One of his hobbies is making deals to buy and sell classy cars: Ferraris, MGs, Mercedes, and so on. "I trade them more than I have them," he grinned. Sometimes he has ten sitting around. At the moment he was down to four.

His preferences for food tend to be simple: tuna fish salad, meatloaf. Though he is often in New York, he tries to avoid both the elegant restaurants and the social scene. He does have a $6 million mansion where he sleeps while in Manhattan, but he thinks of New York as just a branch office.

Columbus is ideally located for anyone searching for a distribution center for a national chain of stores, but it also happens to be where Leslie Wexner was born and raised. His parents, orthodox Jews, ran a clothing store named Leslie's, named after their only son. The son took some courses in merchandising at Ohio State and dropped out of law school there to work at the store. His father was shy, contemplative, his mother assertive and action-oriented. A former professor suggests Leslie somehow managed to pick up both traits.[16] He himself has said he suffers from terminal "antsiness," a constant drive to try something new.

Anyhow, father was soon viewing son dubiously as a fountain of impractical ideas. Son Leslie wanted to limit the store to fast-moving, profitable items such as women's sportswear. (Hence the name of his chain, "The Limited.") Father knew the tried and true way was to offer the public a wide variety of items in order to attract maximum customers and sadly told his son, "You'll never be a merchant."[17]

Son Leslie set up his own specialty store, prospered, and soon he was setting up other stores in other areas. Father relented and both he and mother joined Leslie's operation. But all was not happiness. Some of his stores were in shopping centers operated by Alfred Taubman of Detroit. (Estimated personal fortune 1986: $800 million.) Mr. Taubman took Leslie by helicopter to a center near Detroit, strode to The Limited store, and talked about its appearance. He said in effect that it was a blight on his shopping center. Leslie Wexner recalls:

"It just simply was a store. It took me a while to come to grips with the fact that he was right. If I was going to be in the retail business, we should have excellent, innovative designs that add value. I began traveling around looking for inspiration, a store to copy or an idea."

Leslie Wexner still spends a lot of time, often with camera, traveling and looking for ideas by jetting all over the world (and leaves administration to a large extent to his associates). He may get ideas for interesting uses of color in a museum or by flipping through lots of magazines. He has gotten ideas for merchandise display from a flower-stand vendor in Paris. What he likes best are fresh, exuberant variations on classic designs. Since he can't patent a look, he seeks to move fast. In 1986, for example, one of the things he featured was Outback Red, in a safari look. He ordered that 500,000 garments colored "Outback Red" be in his stores within ten weeks.

Mr. Wexner still tries to keep to the "limited" idea. One of his chains sells clothes to overweights, another sells sexy lingerie.

And in pondering what women want, he recently expressed concurrence with the theory of Charles Revson, founder of Revlon, that what women want often requires them to assume a horizontal position.[18] In short to use their scent and appearance to prove to themselves that they can tempt men greatly. In Mr. Wexner's view, the average woman has enough clothes to last a hundred years; he sells excitement. (Recently he has made a few moves into specialty apparel stores for men.)

"I'm kind of a lousy businessman," he explained. "I'm not that organized and I don't have a great facility for numbers. But I've come to understand ... that I'm a creative kind of person, so that doing things in new ways or putting little twists on things is fun for me."

As for cashing in and turning to his numerous other interests, no way. "The fascination with wealth isn't what drives me. I really like my work. . . . The analog would be to Picasso. You've painted enough pictures, you don't have to do this anymore. Well I like painting pictures." As for the charge that he has a burning desire to dominate women's retail, he says, "Yes, in the context of it being a quality business and fun to do. . . . But some make it sound like Alexander the Great, you want to own it all, and I'm not that acquisitive."

He takes at least four days off every month to escape. Often he goes to the Colorado slopes to ski. For seven years he had a place in ultra-exclusive Vail, but recently has been building a place on seventy acres in Aspen because he can land his jet in Aspen, which he likes just as well, and he couldn't land in Vail.

Or he may get on his 140-foot boat, *The Limitless,* for a spin, wherever it may be. But most often he is at Palm Beach.

In 1985 he created a minor uproar at that totally elegant resort. Some dowagers were indignant at what he was doing to one of their grandest landmarks, the famed Wrightsman House, which is on the ocean. The house alone would take up most of a football field.

Wexner already had a $3 million place in Palm Beach, but he felt cramped in it because of the size of the lot, so he bought the Wrightsman House for $10 million. The house was featured in *Town & Country* for its grandeur and its beautifully furnished rooms and terraces. Soon after the purchase word got out that Wexner planned to tear it down and build a house more to his style.

When I saw him in Columbus he still had both properties. Regarding the Wrightsman place, he explained: "What I liked best about it was the landscaping and the site [seven oceanfront acres]. The house [being torn down] was kind of a funny house. Individual rooms I thought were quite beautiful but the house had been added on to so many times that it didn't flow very well. I thought the house faced the wrong way. The gardens ... had no orientation to the ocean.... [There were] little windows looking out at the ocean. You had this great view but you couldn't see it.... Mechanically the house was pretty shot. Half the space in the house was servant rooms. It must have had twenty-two servant rooms, so it was for a life-style that wasn't mine. I'm building a more contemporary house."

His action may have shocked a lot of townspeople, but he insists it didn't shock the Wrightsmans. "They had filed a plot ... with the city council to divide the property into nine lots and the subdivision plan had a road running through the house." He said that if the Wrightsmans had torn down the house, it would have been okay, but his doing it was almost a sin.

Why did he go to Palm Beach anyhow if he didn't covet the social scene? Was it, I suggested, just an effort to create for him and his company an image of glamour? He laughed and said, "What you see is what you get.

"I always have to apologize. People say it doesn't seem like you. I've had a house there for three years. I've gone to one dinner. I like Palm Beach because it's convenient to get to — two hours from Columbus, two hours from New York. I have some friends who live there. The traditional Palm Beach social part I just don't participate in. I really enjoy my privacy." He said that his old mentor, Alfred Taubman, lived there and was "a very social person. I'm more reclusive."

(Mr. Wexner talked at considerable length about what he planned to do with all his money. We will resume our visit with him on that topic in chapter 16.)

CHAPTER 11

TRYING ELITE PLAYGROUNDS AND PASTIMES

"I think it's a kind of closed ranks mentality that still attracts a lot of people to Palm Beach."

— SHANNON DONNELLY,
society writer, Palm Beach

Of the thirty ultra-rich people I visited, only seven had spent much time at elite resorts. Five additional people had taken up money-gobbling hobbies. And two additional people could conceivably be viewed as members of the international jet set. In short, a majority had almost no experience with any of these fun-seeking categories. So much for our concept of the immensely rich typically becoming pleasure-seeking sybarites.

Still, in large numbers people with relatively substantial wealth — say, those with net worths of more than $25 million — do frequently try to live it up. And in the resort category it appears that the playground that has the greatest claim to be singled out for close inspection is Palm Beach. Its isolated location and its size promote exclusivity along with competitive display by many of its residents. It is protected from the gross mainland by Florida water, yet its beach is little more than ordinary by Florida standards. Even so, in 1986 nine members of the *Forbes* 400 listed Palm Beach as a principal residence (more mentions than any other resort area listed). Two others listed Manalapan, a kind of suburb just down the spit from Palm Beach. In addition, many others on the *Forbes* list, like Leslie Wexner, have residences there but don't call it home.

The publisher of the *Palm Beach Daily News* advised me that she was at a big luncheon after a *Forbes* listing came out. "I looked around the room and counted twenty people who should have been on that list and were not." The *News* is called "the shiny sheet" because it has long been printed on glossy paper so that the type will not rub off on white gloves.

A local society writer, Shannon Donnelly, said: "In Palm Beach people don't have any qualms about flaunting their wealth, especially the new rich." She added that the wealthiest people kept the lowest profile, and treat you the nicest. The director of the weekly *Social Pictorial* said, "The flashier ones I would really put in the $25 million to $50 million group."

Palm Beach has broad boulevards lined with palm trees, and expensive shops with no neon lights. People can feel fairly safe wearing their real jewelry to parties in Palm Beach because of the heavy emphasis on security. Anyone holding a service job in Palm Beach has long been required to carry a photo identification card issued by the police, a requirement that has bothered some people because most service people are black.[1]

The town seems obsessed with partying. Charlotte Curtis, the noted follower of high society, wrote of one very wealthy couple in Palm Beach: "Neither he nor his wife feel they have to be out every night whooping it up, as many Palm Beachers do. They have been known to go ninety-six hours without climbing into the required black tie and ball-gown."

If you want to stage a sizable party yourself during the winter months, the first thing you do is check "the shiny sheet." At the beginning of the season it devotes a full page and a half to a "social calendar." Its publisher said with a laugh, "It's a sort of social clearinghouse." In a normal February there will be a couple dozen charity balls for diseases and causes. Admission is commonly $200 per couple. In 1985 Mrs. Sue Whitmore, a plump Listerine heiress, was chairman of six different balls and spent five solid months working on nothing but balls.[2] The *Social Pictorial* is filled with photos of who was talking to, or dancing with, whom among the more prominent attenders of the better balls and large parties.

Sometimes a charitable reason is given for a grand party even though tickets are not sold. The Arthur Lyttlesdorfs of New York staged a party to generate enthusiasm for the local symphony. It was a monumental affair at their vast house for 300 guests, with lots of pomp and celebrities. The Lyttlesdorfs just picked up the bill.[3] Some thought that a little bit flashy.

Certain local rich Germans have also contributed samples of flashiness. A baron from the Krupp fortune has often employed several housemen in Thai livery along with having a stretch Rolls-Royce, and he is great at kissing feminine hands. A baroness had a hundred people in to celebrate the birthday of her poodle.

Despite its celebrations, a sense of unease hangs over this famed retreat for the wealthy. There is fussing about people being allowed to walk on the streets in shorts or T-shirts, and rich Latin Americans trying to get in. When I was in Palm Beach twenty years ago to give a lecture I saw lots of Rolls-Royces and chauffeurs. In my recent visit I saw few of either. The publisher of the *News* advised my associate Joann Stern: "Very few people here drive a Rolls anymore.

Almost everyone drives either a Mercedes or a BMW. A Rolls is a big car and it's hard to drive and hard to park. Everybody's driving their own car, so maybe that's why they've come to the very very expensive Mercedes . . . and the BMW, which is a very expensive car."

The head of a local employment agency confirmed that chauffeurs were a disappearing breed and that house staffs in general were being cut back. If a family has a chauffeur now, it may expect him also to tend the pool and do house chores. Archie Peck, a realtor, laid such changes down to the fact that "people are simplifying their lives now. It's difficult for us to sell some of the bigger Spanish- or Mediterranean-type houses." The *Palm Beach Post* has reported that the "straight" butler also is disappearing. The "straight" butler is schooled in reception of guests, food and wine service, staff management. But now there is little staff to manage. Most surviving butlers are "working butlers," meaning that they also chauffeur and even help with house chores.

Also disturbing to many old-timers is the appearance of condominiums, even on the grounds of the long-revered Breakers Hotel. You can pick up a condo there for less than $2 million. In the northern part of town you can still be pretty sure that any neighbor is worth at least $15 million, but to the south there are islands of condos for mere millionaires or less.

The big surprise, which made the *New York Times,* was that in 1984 two old-guard incumbents on the town council were ousted and the council got its first Jewish member. Historically Palm Beach was viewed by its guardian members as a place where exceptionally affluent Christians might congregate and cavort amongst themselves. Today, many of its most affluent and prestigious residents are Jewish. During my visit I dropped in on a man whose family had long been prominent in Palm Beach. A couple of neighbors were there. Without any priming from me they commented that there had been "an awful lot of feeling" about the way recent elections involving Jewish candidates were going. There was discussion as to whether two of Palm Beach's most prestigious clubs, Bath and Tennis (initiation fee $15,000) and the Everglades country club (initiation fee $20,000), should be opened up to Jews, and if so how much. A man's name was mentioned and one of the women explained, "He's a Jew." We talked about the rough-cut Cleveland auto-parts maker buying one of Palm Beach's grandest mansions. A woman spoke up in favor of his entry to Palm Beach. "First of all, he's a Christian."

Any happiness created by vast wealth would appear to be diluted if your worth is in the hundreds of millions and you are still scrutinized for club membership by three old-guard members, who themselves are down to their last few millions, pondering the way you spell your name.

Palm Beach has a fine golf club to the north that is often referred to as "the Jewish club." It has tougher tests for admission than the two clubs cited. You not only have to pay an initiation fee in the area of $50,000 but you have to show that you have contributed more than $1 million to philanthropy.[4] That requirement really promotes exclusivity!

About twenty miles north of Palm Beach there is a smaller, tighter enclave of very rich families, mostly "old family." People who live there usually say they are from Hobe Sound. That is an "in" joke. Hobe Sound is a mishmash of social levels. The really elite area doesn't start until you cross the bridge to Jupiter Island.

After you have been to Palm Beach, Jupiter Island really isn't much to look at. There are about four hundred houses along two roads, with a nice golf course occupying much of the space between the roads. People mostly have their names on their mailboxes. If they go calling at night it may be in a two-decades-old wooden station wagon. You can see most of the houses and the houses you see are mostly handsome well-tended one-stories, some spread out but very few awesome by Palm Beach standards. About the only thing an outsider can buy on the island is a newspaper or liquor. The main island dock is too small to handle jumbo yachts.

Yet over the decades Jupiter Island has been populated

by people who have such names as Mellon, Marshall Field, du Pont, Harriman, Whitney, Ford, Duke, Doubleday, Heinz, Dillon. Laurance Rockefeller's daughter Laura vividly recalled to me summering there as a youngster. Average per family net worth certainly would be more than $15 million.

One of the things residents dreaded when I was there was that George Bush, whose wealthy family has long-time ties to Jupiter Island, might be elected U.S. president. The publicity would be dreadful.

You don't have to go through any gate to get onto Jupiter Island, but as I was cruising down Gomez, one of the two roads, I was going slowly to check out the houses. Within moments a police car pulled up behind me. I resumed normal speed and was not bothered. There is a policeman for every sixteen houses. If you stop to get out and walk past some trees to get a better view of the outer shore, you are apt to have your car towed away. Sensors along the roadside, I was told, notify a central police monitor if any car has stopped along the road. All people who work on the island must be fingerprinted and have a variety of identity cards.

If you have a zillion and want to buy on Jupiter Island and get into the swing of things there, you had better be sure you will meet the approval of one woman, Permelia Reed. That at least has been the situation for decades. She has been a not particularly benign dictator of the island. Only recently did her grip start to weaken. Her family bought the island, began selectively selling plots, and created the Jupiter Island Club around which most island activities center. Two-thirds of the island residents — including virtually all the prominent old families — belong to the club. Theoretically there is a normal, democratic procedure by which applicants for membership are inspected and processed. But stories abound on how Mrs. Reed has done the picking. Two residents of the island gave me varying versions, and I heard several other versions from people living nearby. All the stories have had Mrs. Reed at the meeting as an observer, listening or watching while crocheting. The most common version was that if she picked up a green scarf to work on, the candidate was okay; if she began working on a black scarf, the membership committee was being advised to vote no.

Palm Beach and Jupiter are two of the more interesting playgrounds for ultra-rich people. I'll simply list some of the other places where you find heavy concentrations of very rich people:

- La Jolla, California, which is really a part of San Diego. There are usually a half-dozen *Forbes*-type people in residence. During the first week of August, rich, socialite Texans start arriving by the hundreds and sometimes swamp clubs such as the La Jolla beach and tennis club. Texan Harold Farb spoke of the Pacific Coast between San Diego and Los Angeles as the American Riviera and mentioned that one reason he preferred it to European seaside resorts was that the natives spoke English.
- Palm Springs area in California. Palm Springs itself, once glamorous, is now mostly middle-class sprawl but down valley Rancho Mirage has attracted such wealthy notables as the Walter Annenbergs, the Leonard Firestones, the Bob Hopes. And a $500 million resort at Indian Wells has been catching the eye of some super rich.
- Southampton gets strong support from very rich New Yorkers.
- Newport, Rhode Island, despite being burdened by huge aging mansions, tour buses, an attempted-murder scandal, and the current departure of the America's Cup races, still has a very loyal following among many old families of wealth and people such as Doris Duke, who has spent and raised many millions of dollars to renovate exceptional aging mansions.

In addition there are such notable watering places as Mackinaw Island for midwesterners, Fishers Island off the

Long Island Sound, and Bar Harbor, Maine. And for athletic types there are Vail and Aspen, Colorado.

The very rich I have encountered have shown little interest in European resorts. Perhaps they are uncomfortable not knowing the language. But great spots for the international rich are certainly available in inland places such as St. Moritz and Gstaad. America's rich seem more inclined to cover the top spots in the Mediterranean by dropping in at the Aga Khan's posh coastal-area Costa Smeralda in Sardinia, Marbella in Spain, or the Monaco area in France by boat, their own or a chartered one.

Some rich Americans, particularly Texans, maintain places at spectacular Acapulco, Mexico, including a preposterous "baron" from Texas, Nicky Portanova, who was forced by a court decision to get by on less than $25 million a year. (We'll get to him later.)

Closer to home, many very wealthy Americans maintain places in the Bahamas. Lyford Cay, often called a tropical paradise, has a handsome stretch of beach with a gloriously sited golf club and marina near Nassau, and is widely regarded as one of the most exclusive resort spots in the world. It is heavily guarded not only at the gate but often with patrolling German shephards so that, until recently, there has been little concern about restless natives. However, employees of the Lyford Cay Club, which dominates the Cay, have joined the nation's largest union. When I was there my host changed plans to take my wife, Virginia, and me out to a club restaurant and instead had us dine at home because of fear that club employees would join a strike then in progress. They did not.

This cay has been favored by high-level British royalty including the queen herself and by Prince Rainer of Monaco. The Aga Khan chose it for a honeymoon.

It harbors at least two American billionaires (Jay Pritzker and Walter Annenberg) and more than a dozen other U.S. centimillionaires, along with the enormously wealthy Greek shipping tycoon Stavros Niarchos, who has a relatively modest house.

Rich Pastimes

On the *Forbes* 400 list the person who most vigorously seeks to have fun by dipping into his hundreds of millions is, as indicated, the publisher himself, Malcolm Forbes. For weekend retreats when he is not at his Far Hills, New Jersey, mansion, he can go to his great château in Normandy, or his castle in Morocco, or his house in London, or his place in Fiji in the South Seas, or one of his U.S. ranches. Visiting those playgrounds is just the beginning of his ways to have fun.

At auctions he collects Fabergé eggs made for the Imperial Russian family and is pleased that in his multimillion-dollar collection he has two more eggs than the Kremlin's.

Don't think he is stuffy, though. He loves the feeling of riding motorcycles, has gone 130 miles an hour on one. In his various garages he has about seventy gorgeous motorcycles and is the first Westerner to have crossed the U.S.S.R. and China on a motorbike.[5] In each case he led a caravan of bikers he had assembled, and wore a red vest with "Capitalist Tools" printed on the back.

Coasting in a balloon also gives him a marvelous feeling. Each time he comes down from the heights he may have to vent hundreds of dollars' worth of helium before resuming. He has a multitude of large balloons of various shapes and splendor and made the first coast-to-coast crossing of the U.S. in a helium balloon.

He splurges occasionally on a rare Maserati or Lamborghini; and has fun with his Boeing 727. Recently he has gotten the most attention for his latest boat, the 151-foot-long luxurious *Highlander,* complete with bagpiper, helicopter, a couple of speed boats and white padded leather ceilings to mute any noise. It reportedly cost $5 million.[6] If so, he picked it up at a great bargain because by late 1987 *Time* reported that new jumbo yachts — those over 100 feet in length — ranged in price from $5 million to more than $40 million. The number of such jumbos with U.S. owners, it reported, had increased by 60 percent in just one year. The annual upkeep of a 100-foot-and-up boat would start at about $500,000, plus the salaries of people on the crew.[7]

Along with an assumption that super-rich people have super-grand houses, there is the widely held assumption that the richer you are the more you splurge on the accoutrements of super-costly pastimes. That assumption got only small support from the super-rich people I visited. Only three of my thirty interviewees had spent much on a boat, say, more than $75,000. And only three had gotten involved in raising Thoroughbred horses, which can be an expensive hobby. At the Keeneland Selected Yearling Sale near Lexington, Kentucky, where many of America's and Europe's very rich gather every July, a horse of prime lineage can go for $10 million. The connoisseurs of Thoroughbreds had cause for deep chagrin in 1985 when Spend a Buck, which had cost its owner $12,500, won the Kentucky Derby. Worse, it was owned by Dennis Diaz, who freely called himself an outsider, an ethnic snubbed by the racing establishment. When it was pointed out to him that if he played his cards right he could eventually make $40 million from the horse, he replied, "I can't spend that much anyway."[8]

Using fine horses for fox hunting has virtually disappeared as a sport outside Virginia, the Carolinas, and small tracts in New Jersey, because suburban sprawl has been wiping out both foxes and appropriate hunting grounds. If foxes are chased, they are frequently ranch-raised and not too foxy about eluding chasers. Polo, however, has been undergoing a resurgence, especially in the Palm Beach area and in Texas, Connecticut, and California. To finance a four-man team with six ponies per man can cost at least $200,000 a year. Possibly one reason for the resurgence of interest is that a polo field, a symbol for poshness, has been used often in recent years as the centerpiece for a very expensive real estate development.

A very rich Texan, Norman Brinker, who made tens of millions from food chains, became a crusader for polo in Dallas and formed what was at first a very small club, the Willow Bend Polo and Hunt Club. To stir up interest in what a gala event polo could be, he began showing movies of matches at his club and elsewhere. Gradually polo caught on and the matches have become major social events in Dallas.

Ten of the thirty persons I visited have private planes reserved for their use. Most others make some use of business-owned planes for business or personal travel. Whatever the technical ownership, the cost of suitable planes for personal use is in the $1 million to $13 million range. Many have intercontinental range. An attorney who deals with very rich clients told me of a wealthy New York industrialist who, with his wife, has taken up cultural pursuits. They have an intercontinental plane. However, when they choose to fly to Europe they consider their plane too slow. They take the Concorde to save three hours' flying time. Their own slower plane follows with their extensive baggage. And it is perfectly adequate for hopping around Europe.

Another hobby that many very rich people take up is buying a controlling interest in a major league ball club. The purchase and upkeep of such a club can quickly get into the tens of millions, and offers less prospect of profit than putting the money into sound corporate bonds. Since the big thing the buyers are getting, in their mind, is an owner's box (and all that goes with it), they don't need to be too concerned if they lose money. It can be written off against their other profits. Ball clubs used to be marvelous tax shelters because you could depreciate the players! But the IRS fixed that. Meanwhile, the fierce bidding by owners for stars ran the average salary of big league baseball players up about 700 percent in the ten years ending in 1985. TV money had something to do with this. But in 1985 ten baseball teams reported losses of at least $2 million.[9] All but four of the twenty-six clubs were then owned by wealthy individuals.

The Ewing Kauffmans of Kansas City, whom we have met, were frank in relating their motives and rewards in buying a controlling share in one of these clubs, the Kansas City Royals. Why did they buy the team in the first place, when it was just an expansion team?

Ewing Kauffman: "She told me to."

Muriel Kauffman: "Well, I thought he was working too hard. I thought this would be a hobby for him and he'd live twenty years longer. Also, it could be great for our community. . . . People come from the four-state area and stay overnight and spend money and it turns over at least three times before it hits the bankers."

Mr. Kauffman: "Owning a baseball club is not a wise investment. You buy it either for your community or ego or to get yourself known or because you like baseball." He continued: "Last year six teams out of the twenty-six made money. The rest of them lost money. We were one of the six that made money. But when [your investment] is worth $25 million you should at least make $2.5 million, after taxes, as an economic investment, and we don't make that kind of money. We've lost as much as $4 million in one year." (This was while the team was winning six division titles in ten years, which he called "the best record of anybody in baseball.")

Which team sports are most and least attractive in terms of money? Mr. Kauffman: "Football's the best. Basketball's probably the worst. Or baseball. In football all the teams share their TV revenue." Also, he pointed out, football gets its players already suitably trained by colleges, whereas baseball clubs have to support farm systems.

Georgia Frontiere
and Her Goliaths

Mrs. Frontiere is the only woman ever to own and actively direct a big league football team. Of the four people I visited who happened to be using some of their great fortunes to be team owners, she had been most energetically involved — more than fifty hours a week during the season —in a notoriously male-oriented, muscular field. Still a cheerful, wholesome platinum blonde beauty in her early fifties, she by choice took charge of several dozen tough Los

Angeles Rams. They typically tower a foot and a half above her and on average are about two and a half times heavier than she is.

When the sixth of her seven husbands, Carroll Rosenbloom, died by drowning, she found herself owning an empire with a net worth of more than $100 million. This fortune came from textiles, oil, land, securities. She told me she had "competent tax attorneys" to take care of such matters. But she also inherited a controlling interest in the Los Angeles Rams.

Despite admonishments that there were a multitude of better ways to invest the tens of millions tied up in the team, and that it would be a brutal business for a lovely female to mess with, she elected to keep and run the team. She had greatly enjoyed following the team on virtually every road trip and saw it as an interesting, philosophic challenge.

Mrs. Frontiere said she saw herself as a "female warrior." Too many women put themselves down and think that after the age of thirteen if they mix it up with males they won't be considered "feminine." Mr. Rosenbloom had always urged her to fulfill herself and not just be another woman.

At first glance her life story might look like that of a husband-hopping female who hit the jackpot on number six. The real story is more interesting and complex. She has explained that she had so many husbands because she was an old-fashioned person who felt she had to marry a man if she slept with him.[10]

Her father at one time had been an affluent broker who had done business with the senior Joseph Kennedy, father of the president. Her father went broke during the depression and later divorced Georgia's mother. Mother and daughter migrated from St. Louis to Fresno, California, when daughter was fifteen. That same year daughter had her first marriage, which was quickly annulled.

She took up singing, became good at light opera in a troupe and at supper clubs. Later she became a TV weather girl and briefly a co-anchor on the TV network *Today* show, all the while going in and out of marriages quite rapidly. In her second marriage her husband was killed in a bus accident. Her husbands have been mostly from the world of entertainment. Meanwhile she had gotten to know the wealthy Kennedy family very well. And in the mid-1950s Mr. Kennedy senior introduced her to a friend, Carroll Rosenbloom, also enormously rich and a couple decades older than she was. They gradually became good friends and when his marriage soured, they became constant companions. By the time he finally was able to get a divorce they in fact had started a family.[11] The daughter and son now are in their twenties, and Mrs. Frontiere is a grandparent. Mr. Frontiere, her seventh husband, is a noted composer.

Taking charge of the Rams after the death of Mr. Rosenbloom did indeed provide a rough time. Sports writers hooted that she thought Red Grange was a Communist farm union. Several star players staged a brief walkout. Then there was the problem of Mr. Rosenbloom's son by previous marriage being high in the management of the team, presumably being groomed to take over. She felt that to take over effective control it was necessary to weed out the stepson along with other management people she wasn't sure would be rooting for her.

She confessed she ran into a lot of prejudice even from other owners. They were nice and polite and everything but "they had never looked upon me as one of their equals. I was someone's wife and that was a different thing." Now she speaks of the players as marvelous. In most years she has managed to keep the Rams a winning team that has frequently made the playoffs. A winter for the *Sporting News* complained that by 1987 she had become more interested in her elegant parties than in spending more to get and hold on to more top players.

The Frontieres have a ten-room Colonial-type house in elite Bel Air, plain looking for that area. She fussed about the smallness of some of the rooms. They wanted to dress up the front but had never gotten around to it. The day I saw her she was more than a little distracted because at another house they have north of Malibu, a boiler had blown up and caused a fire.

Their third house was on a golf course in Newport, Rhode Island, and the Frontieres have had a problem shared by at least one other centimillionaire I visited. Having great wealth doesn't necessarily get you into the country club even if you live on the grounds or face the course. The keepers of the gate may, for example, not like the way you spell your name, or not like your profession, or your marital history. She explained:

"I thought it would be nice to have a house on the golf course because I like to play golf but so far we haven't been able to get in. I'm not one to go where I might not be wanted so we'll probably end up selling it unless they decide to accept us. I think they're a little afraid we might bring the football players in, even though I don't play golf with them."

Some local powerful matrons also might not feel totally comfortable having a still very handsome woman who had attracted seven husbands in their midst. At any rate, Georgia Frontiere is not distraught.

"I'm a happy person. I always look for the bright side."

CHAPTER 12

LIVING HIGH
BUT CRAVING
SOMETHING ELSE

"I like to get paid for what I do. I made
$7,000 last year. That isn't so bad is it?"

— ELECTRA WAGGONER BIGGS, whose net
worth in 1982 was put at $150 million,
commenting soon after she began
sculpting[1]

Perhaps the women's movement
had something to do with it. In any case, a number of extremely rich heiresses are no longer content to devote
themselves wholly to basking in affluence, dropping in at
the better international watering places, sampling marital
partners, appearing at the best balls, riding in the chases,
and doing occasional good works. They may like much or
all of that but they also want to prove they can make it on
their own in a challenging field totally apart from the source
of their wealth.

Heirs of the Pulitzer newspaper fortune are worth about $450 million, but Lilly Pulitzer has built and run a chain of fashionable women's apparel stores. Cindy Firestone of the tire fortune has been a movie maker and has won acclaim for such hard-hitting films as *Attica,* a documentary on the prison riot.

Here we will look in on two other very wealthy heiresses.

Home on
the Waggoner Range

Electra Waggoner was called the Doris Duke of Texas, only she was regarded as more beautiful, with her honey blond hair and big brown eyes. Her grandfather, the legendary W. T. Waggoner, led a great cattle drive up the Chisolm Trail and from one trip came back to Texas with $55,000 stuffed in his saddlebag.

He used it to start assembling, in north central Texas near the Oklahoma border, a ranch that is still the largest inside one fence in the United States. Half a million acres. It is about forty miles long by twenty miles wide. In land area it is close to the size of the state of Rhode Island. It covers or spills into six counties. Soon after the turn of the century, he hit oil. Electra recalls:

"He was looking for water desperately for his cattle and he was furious when he hit oil because they didn't know what to do with it. Nobody around there used it except to fill lanterns. You gave it away."

Soon oil was in great demand and it turned out that the oil field, which he called Electra after his only daughter, was enormous. When W. T. Waggoner became inactive, the ranch passed into the hands of a professional management organization. Two of his children, Electra I (aunt of the current Electra) and Guy, paid relatively little attention to anything about the ranch except the money it spawned. Guy went through a lot of divorces. Electra I got a reputation for going on $20,000 shopping sprees at Neiman-Marcus in Dallas, and of being a super-lavish entertainer. The second son, E. Paul, got interested in the ranch only belatedly, mainly because of his interest in horses. He built a 10,000-seat rodeo stadium a dozen miles from the ranch, outside Vernon. At the stadium he had his own house, complete with servants and hunting dogs. He got together there with his male friends for poker. His daughter, Electra II, called the rodeo stadium and house his "playpen for himself." He still lived officially with his wife at the ranch. His prize horse is buried, standing up, in a special little park near the entrance to the Waggoner ranch.

Electra II, Electra Waggoner Biggs, whom I talked with, was Paul's only child. She was a celebrated international socialite, while also becoming a respected professional sculptor. And now, in her sixties, she is a handsome, dashing, cheerful woman with a bouffant hairstyle.

Electra II has rarely ridden a horse and she was in her fourth decade of life before she came near the ranch for anything except a visit. Now she uses it as her home where she sculpts and from which she does her world traveling. When she is around she attends the monthly business meeting. She professed not to know how many cattle the ranch now had but knew it was in the thousands. Electra Waggoner Biggs shares the ownership of the "estate" that runs the whole spread, including her spacious home, with her cousin Bucky Wharton.

One of the roads leading to the ranch starts at the town of Electra (population 4,000). You go through slightly rolling countryside where cattle and horses are grazing, tractors are harvesting crops, and lots of oil rigs are pumping. After about a dozen miles there is a formal stone entrance to the ranch proper. From there a winding road goes past buildings and houses for about three more miles until, on a rise, you see a vast hacienda with red tiled roof. It faces, beyond a long lawn and gardens, a great 1,400-acre lake made to water livestock.

An immediate problem was how to get into the house since the parking lot faces the kitchen. There is, I later learned, a front door facing the lake. I tried a couple doors until Electra II noticed and hailed me. People usually come through the kitchen.

Inside there was a nice sweep of space, with a grand piano the main feature. It was almost completely covered with family photos. She said in jest: "I've got so many pictures that I'm going to have to get another piano." There were plastic-covered chairs.

"Daddy," she explained, "built the original small house and thought he would surprise Mother. And he brought Mother up from Fort Worth where they had been living for years, and she said she thought it was very nice. But like all women she wanted a little more. So she kept adding and adding and it has no rhyme or reason. It just rambles on."

Electra II still loves to dance, to eat caviar, and to wear $2,000 outfits by Oscar de la Renta. She was dressed in a chic traveling suit and said she would be traveling down to Wichita Falls after I left. She was going by car. Did she have a chauffeur?

"I wouldn't know what to do with him. He'd drive me crazy. If I didn't drive myself I'd be sitting here forever. I drive everywhere." She once even got lost on her own ranch.

What about the ranch's company plane, a Citation? She uses it but only if there is a business reason. "The government has made it impossible to use it on pleasure. It's so darned expensive, you know. Under this new law if you ride on your own plane, unless it's company business, you pay three times what the first class fare is."

Electra II was born and raised in Fort Worth. Her mother took her to Europe every year and saw that she became fluent in French and Italian. At age twelve she was shipped off to a finishing school on the Main Line outside Philadelphia, which she considered a kind of prison. "And then I never came home."

She made her debut at the Bachelor's Cotillion in Baltimore, then judged to be one of the two most exclusive debutante balls in the country. And in about a year, without benefit of college, she married a nice boy from Williams College whom she had met on a boat from France. His father ran one of the nation's top accounting firms. At the wedding she wore a $10,000 gown with a magnificent train. They lived in an apartment in the posh Carlyle Hotel on Manhattan's Upper East Side. They often dined at the Stork Club. She recalls:

"It was one of those things where I was much too young and he was too young and it just didn't work. I just wanted out. We were married two years or whatever. I've pushed it out of my mind."

Before marriage she had been going to a residential school for girls right across from the Metropolitan Museum. You could take whatever you wanted. She fell in love with sculpturing and began taking a bus to Greenwich Village to study with a little old lady there, and became quite good with her hands. After the divorce in Reno, her mother took her to California and one night Electra found herself at a house where there was clay and she began working with clay. One of the people present, the world-famed actor Ramon Navarro, showed interest and the upshot was that a few days later he posed for her at her hotel. She related:

"It was good. It looked like him. So that gave me an interest and I didn't know what to do with myself and I was young and divorced and didn't want to go home so mother got me a penthouse apartment back in New York at 53rd and Park. It had a little studio. I started to work, and to study again. I took drawing and casting at the Metropolitan and had a lovely old man come in and criticize for me. I carved cuff links in gold."

Soon she was in Paris learning how to cut marble and won a third prize in an art show for a bust called *Enigma*. One summer in France she worked in a bronze factory. In short, she did a lot of hammering as a part of her work.

Over the years she did busts, usually bronze, of such notable people as Harry Truman and Knute Rockne. Her most monumental creation, a commission that took several years, was a fifteen-foot-high statue of Will Rogers on his favorite horse. General Dwight Eisenhower was at the unveiling of it in Fort Worth.

She took on any size carving. For example, she was also commissioned by actress Mary Martin to do tiny medallions of her for members of the cast of *South Pacific.* When I saw her she had recently, on commission, completed three enormous heads of people who had bequeathed a library in Fort Worth.

Back in the World War II period while in New York, she fell in love with a fellow Texan, Johnny Biggs of Sherman. He was a fine baseball player but turned down the pros to work as a manager for the International Paper Company. On their first date, as a lark, he insisted on taking her to Coney Island. They married. He became a captain in the army. And after the war, with two small daughters, they decided to settle down back at the Waggoner ranch. The ranch manager was about to leave and Johnny took over the job. He loved horses.

It took Electra II quite a few years to feel comfortable with ranch life and to adjust to the social life of nearby Vernon (population 15,000). When she got restless she would take off for Paris or San Francisco.

She had a governess for the daughters but when they got to school age, but were still too young to be shipped off to a good private school, they went to the Vernon public school. Mother Electra felt that had not been a good experience. "I think there is a great deal of pressure put on them because their peers are not the same. And the children are very cruel. . . . Girls especially. . . . They make fun of you if they think you have more than they have." The experience, she has suggested, made them tend to be shy, particularly Electra III.[2] At any rate, she was relieved when they reached the age of twelve and could be sent off to Dallas's elite Hockaday School.

The daughters, both very attractive, never showed much interest in getting into the international social set. Electra III married a Houston dentist and moved to a quiet life as homemaker and artist in Santa Fe. The other daughter,

Helen, married and returned to the ranch with her husband. He works on the ranch, has an office in town, and is mostly interested in the horse operations, taking the best horses to the big quarter-horse shows.

Mrs. Electra Biggs proudly showed me pictures of her cute grandchildren from both her daughters' marriages, but she had again been uneasy about the effect that classmates at local public schools had had on Helen's daughter before she was old enough to be sent off to Hockaday. A grandson was still at the local school, but "he couldn't care less" about peer pressures.

Daughter Helen, folksy and informal, and her children have been active in local agricultural activities such as 4-H. She is much involved in Vernon community life and led a fund-raising drive to build the Red River Valley Museum near Vernon. It had just opened, and one whole room was devoted to Electra II's sculptures.

The fact that neither of her daughters has shown interest in living the glamour-filled, jet-setting life of an heiress — the kind of life into which Electra Biggs's mother carefully guided her — may indeed be partly due to hurts experienced in the Vernon public schools. But perhaps a better explanation is a change of values instilled while they were growing up in the counterculture. New concepts of a satisfying life began emerging. Pursuit of happiness took a new turn, even for the rich.

Ever since Mrs. Biggs's husband John died of cancer of the throat in 1977, she has kept herself from going stir-crazy, as she puts it, by doing extensive traveling between interludes of sculpturing, and some occasional home partying. She has a big annual New Year's party to which people come from many parts of the country. Also people come from all over for her January hunting season: "quail, duck, turkey, geese, deer, wild hogs, you name it."

Mrs. Biggs has no other home but keeps a hotel suite in Houston. She added: "To own a home today is a lot of trouble and you can't get help.... You're tied to it if you own a house. You have to go there. This way I go where I please. I go to Hong Kong every spring if I can get somebody to go with me. I've gone thirteen times. I have many friends there of all different nationalities.

"I've done Bangkok and all that and I don't like Honolulu and I love San Francisco. I've sort of narrowed it down. I mean, you know, Palm Beach to me is getting so that you can't walk down the street without seeing ugly sights and people half-dressed and, of course, New York's the same. . . . This summer I went to Paris and Venice. I like Paris. I go to New York twice a year and I'm going to Washington on Friday. And from Washington to Atlantic City to spend two days [mostly] to go to the shows. [When] I came back from Europe . . . I went to La Jolla and I went from there to San Francisco. That's my favorite of all. Then I went to see my daughter Electra in Santa Fe.

"So I don't get lonesome," she said.

Despite co-ownership of a half-million productive acres and other investments, she was not feeling particularly rich at the time of my visit because oil and agriculture prices had been down lately. (Both were up by 1987.) She had no major philanthropies of her own but as president of her parents' foundation (with assets of about $5 million) she feels she and her children, who are foundation officers, have done a lot of good around Vernon.

Since her house (but not what's in it) is owned by the Estate and the Estate takes care of the lawn and gardens, she does not have a lot of domestic upkeep expense, even with a couple of girls in the kitchen. So despite her expansive life-style, "I live on a lot less than a million a year, I can tell you right now."

And many weeks at a time, each year, she gets upstairs to her studio. She said: "It's hard work, sculpture. It's not easy. I [still] have an ambition to be the best."

Terry Allen Kramer,
Who Took Up Gambling

Of all the people I encountered, Terry Allen Kramer comes closest to matching the public's concept of how super-rich heiresses are supposed to live. She is truly one of the international beautiful people and she likes "nice houses."

Her father, Charles Allen, who was eighty-four in 1987, had long been considered on Wall Street as a genius at picking unlikely stocks. At the securities investment firm Allen & Co. in uptown New York, he has been surrounded not only by his brother but by his son, by his nephew, by Terry's husband, Irwin, by Terry's son (in training) — and Terry herself when she is in town. As a group they had a net worth in 1986 of $700 million at the very least.

Terry, a tall, slim woman in her early fifties with a colorful mane of hair and a voice that has variously been called smoky, husky, and raspy, has nothing to do with stocks. In fact she has always left her securities investments to her father. Her office jumps out from the rows of staid offices with its posters around the door and the interior done in vivid grays. When I met her, she was in a slacks costume. In one corner were a pile of colorful sweaters. She had just gotten back from salmon fishing in Iceland. In a moment we will get to the impressive independent career that she pursues from that office.

I had heard a report that her father at some point had given her a fourth of the company. She said, "We never talk about those things." She did agree she was a very rich person in her own right "by the good grace of my father." And she had married into a wealthy family.

Terry Allen Kramer does most of her traveling in her blue Rolls-Royce or in her husband's transcontinental Gulfstream II, which is worth a few million dollars. (Husband Irwin was an Allen clan member on the board of Columbia Pictures a decade ago when the company was wracked by upheaval. David McClintick, in his best-selling account of the turmoil, *Indecent Exposure,* depicts Irwin Kramer as a stubborn and sometimes belligerent negotiator.)

By chance I saw one of her "nice houses" before I met her when I was checking out Lyford Cay in the Bahamas, which, as indicated, may be the most elite watering place in the Western Hemisphere. Her father was a founding member of the Lyford Cay Club. Soon after the car that I was in passed through security gates at Lyford Cay, I saw on the right a great gate surrounded by two massive gatehouses. And off in the distance on the ocean was an extraordinarily wide house under construction. My host said it was being built by someone named Kramer from New York. One published report called it the biggest mansion on Lyford Cay.

Later Terry Allen Kramer explained to me how she and her husband came to build it. They had gotten tired of the transportation problems involved in flying out to their place at the Racquet Club in Palm Springs, California, and they had some money from selling their thirty-room place on the North Shore of Long Island, out on Sands' Point. They were vacationing for a couple weeks at a rented house on Lyford Cay and had "fallen madly in love with the whole thing." It was "marvelously" well protected. And their rented house was so delightful that they tried to buy it from its English owner by offering something over two million dollars for it, a figure her father called ridiculously high. The owner declined (and later sold it for more than $3 million).

This left her depressed because there were no more good places left for sale on this lovely spot. In that mood — and it was raining — she was on her way to play golf and encountered another English friend. When she lamented the real estate situation, he said it was funny she should say that because an eight-acre piece of land right on the ocean had just become available that day. Mrs. Kramer recalls:

"I said whoopie and bought four of the acres. And when my husband came back from golf, I said, 'Guess what I did?' And we got in the golf cart and went over and he said, 'I'll buy the other four.'"

She explained to me that the place probably looked bigger to me than it actually is "because it is only one room wide. I want to build along the whole ocean so that every room faces the ocean ... so it [the house] looks like it goes forever." As for the two massive gatehouses, she explained, one was the garage and the other the butler's house.

This new house has created quite a furor. *Forbes* in its October 1987 article entitled "There Goes the Neighborhood" reported unease in the Lyford Cay paradise. Not only were the natives unionizing but the old-guard members of the club didn't like the taste of some younger members and were reported particularly upset by the Kramer spread. It was said to have cost $4.5 million and was painted what was considered to be a shocking pink. The report said it was locally being referred to by some as the "Kramertorium."

To continue with Mrs. Kramer's account, she said the situation was "crazy" because they were also building a place closer to home in Southampton, Long Island (another famous resort). And the two were supposed to be completed in the same month, October. She was confused, didn't know what furnishings would be going where.

They had been renting in Southampton for some years. Rent ran around $50,000 for the season on a house with a reported asking price of $3.3 million. She once staged a birthday party there for Irwin that was attended by several hundred people and reportedly cost $100,000.[3] She says she always gave large parties in those years. But how did she know several hundred people to invite? She didn't, necessarily. "In a place like that on a summer weekend everybody has houseguests. What are you going to do, say: 'You can come but your houseguests can't'?"

At any rate, in the mid-80s she felt rentals at Southampton were really getting out of hand. She mentioned one guy who was charging $125,000 just for a month. So she started looking around, and again the situation was depressing.

"I was walking on the beach one day and realized that there was almost no beach property left in Southampton and wouldn't it be nice to have [the] one little piece left ... two and a half acres. So I went off and bought this piece of property which was beautiful. There's a pond on one side and the ocean on the other, on a private road so no cars can go by. My husband said, 'You're crazy.'" But she or they went ahead with it. The house that resulted, she said, had plenty of bedrooms and was really gorgeous. *Hamptons* magazine, which must by now be pretty blasé about big houses, calls it "palatial."[4]

Also of course the Kramers have their main residence back on Park Avenue, complete with chef.

One interesting aspect of Mrs. Kramer's great passion for being on the water is that she not only has no boats but hates them. "I don't go on other people's boats either."

But they do travel a lot. They're getting to Europe more often than they used to.

The above is one half of the story of Terry Allen Kramer. The other is her belated, dramatic career in the theater.

At age seventeen, she was in California with her mother when a movie producer, taken by her beauty and quick wit, did a screen test on her. She recalls: "I'm sure I couldn't act. But ... Mother made one frantic call to my father in New York, who made a few less frantic calls to the movie moguls, and that was the end of the story. I was back to Vassar in the fall. I wasn't allowed to work. No way. You get married. Girls in my day just didn't do that [work] unless you wanted to be a schoolteacher."

So within a year she got married. The marriage was brief. "Yes, I was divorced. Who hasn't been divorced?" Soon she had settled down to a long-term marriage with Irwin and occupied herself by raising children, taking care of their houses, having big parties.

By the time the three children were in high school she was getting bored and becoming infected with the new feeling that women, including heiresses, ought to be doing something on their own. "I do think there's been a great change in a woman's life, rich or poor, and I do think that young women feel they have to be doing something other than children."

Father and husband, being aware of her restlessness, agreed the time had come for her to get active in something. The theater was a natural place because the family had had a long interest in it and an old family friend, Harry Rigby, was a well-known Broadway producer. Mr. Rigby and Terry Allen Kramer became partners. Mrs. Kramer had more to contribute to the partnership than might first seem apparent. She was not only a person of wealth but had access to lots of rich friends as backers. Play-producing is a gambling business. Many promising productions die for lack of cash. Mrs. Kramer explained: "You know, Harry would get a guy for $500 or something. I'd go to the tycoons. No, I didn't have that many. I think I have about twenty." The tycoons she tapped included centimillionaires such as Edgar Bronfman, Jr., and A. Alfred Taubman.

Being a mother, she thinks, also helps in her job. "All producers should be mothers. A lot of people in the theater are children."[5]

Still, for the first several years she and Mr. Rigby had more flops than successes (not unusual on Broadway). One of the successes was *I Love My Wife,* which ran for two years and got six nominations for Tony Awards. But the fact remained that after a half-dozen years as a producer she had to face the *New York Daily News* headline, "Queen of the Flops?"

This unpleasant article opened with, "Dubious distinction of the week goes to Terry Allen Kramer who may well have become the first Broadway producer to have three shows close after one-night stands. Shows with losses close to $3 million."[6] The shows appeared over a three-year period. The article did mention some other plays she had co-produced that had "respectable" runs and one solid hit still going, *Sugar Babies.*

Actually the musical *Sugar Babies,* starring Mickey Rooney and Ann Miller, went on to become a smash hit, running for more than 1,000 performances. While it was still running on Broadway, a roadshow starring Robert Morse and Carol Channing was launched, a venture that Terry Kramer says she opposed. At any rate it bombed, with about a $1 million loss.

When I saw her she claimed that on balance her investors were ahead. She was tracking *Sugar Babies* starring Mickey Rooney on its new road tour across the country and holding her breath. The show and Mickey were one and the same. If he caught cold or took a few days off, it was over. The public would accept no substitutes.

She has called him brilliant but a "tiny terror." He kept wanting more money, claimed he couldn't live on the $35,000 a week she was paying him, wanted $50,000.[7] When it became a demand, she closed the show.

Meanwhile her partner had died and she had gone in with a new partner, James Nederlander, and they had also gone into owning or operating theaters. They owned two in London, and one was playing a musical revival that she thought was marvelous, *Me and My Girl.*

She said, "We're trying to figure out how to bring it over here." They succeeded in working out the expensive details and brought it over to New York. It was an immense success. As a part of launching *Me and My Girl* in America, they took over New York's most spectacular new theater, the Marquis.

She was pleased meanwhile that, with encouragement from her, one of her daughters, mother of two children, had opened a little French restaurant; and another daughter was in the business of designing and selling costume jewelry. She added: "It's so different now. It isn't fun anymore not to be involved."

As for money, could she visualize a time when she had so much in net worth that she would want no more?

"No, I never think of those things. Listen, the more you have the more you can leave."

CHAPTER 13

MAINTAINING

A JUST-FOLKS

LIFE-STYLE

"They have so much income I have sterilized them from any ambition."

— WALTER W. CARUTH, JR., speaking
of his four sons

We have visited with some
centimillionaires who live in regal mansions and lead the
ultra-high-society way of life. But, as already indicated, they
are far from typical. Most centimillionaires and billionaires
don't try to lead life-styles one might assume would go with
their incredible wealth because it doesn't come naturally to
them and in any case even trying would require a great
preoccupation of one's time.

The richest man in America in 1987, Sam Walton ($7-
plus billion then), the discount chain operator of Bentonville, Arkansas, rides around town in a beat-up Ford pickup.

He lives in a large ranch-type house, and does a lot of his chatting with friends at a local coffee shop. He politely declined to see me.

The fifth richest man in America in 1986, billionaire Warren Buffett of Omaha, declined to see me in a long friendly letter explaining he had been forced to invoke a flat rule against interviews. He did offer to make an exception by visiting with me over the telephone, but that would have broken my rule about how visits were to be conducted. At any rate, Mr. Buffett, a wizard at investing, lives in the same upper-middle-class house he has lived in for thirty years, or since long before he was even moderately rich. His office is said to be plain, with linoleum floor and throw rugs. He spends much of the day sipping cherry-flavored Pepsi.

Mary Hudson of Kansas City, who built a nine-figure fortune operating a gas station chain, achieved her wealth largely by penny-pinching, and the habit apparently carried over to her private life. Although she has a thirty-nine-room mansion on a hill in the Kansas City area, she has reportedly made a considerable effort to keep unnecessary lights turned off. Once when she was preparing for a large dinner party she bought off-price liquor, and brownies for dessert. She didn't see any reason for using a separate dessert plate for the brownies.

The Centimillionaire
Who Prefers Biscuits and Gravy

The remarkable man we are about to meet illustrates a number of relevant points about great net worth. Wealth can be wildly superfluous to one's preferred style of living. And great wealth can promote a real loss of satisfaction in one's life by making it harder to find true friends . . . by promoting family acrimony . . . and by causing chagrin about expectations from one's offspring.

Walter W. Caruth, Jr. was the first super-rich Texan I visited and I expected, perhaps unreasonably, something pretty spectacular. I knew very little about him except that through his family he controlled about $600 million and that North Dallas was sometimes called "Will Caruth's backyard." I was told, incorrectly, that he was a big figure in the John Birch Society. It turned out to be a son with the same name, Walter W. Caruth III.

Also I knew he had an MBA. This turned out to be a very interesting fact. Conventional wisdom is that having an MBA is virtually a must for anyone who hopes to succeed in business. When I had completed my visiting with people of vast wealth, I reviewed the educational backgrounds of the thirty people. Only two had attained MBA degrees, Mr. Caruth and Sam LeFrak. Both had inherited very substantial businesses from wealthy fathers. Not one of my self-made persons of great wealth had an MBA degree.

Rich newcomers to Dallas searching the society pages for clues on who is who can look back for twenty years and find few references to Will and Mabel Caruth. Charity balls? They are invited to them all. Mr. Caruth: "We've gone to one, maybe two over the decades, just to hear the orchestra or something."

Forty years ago the Caruth family owned 30,000 acres of land in Texas, just a moderately large spread by Texas standards. But the Caruth spread had something special in its favor. It was situated just to the north and northeast of Dallas, then a small city of about 200,000 people.

After Will got back from college he took the $1,000 his father had given him for not drinking or smoking during adolescence and put it into a small construction company. He was starting to make a go of it.

One day his father, gruff, stubborn, and taciturn, came into his small office and without a word tossed him a document conveying to him total control over the Caruth land holdings. The astonished young Will asked:

"Why are you doing this, Dad?"

"I think you have grown."

With that he walked away.[1]

Slowly and shrewdly Will began selling off the land. He is quick to say it didn't take a genius to make a fortune, given the location. Typically, he sold land cheap and kept a 50 percent interest in development. He still owns 30,000 acres of land but it is mostly located elsewhere.

Will arranged, for tax reasons, to take himself substantially out of his father's will and to set up generation-skipping trusts that eventually put the title to most of the family assets in the names of his father's grandchildren (Will's four sons and the two children of a sister). Meanwhile, he followed his father's order to maintain management control. Despite all this he has a fortune in his own right, which he sees as more a bother than a bonanza.

I assumed that being a centimillionaire he would live in the area strongly favored by the big rich, Highland Park. Instead, I was directed to a fairly new area in University Park, once Caruth land. Most of the houses, while handsome, were fairly close together along the streets, presumably designed for up-and-coming corporate executives. The Caruths were in a corner house, somewhat larger than neighboring houses. No walls, circular drives, and so on. The house sat back from the road by about thirty yards.

It was early evening. As I walked toward the quite ordinary front door, I could see Mr. and Mrs. Caruth, through the picture window. They were in lounge chairs in the two front corners of a living room. The chairs were aimed at a TV set. Mrs. Caruth, a pleasant, blonde woman from an old Boston family, greeted me. They had been married about fifty years. He apologized for not getting up. He had a bothersome leg. His voice was cheerful but a bit raspy; his body was now comfortably rotund. He was dressed in shirt, pants, and slippers. (In an early picture he had looked the erect, solemn businessman.)

It was a comfortable, but not large, living room. The main features besides the TV set were a glass enclosure of stuffed pheasants and a small shelf about a foot from the ceiling around most of the room on which sat awards given to the Caruths over the decades.

They turned off the TV. Were there particular programs they liked?

Mr. Caruth: "We like all of them. Both of us seem to enjoy these educational programs on Channel 13 but she gets quite annoyed with my flipping from tennis matches to football."

Mrs. Caruth: "And baseball."

Mr. Caruth: "You can't find anything more tranquilizing. I can go to sleep on a baseball game just like that!"

He got to talking about money fairly directly.

"I am not impressed by people that are lavish about throwing money away without getting value for it. Right now I am in a critical situation. My car has sprung a leak in the radiator. It's only thirteen years old, and it's a beautiful car, a 1972 Chevrolet Caprice." (I had seen it to the rear and assumed it belonged to a servant.) "It's the last model that did not have a catalytic converter and it's got a 400-cubic-inch engine." Did he drive it himself? "Of course I do.

"The beauty is with that 400 cubic inches you can just walk off with a horse trailer without even knowing you have it on there. You can drive it over these prairies I own without setting fire to them."

Mrs. Caruth said regarding a household staff: "Well, I do most of the work around here. I thoroughly enjoy my house. I had a maid for a long time. She retired about five or six years ago. So I have a maid that comes in and cleans if I want her to, and if I stay behind her. But if we have company, I do the work. It doesn't bother me."

No cook?

Mr. Caruth: "She does all the cooking."

What had they had for supper?

Mrs. Caruth: "I made him a steak tonight 'cause he mentioned it. Squash, rice, gravy and biscuits, and salad."

Mr. Caruth: "I don't eat too much steak. I've been living on chicken, especially barbecued, and meatloaf. What's better than meatloaf?"

Mrs. Caruth: "He likes plebian food. He likes hash and stew, chicken and dumplings."

Did they go out much to the many fine gourmet restaurants in the Dallas area?

Mr. Caruth: "Not at all."

Mrs. Caruth: "I go when he is out of town because he really does not care for them. We go to the barbecue place. We go to the Mexican place. We go to a Chinese place, things like that, maybe once in two weeks."

Mr. Caruth: "After all these years we found a good place to get fettucini right over here on Greenwood Avenue."

How often did they have catered meals? Once in the last fifteen years.

They asked me where I was staying. I said The Mansion, owned by Caroline Hunt of H. L. Hunt's "first" family and, as indicated, reportedly the world's richest woman.[2] (I was expecting to see her but the visit was canceled because she had a sick child.) Mr. Caruth guffawed at the money she had poured into the hotel, $175,000 a room. He had built a fine hotel-type place over in Florida for $14,000 a room.

Mrs. Caruth: "Caroline and I used to have play-groups with our children together once a week when they were young. Her two oldest boys are the same age as our two youngest ones."

Our talk got onto church-going.

Mr. Caruth: "I was a deacon over at the Highland Park Presbyterian Church and I just got allergic to all those dog-gone fur coats that were hanging around."

Mrs. Caruth: "And parking a mile from the church."

They heard a minister at their son's graduation that they liked very much so they joined his church, Congregational, at the time. After a while he died and there was a successor that Mr. Caruth didn't take to. "He spoke in such a high tone of voice I couldn't even hear him. I got sawmill ears. When I was working down in east Texas in sawmills, why your ears actually just sort of close up. You don't hear any highs. So anybody that tries to sell me high fidelity sound equipment is a fool. But anyway we had a little trouble [with the minister] so I had an opportunity there to pay off the mortgage and I don't think we ever went back."

More recently the Caruths had not been active church-goers. They had become fond of an "extremely religious"

Methodist minister in Fort Worth who broadcast his sermons over television, Barry Bailey.

Mr. Caruth: "It used to be I would set the tape recorder to pick him up here and record his sermons and take the tape to Florida. Don't have to now. We pick him up direct.

"Anyway, my own philosophy, I think mundane, involves all of Christ's teachings. Try to be proud of what you're doing for your fellow man. Rather simple. And as for the hereafter, I've found amusement in the last year or two in metaphysics. . . . There are certain natural laws that we're not smart enough to understand yet. And we can't tune in on those frequencies.

"But a great deal has been done toward research in recording voices of the dead. . . . It seems you can tune a tape recorder onto a white sound like in between the stations and some way you can get voices on that if you play it back. Anyway, we think it's quite interesting the way that those things can happen and we've funded a research scientist." The man had been brought to nearby Southern Methodist University (largely built on Caruth lands) for study and research.

Mr. Caruth spent a good deal of time talking about the woes that had befallen him as a result of being in control of a large fortune.

"I don't think there are any particular rewards of outstanding affluence because I don't need all these resources to make me happy. What I want is a bulldozer and a piece of land that I can beautify."

Mrs. Caruth: "And the rewards to you that come if you can help other people."

His woes arising from wealth seemed to fall in three categories.

One. Finding real friends. He was hounded by people he hadn't seen in years who wanted him to go in on deals.

"It's been very hard for me to have friends because they'd come in the door and I'd wonder, because everybody was looking for something for quite a time. They would really get very annoyed when I wouldn't sell them a piece of land for less than what it was worth. One guy said, 'I can liquidate the whole thing over here for you in two years.' I said, 'Hell, who couldn't.'" It was something that should not be done for another ten years and then "done proper."

He felt he was forced to be a loner. Gradually he learned to reject everything that didn't really intrigue him. He said he would respond: "Hell, I don't see anything in it but money, and I got that. So why bother?"

It was this problem of wariness about who could be a friend that caused them to become enthusiastic about setting up a base in Crystal River, Florida, north of Tampa.

He said that he and Mabel had had a lot of fun overhauling a resort inn there called The Plantation and developing it into "a little diamond." With considerable fondness he talked of their many friends in Florida and the pleasure the Caruths had had in introducing these friends to Mexican cooking.

"We've got some grand people down there.... They're awfully nice and they accepted us just as individuals rather than looking at us as big money people." He has explained his enthusiasm for the Floridians in these terms: "I'd rather be known as a person rather than an institution.... That's why I like Florida. The name Caruth doesn't mean a damn to those people down there."

The major extravagance of the Caruths in the past decade or so was their purchase of a Citation jet airplane to get back and forth to Crystal River. It is the only jet certified to land at the small airport there.

Mr. Caruth: "It's a little bit annoying to go out here to the Dallas/Forth Worth Airport with my emphysema and gimpy leg and walk from one end of that thing to the other. So Mabel and others finally persuaded me." It also saves the two-hour ride up from Tampa.

A second source of woe was created by the control given to him by his father to manage the estate. He found himself on the receiving end of fierce discord with a sister and her husband. He said they tore into his careful plans for selling parcels of the family's 30,000 acres of super-prime land, especially parcels owned in common. And in the process they apparently succeeded in setting his own mother against him. This is the only aspect of the Caruth saga that at all resembles the TV melodrama *Dallas*.

It still brings pain to Will and Mabel Caruth.

Mr. Caruth: "There was a pressure there from inside the family, from my sister's side of the family. They practically alienated mother from me, [claiming] that I'd stolen millions of dollars. I offered to open every transaction I had made over the years and put it to arbitration. If the arbitrators found that I had not paid full value for what I received, I would gladly pay it. But if it was found I had overpaid, I wanted it back. All of it was just a bunch of mouthing, mouthing, mouthing [by kinfolk] who kept trying to get more control.

"I think that's one of the reasons I am a soft sell, because I had those experiences about the way a . . . wealthy man can act. I think that affected me, don't you agree, Mabel?" And the way his own mother talked to him.

Mrs. Caruth: "That hurt him as badly as anything I've ever known."

The third source of his woes was his disappointment in the way that great wealth affected his sons. As indicated earlier, to minimize inheritance taxes he had passed title of great wealth to each of the four of them (as well as the sister's children).

The Caruths seemed fond of their four sons (and their nine grandchildren) and see them often. And two of the sons have had some built-in problems. One was thrown from a horse and suffered a long-term effect. Another was required to be on strong dosage of a drug for an ailment.

William Walter III has been a full-time worker for the John Birch Society, giving lectures to the Daughters of the American Revolution and so on, and also works at photography. Apparently early on he had confirmed to his father, in a talk while on an auto trip, that he was not interested in any major role in the family enterprise. Son Bob raises quarter horses. Mr. Caruth does not hide his disappointment that his sons are all either uninterested in, or incapable of, managing the family empire. And he wonders about the wisdom of thrusting wealth on young people.

Mr. Caruth: "I think that one of the main unfortunate things is that our younger generation doesn't have enough responsibility. There's no motivation like a growl in the gut. I set up these things here in my different businesses where it could be split in four different pieces and my boys wouldn't have to compete with one another. They could each have a business of their own. It could be a beautiful setup.

"But by managing Dad's and Mother's estates to the best of my ability, they have so much income that I sterilized them of any ambition.... And now, why none of them has any competence to run a business. None of them is inheriting anything from me.... They're already so well taken care of they couldn't use any more money if they had it. So all of my estate goes to the Caruth Foundation when I die, for education and scientific research and public safety.

"I was able to salvage something. Since my kids didn't know how to run their financial affairs ... I made a bargain with them, a contract really." In return for funds he is passing to them each year through a trust, they agree that upon his death they will put their trust money in another trust "that will last for their lifetime where the bank would have the fiscal management. They would have the income and everything else but they would not be in a position to squander the capital." Mr. Caruth seemed to be gambling that some grandchildren might be more interested in the management of wealth.

So finally we turned to how much it took the man controlling a $600 million family empire to finance his own life-style. Could he and Mrs. Caruth live on $1 million a year?

Mrs. Caruth: "Oh, good grief!"

Mr. Caruth: "We're living on a hell of a lot less than that. I would say that with all of our extravagances, all of Mabel's traveling, and all of my fishing tackle, there would be less than $200,000 expense a year."

Mrs. Caruth: "I'd say closer to $100,000."

Mr. Caruth: "That's leaving out the airplane, which was a one-time thing. This house isn't green-stamps, you know." Analysis of family finances continued. They seemed to concur that living costs probably ran at least $150,000 a year.

The Just-Folks of Hallmark

Donald Hall and his sisters Barbara and Elizabeth have a net worth of close to a billion dollars, most of it coming from Hallmark Cards, a private company founded by their father, Joyce Hall. They comprise one of the wealthiest families in the Kansas City area.

Donald, their business leader and holder of half the family fortune, lives in suburban Mission Hills in a house not far from the grand guarded hilltop mansion of Ewing Kauffman. Hall's house is on an upper-middle-class street and is the kind of house a sight-seer would not look at twice. Right on the street. No fence. A ranch type built on three levels.

Mr. Hall, amiable but shy, taciturn, and rather proper, recalled he and his wife had designed it themselves, with no knowledge of architecture, twenty-seven years earlier. "It's been a very nice home. It is where our kids all grew up." The house originally had three bedrooms but they had to add "a little offshoot" when their third youngster was born. There was no swimming pool. He guessed the market value was less than a half-million dollars.

Was he ever tempted to build an estate more appropriate to his wealth?

"Well, my wife and I are starting to talk about building another house because all the kids are out of the house and it's not right for us anymore. We'll probably build a house, probably not bigger. It might even be smaller."

Was it true he still drove his own car to work?

"Yeah. I'm not too old to do that yet. I drive a Buick."

He had just flown in from Washington. The huge company has one airplane, but since his trip was not business he had flown commercial.

Any boats?

"We have an eighteen-foot boat that we take to a lake out here and water-ski behind."

Did he have other homes? "We have a little place in Hawaii. It's a condominium."

How big a staff at home? "Well, my wife has a woman who helps her about two-thirds of the day on weekdays." Who cooks? "My wife. It's the only reason I have trouble with fat."

He greatly enjoys playing golf at the nearby elite Kansas City Country Club but "is terrible at it." His wife and he also like to ski. "We used to go to Aspen a good deal, but Aspen got very social so we go to the old place in Utah, Alta (near Salt Lake City). The snow, I think, is better there."

Is it possible that he was living on less than a million dollars a year?

"I would hope so. Yeah, I would sure think so. You could play a lot of golf on that."

Donald's father, a dynamic, strong-minded man, wanted his children to grow up knowing the value of work and so though the family was already wealthy, the children were raised on the family farm. Donald stacked hay, planted, raked, hoed corn, owned his own flock of chickens.

His two grown sons and grown daughter all work for the company. He didn't know the title of Donald Jr., the oldest, but knew he was a manager of color separation in graphic arts. None of the children can reasonably expect a fast series of promotions to be chief executive of the company. With Donald Hall's blessing an outsider had recently been brought in and made chief executive officer.

The company was a pioneer in adopting a plan that encouraged employees to own shares in their company. And it has been rated as being near the very top of the 100 best corporations to work for in America.[4]

The Wealthiest
Self-Made Woman?

Sarah Korein may well be the richest self-made woman in America. Many women are ahead of her in net assets, but most inherited their fortunes or were able to build exceptionally on enterprises already well started. Others had significant help from male relatives: fathers, brothers, or sons. Estée Lauder, founder of the company bearing her name, is a lot richer, but *Forbes* said in 1985 that son Leonard had long been instrumental in the firm's growth. Mary Hudson, the tight-fisted gasoline chain owner, possibly may be as rich as Ms. Korein but in one phase she was working closely with her brothers. There have been no male relatives helping Sarah Korein in any significant way. Her only help from relatives was, at the beginning, from her mother. She got into the high-rise business almost accidentally as a young schoolteacher.

Ms. Korein, when I saw her, owned a dozen choice skyscraper-type buildings in Manhattan. Though of gentle nature, she has played hardball successfully with some of New York's more fabled male real estate operators.

Forbes listed her as being worth at least $100 million in 1982. The next year it dropped her solely because its cutoff for making the list had jumped to $125 million.

She had rarely, if ever, been interviewed. Even contacting her required quite a search. The person to talk with, it turned out, was a friend who managed the elite Delmonico Hotel on Park Avenue, which she owned. She was living quite a few hundred yards away in one of several big buildings she owned on Central Park.

Her choice for residence, interestingly, was not in any of her several elite residential buildings and hotels but in a relatively ordinary apartment building for the area. It was a forty-five-year-old building. In it, at street level, a store was selling such things as dish towels and men's shirts. Security arrangements in the lobby appeared to be quite casual for the area. The main part that I could see of her apartment was low on grandeur. Tens of thousands of New Yorkers have living rooms at least as large. The walls were thickly covered with paintings, which she assured me were not Old Masters. There was a handsome sculptured horse and small Oriental tea tables.

Ms. Korein was a surprisingly youthful-looking blonde for a woman past seventy. She was frail, perhaps because she was still recuperating from injuries of a bad fall, and was dressed in a long white lace gown, sandals, a string of green beads, and dark glasses. Her laugh was warm, but her voice was the big surprise, since she has faced up to some of New York's most super-dynamic realtors. It was soft, in fact so soft that at times both I and my tape recorder had trouble hearing what she said. A part of her legend is that she didn't need to do much talking. She did her homework thoroughly, set her price, and typically scorned bargaining.

Born in Germany, she married a Hungarian-born civil engineer and they came to the Bay Ridge area of Brooklyn. He rarely showed any interest in real estate.

Sarah Korein went to normal school to get a certificate and began teaching school. She and her mother together had $16,000 and a lawyer suggested they put it in second mortgages paying the then high rate of 6 percent. She described her mother as "a housekeeper, a very sweet woman." And she summed up what happened as a result of the hard times of the 1930s:

"There were a lot of vacancies. The houses were neglected. By accident we came into the real estate business. The first one we acquired was a six-story apartment building in Astoria."

They obviously didn't have enough money to take over the building themselves. Instead, they made a deal with Prudential Insurance Company, which was stuck with the building. They threw themselves into cleaning out the place, sprucing it up, painting the floors, cleaning out the lobby. All this brought them a good loan from Prudential, and they found themselves holding title to a sixty-apartment building. By a shrewd pricing policy and advertising in German-language papers, they gradually got their building to be a money-making proposition. The insurance company was very happy and impressed. Thenceforth they had a good source of credit for future ventures.

Nowadays Sarah Korein typically wants "equity" or unfettered ownership. "On some buildings I have no mortgages at all. . . . I learned that it should not be on a loan. If you own your realty no matter what the times are you are always better."

Another of her secrets: "I always look for good location and good quality building." Hence her strong emphasis on Central Park, Park Avenue, Wall Street. The land values will rarely go down, will almost always go up.

Had she ever gone back and taken courses in advanced management or real estate?

"No. I'm going to tell you something. In my days I stood up and a lot of these giants fell by the wayside. I learned the business so well, I mean I learned every phase of it . . . by involving myself, by experience." To her, the land under the building is the main consideration. "No matter what happens the land will always be there and so will the value of the land if you have a good location." In high-rise economics, I gathered, there are four elements: the land, the building on it, the lease on the building, the management of the building. She cherishes them in descending order. The conversation turned to William Zeckendorf, Sr., the fabulous developer I visited three decades ago. (See chapter 3.)

"He used to come and visit us every Friday. . . . He was a great man. I happened to be very friendly with him and also became a partner with him [on a well-located office building] so I knew him. He would have the lease and I would have the land and building. The problem is that [later] in the early seventies things were not so good for him and he hocked his lease." And hence they got into a lot of problems. Sadly she said, "He was excellent at buying and selling, financing, building. But when it came to management that was his biggest problem.

"And I had another piece where Harry Helmsley [who became the famous billionaire] had the lease. But things were bad and he stopped paying his rent too when things were bad." She described the complications and how she had ordered him and his friends out. She continued: "He said, 'Sarah, you're not going to take away management from us. We're all together.'" Ms. Korein chuckled. "I said no." This was a fine building on Madison Avenue. She said she still owned it.

She was still very active in New York real estate. "I'm trying not to be, but you know I'm not really a club woman and I cannot sit down and play cards because I have no patience for it. So my life is really involved in the business. And to me ... to make a deal is very important and especially when I work it out, work around it until it is a good deal. Maybe I sound silly."

Her beloved husband the engineer died about a decade ago. She led me to pictures of her two children and grandchildren. "This is my son, who is a professor in neurology at New York University Medical Center.... And my daughter here is an associate professor at the John Jay College of Criminal Justice. Even my grandchildren are scientists." One grandson, she said, wrote a textbook on computer robotics that is used for instruction at MIT.

She said she would have welcomed them all in real estate but saw they had different aims, goals.

Sarah Korein's main extravagance is that she owns a house in a fairly elite area of south Florida. It is not on the water and it is not a big spread — just four bedrooms on a court. She likes to go there occasionally. Ms. Korein said she used to be a gourmet cook but now cooks only when the children come. "I don't spend excessively. You know you come to a stage in life when you don't need so much. I don't believe in showing off."

Her philanthropy mainly involves gifts to hospitals, universities, orphanages. "Those are my favorites." She gave a million dollars to the Einstein College of Medicine of Yeshiva University, which honored her with a doctorate.

As I was about to leave she graciously asked me to take her arm so that she could walk with me to the door.

CHAPTER 14

PLAYING

THE POWER

GAME

"Witt doesn't mind judges who know
their place. He just doesn't think they
should get uppity."

— A Little Rock, Arkansas, politician
some years ago[1]

Uppity judges could be both-
ersome to Witt Stephens if, for example, they disapproved of
some of the ways he and his younger brother Jack have run
public utilities: water companies, gas companies, telephone
companies.

Witt and his brother have also been buying and selling
dozens of other companies. And during all this they have
created in Little Rock the largest investment banking firm
in America outside New York City. Recently they shifted
more to making their own deals.

Corporations may finagle to influence prices or public policy; and occasionally immensely wealthy individuals such as Leonard Stern, Rupert Murdoch, Ivan Boesky, Lester Crown, and Jack Simplot may gain a reputation of using their fortunes to play rough. But the legendary predatory figures who stalked the American landscape and used politicians to enhance their power are much less conspicuous today. For a few decades Wilton R. Stephens of Little Rock was recognized as one of the last of the stalkers working through political clout. When I saw him, in his late seventies, he still was a man to reckon with.

Witt Stephens, Power Player

In his downplaying country-boy way of talking he explained to me, "I'm really a farmer at heart, and uneducated. I couldn't make it as a farmer and so got into the investment business and started trading." It is true that he was born on a farm and does virtually all his vacationing on the family farm and that he never finished eighth grade. He also modestly attributed most of the success of their network of companies to brother Jack, who is fourteen years his junior. "He sits back and does the work . . . and I trade." Jack looks more like a typical businessman. In mid 1987 their net worth was put at a billion dollars.

The Stephens holding company empire is run from a plain gray three-story building in downtown Little Rock. Some of the 250-odd employees overflow into nearby buildings.

The Stephens investment banking company also has an office in Hong Kong but Witt has never been there. And he said it had been about twelve years since he had been to New York City.

Witt Stephens is a tall, shambling man in a chronically rumpled suit. His voice is gravelly and usually heard from behind a well-chewed cigar. His office is small.

He was slumped behind a phone taking a call when I arrived, and then there was another call. The secretary advised: "You rush in when he gets off the phone or he'll be on the phone again. He does a lot of his own dialing." (I did.) His calls mostly seemed to be with cronies.

When young Witt decided he was not cut out to be a farmer, he started selling belt buckles that gave one a military look. He also sold jewelry to Indians. And he sold Bibles door to door. In approaching housewives with his Bibles, it is said that he sometimes would suggest that they kneel in prayer.

While Witt's father was a farmer, he also was a trader. And he had spent time in the state legislature. Father and son were definitely not bumpkins. It was father in fact who suggested to son that he might find it profitable to get together some money and put it into municipal bonds. The depression had run them down to twenty-five cents on a dollar. State bonds in fact were in default. Father thought they could only go up. So Witt got together about $15,000 and started buying and selling bonds, and within a few years they indeed were paying off at par.

As he found himself getting into high finance, I asked, did he consider going back to school and enhancing his capabilities by getting a college degree and maybe an MBA?

"No. That's a bunch of horseshit. You know that.... I didn't go to school but I knew the way to make money for me was to make it for other people."

Taking off from his trading he was soon buying and selling larger and larger companies, usually gas, water, or telephone utilities that required some sort of government approval to be bought or sold. With a small operation he could move fast but had trouble getting people to take him seriously. He had to go all the way to Philadelphia to a Securities Exchange Commission hearing when he wanted to pick up a gas company in Fort Smith, Arkansas. An SEC lawyer at the hearing was really working him over.

"This nice young fellow from Harvard was questioning me awful hard about where I was going to get the cash for the deal." After the lawyer had pressed him quite sternly for a while, Mr. Stephens looked up at the judge and said: "I brung it with me." He reached in his pocket and passed up a cashier's check for the full amount. "We had a lot of fun in those days."[2]

Witt Stephens concluded fairly quickly that when you are buying and selling utility companies and operating them it is helpful to have a favorable political environment (i.e., friends at high levels). Mr. Stephens is a friendly fellow and he quickly learned to be not only friendly but extremely generous by Arkansas standards with his favorite candidates for high office. Witt Stephens was a longtime ally of Orval Faubus, governor for six terms, and as recently as 1983 Faubus referred to the Stephens brothers as "the most powerful single political force" in the state and added that they can "dry up" funds for candidates they oppose.[3]

Political ideology may have relatively little to do with their choices. In a fairly recent governor's race Witt backed the Democrat and Jack the Republican. The Democrat won and the losing Republican went to work for Stephens enterprises.[4]

One major goal of utility owners, of course, is to get permission to charge higher rates. When Witt was actively running Arkansas Louisiana Gas, he was able to get new rate schedules that added millions of dollars to company profits each year. Fellow stockholders included at least seven prominent state officials, among them the commissioner of revenue.[5]

Also while Witt was running Arkansas Louisiana Gas, he persuaded the state Public Service Commission to adopt a new rule that would pass through more of the costs to consumers. Some consumers hollered so much that the state supreme court struck down the ruling. Witt Stephens was really put out. The *Wall Street Journal* explained what happened next. "Mr. Stephens' political machine went into high gear; and within a week of the court ruling a bill incorporating the new rate rule was passed by the state legislature and signed into law by Governor Orval Faubus."[6]

The Stephenses' numerous corporate arms sometimes do business with each other. In one instance that got national attention, a gas utility that Witt owned, Arkansas Oklahoma Gas, seemed to have a sweetheart deal with a Stephens gas supplier, Stephens Production Company. According to one analysis, the Stephens utility was paying Stephens Productions 97 cents per thousand cubic feet while paying outside suppliers 68 cents.[7] Extenuating circumstances were claimed. The Arkansas Public Service Commission simply admonished the two Stephens companies to be less chummy in the future.[8]

Mr. Stephens's life is almost totally absorbed in making money, not consuming it. He has no boats or personal planes, rarely travels for pleasure. Sometimes he plays bridge at night with his brother and a couple of buddies. He offered me directions on how to go to get a look at his house, in Carmack Village just outside Little Rock. It is a handsome Colonial house with a few columns and fine trees on a bluff overlooking the Arkansas River. It sits back about seventy yards from the street. The taxi driver explained to me that where Mr. Stephens lived was no longer the most elite area of greater Little Rock. Mr. Stephens was widowed and remarried and had two grown daughters and a son just finishing high school.

"I don't run with the millionaires. I don't buy that path of life."

He spends almost every weekend at the 2,500-acre working farm the family has long owned about forty-five miles south of Little Rock. Had he thought of retiring and enjoying life?

"The only way I can enjoy life is to work every day, because I've worked since I was seven years old. It's a challenge, you know, to be able to think up deals, recognize a deal when you see it."

As for money: "I like to play the business game and money is a way of keeping score."

Was he much involved in philanthropy?

"No. My brother is."

CHAPTER 15

VENTURING

FOR MORE

THAN MONEY

"I love to work on the ranch, doing the
cattle work, the horse work and the
fencing work.... I've been another
ranch hand."

— EDWARD BASS, regarding the time he
 spends at a vast experimental ranch
 in Australia; *Fortune* in 1987 put his
 net worth at $1 billion

Some say the four Bass
brothers are taking over from the Morgans and Rockefellers
and du Ponts as America's premier rich family. They're accumulating the necessary billions. While their roots are in
Fort Worth, Texas, they are widely judged too quiet and reserved to be considered real Texans. All are Yale graduates
and increasingly they have acquired homes outside Texas.

The oldest brother, Sid, and his wife, Anne, in the mid-
1980s were soaring to the top of New York society, from their
palatial Fifth Avenue apartment, through the usual route of

active patronage of the arts. (Their joint ascent to social stardom was disrupted by publicity about a romantic diversion.)

Brother Bob and family had bought a $4 million compound of houses in the heart of Washington's social center, Georgetown.

Brother Ed, second oldest and a bachelor, had set up a series of home bases around the world. For quite a while he considered Santa Fe, New Mexico, his real home and it was so listed by *Business Week* as recently as 1986. He told me he now considers as "home" whichever home base for a project he is currently visiting. He explained: "People ask, 'When are you going home?' Well, that is not an appropriate question. I now feel at home at each of the places. Each time I go to another place I'm coming home again." One "home" is an apartment in downtown Fort Worth. All the other brothers, including youngest brother Lee, maintain multi-million-dollar homes in elite Westover Hills on the west side of the city.

The brothers' inherited fortune was begun by oil wildcatter Sid Richardson. Childless, he put most of his wealth in a foundation but gave a few tens of millions to his nephew Perry Bass. Perry nurtured the fortune for a decade, while sons Sid, Bob, and Lee all got masters degrees in business administration. Ed started out studying business but did his graduate work in architecture. When his four sons were starting to get out of school, Perry put most of the money into Bass Brothers Enterprises and went off sailing.

Wizards from the nation's top investment firms were brought in to make the money grow. The chief imported genius at deal-making for fifteen years was Richard Rainwater, the investment coordinator.[1] In guiding the Basses he became a centimillionaire himself. The money went into bargain companies, into growth companies, into choice real estate, and as the fortunes got into really big numbers, into playing a cat-and-mouse game where takeover threats were involved. This is a game that extremely rich individuals can play much more effectively than ordinary corporations. Individuals can be more secretive and act more swiftly than corporations, which have to assemble boards of directors, consult unions, and so on.

The game, officially known as arbitrage, has become widely known as greenmailing, and the Bass brothers have been described as major players. They might have no intention of actually taking over the target company, but the target would never know. Quietly, through a network of friends, trusts, and so forth, they would round up, say, 10 percent of a target company's stock then softly say "boo." The simple news that the Bass brothers were buying big into a company would in itself cause Wall Street investors to take note, and hurry to place buy orders, so the stock's price would rise. And the target company might try to buy off the Basses.

Thus it was for example that Texaco gave the Bass brothers a $400 million pretax profit by buying back their Texaco stock, getting in addition a promise that the Basses would leave Texaco alone for ten years; and the Basses made $100 million pretax by cashing in their Marathon Oil stock when Marathon sold out to U.S. Steel.[2] Blue Bell, Inc., maker of blue jeans, gave the Bass brothers a $50 million pretax profit by buying back their interest in Blue Bell.[3]

In 1986 the brothers decided to operate more loosely. They divided their multibillion-dollar empire into four companies; but they still do a lot of things together. And singly or in combination they still have a reputation (some more than others) as heavyweight marauders studying the corporate world for potential takeover plays or other ways to make a company's stock prices jump.[4] In 1988 brother Robert (and his advisers) made a takeover offer involving $2 billion.

The Novel Projects of
Edward Bass

Between 1983 and 1986 the net worth of Edward Bass, the least involved of the four brothers in terms of time devoted to family businesses, rose at a rate of $100 million a year, until it approached the billion-dollar mark.

Most of his money was in clear profit-oriented investments. But his investments around the world in personal "venture capital" projects are what passionately absorb his interest even though, again, he insisted to me that they account for only 5 percent of his assets. He often learns what is happening with the great bulk of his regular investments by reading the newspapers, but says he does try to get to strategy meetings.

It was to learn more about him and his personal ventures that I journeyed to a ranch near Tucson, Arizona, his home that month. Some call him the family oddball. I found him extraordinarily interesting.

The arrangement was that someone would meet me at the Tucson airport and drive me the thirty miles to Sunspace Ranch, where unusual things were afoot on a dramatic plateau near Oracle. Unfortunately I found en route that the plane would be an hour late in arriving. I managed to get a message to someone at the ranch about the delay.

When I finally arrived at the airport, a slim, handsome man approaching forty with sandy hair and a nice-boy look waved to me and, smiling, stepped forward and said, "I'm Ed Bass." He was dressed in shirt, boots, tan pants with a bullhorn belt buckle. Maybe he had planned to meet me but I suspect he pitched in when whoever was supposed to meet me was unavailable because of the delay.

When we got to the luggage area, he insisted on taking the heavier of my two bags and led me a hundred yards or so to his compact station wagon. He apologized for the fact that we would be a bit late for supper at the ranch. As he drove swiftly toward the ranch he briefed me on what he was trying to accomplish. Some of his verbiage left my mind spinning: biospherics, ecosystems. There was a conference center at the Sunspace Ranch and they had just completed an international conference on techniques to preserve the environment.

Meanwhile, considerable progress was being made on a $30 million project to build Biosphere II. I learned that Biosphere I is the planet Earth which we live on and Biosphere II would be man's first attempt, outside of test tubes, to create a miniature planet, a kind of sealed-in Noah's Ark complete with microbes, a variety of plants and animals, miniature jungles, savannahs, bays, deserts. It is being built to occupy two acres and to sustain eight volunteer humans for about two years. A writer in the scientific publication *Discover* has called it the most exciting scientific project to be undertaken in the past quarter century. Currently many male and female candidates are training to qualify as one of the eight humans to board this ark and be sealed off for the two-year stay. At this writing seal-off time is set for 1989.

The project has attracted considerable interest from universities and government agencies, since it offers a quick way to test the impact of changes in the environment, even the claim that nuclear war would produce a devastatingly long winter. Duplicates on a smaller or larger scale could be used to save endangered species. And a biosphere could potentially serve as a long-term life-support system in orbit or on the moon or Mars.

Mr. Bass insists on viewing it as an entrepreneurial effort and suggests that as with any advanced engineering project it might produce profitable spin-offs.

On the journey to the Sunspace Ranch he also got to talking about his projects at the vast ranch in northwest Australia, 150 miles from the nearest town, and a smaller, totally experimental ranch in Australia. He has been spending at least half of each year at the large Australia ranch partly because he found he enjoyed ranch life so much. But there is a serious purpose to his project. The site was chosen as an extreme example of a dry and tropical, monsoonal savannah. There are many such places around the planet, particularly in Africa and South America, and his group is seeking ways to halt the desertification of such areas on the planet. They are developing improved strains of prairie grass for cattle feed, more suitable cattle and horses for that climate, and have the cooperation of the Australian government. Many of the stockmen at the vast ranch are aboriginals.

Ed Bass confessed he hadn't dreamed, when he set up the ranch, that he would get hooked on ranching in a personal way and he has kept arranging his schedule to allow him to spend more time there. He said he kind of started out as a tenderfoot. "Then I graduated to being what they call a jackaroo. I'm approaching being a competent stockman."

When we got to the Arizona ranch center, high on a hill, we found that about a dozen of his associates were in the dining room just finishing eating supper. They were scientists, technicians, administrators, visitors from other Bass-related projects — both men and women — all informally garbed. They found two seats for us near the bottom end of the table and, after I was casually introduced, they continued talking about problems and progress on projects. In a few moments a woman brought us our supper: milk and warmed-over lasagna. A woman from England reported on the Bass-related "October" gallery in London. It is the only gallery in the world that seeks out the great art from all the cultures on earth. After about an hour of reports and questioning, we went to the main lounge for an hour of bull-sessioning before everyone retired. Mr. Bass's quarters were off to the right, mine in a dormitory area on the left.

In the morning while many of us were eating an outside, help-yourself, stand-up breakfast, Mr. Bass arrived on a bike. He had been out riding. Guests who began arriving included the head of the environmental study unit at the University of Arizona, where exotic work is being done in super-efficient foods, and a food-processing entrepreneur from Chicago who was interested in getting in on the ground floor of Biosphere II by being an investor.

Before breakfast I had picked up some brochures on Biosphere II and other Bass-involved projects. I say "involved" because he is far from being a hard-driving out-front leader. Rather, he is persistently a quiet team player on his projects. You have to read deep into the literature on committees to find his name, and his main role usually is in finance.

This team concept occurred to him soon after he left architecture school. He went to Santa Fe, a kind of Mecca for creative people, where he traded with the Navahos and became a designer and builder of adobe houses using indigenous material. Then, he and six friends (male and female), chosen mainly for their imagination and interest in making the planet a better place rather than for their financial worth, formed Decisions Team Ltd., a management team. He is listed as chairman. It plays a role in all of Mr. Bass's favorite projects. At the Biosphere II project the team works under the sponsorship of something called the Institute of Ecotechnics, of which Mr. Bass is simply listed as a "director."

In addition to the Australian projects and an interdisciplinary arts center in London, Bass & friends run an East-West cultural meeting center at a bargain-rate hotel, run on solar energy, that they own in Nepal. They have a handsome meeting center on a large eighteenth-century farming area with manor house in southern France that they are seeking to restore. In the heart of downtown Forth Worth they have the Caravan of Dreams, a glass-domed structure containing, it is believed, the nation's first avant-garde center for the performing arts. And they have been running a tropical rain forest study in Puerto Rico.

After breakfast Mr. Bass suggested we take a tour of the Biosphere II project, a few hundred yards down slope. The biosphere itself, under construction on two acres, was made up of arched greenhouse-type units connected with units shaped like flattened pyramids. Nearby were experimental buildings containing plants and animals that would go into the biosphere.

Tomato plants bearing nearly full-size tomatoes were growing on steeply slanted white panels. Ed Bass lifted a panel to show me wholly exposed plant roots. "Every couple of minutes a nutrient solution is sprayed on the roots of these plants. They have been here exactly one week."

There were also swift-growing kale and eggplants. He said that in the biosphere such plants would be in tiers clear to the ceiling for efficient space use. Nearby in a tank were fast-growing fish. "One pound of feed can produce one pound of fish. . . . One to one is absolutely incredible." In the closed process for purification and recycling of waste, fish waste would go to become plant nutrients. "Rabbit and poultry cages would go above those tanks and the rabbits will be fed from the garden production, and the poultry also. Their droppings will go down and feed the fish. Goats are included as waste cyclers and milk producers. They are more efficient, smaller size, easier to handle than cattle."

The biosphere, in short, will incorporate know-how techniques for living plausibly in outer space that space enthusiasts, including those at NASA, have barely dreamed about.

He insists that all the innovative projects he is tackling are considered as entrepreneurial. He didn't seem comfortable being tagged as an idealist. All or most of the projects have the potential, he said, of becoming valid venture capital projects. However, he conceded that in all he was "looking for more in the way of return than a straight, present value return on the dollar calculation. . . . All of the projects have an orientation toward doing something far beyond the monetary reward."

While he does make contributions to a lot of favorite causes, such as the famed Jane Goodall study of the social behavior of chimpanzees in Africa, he doesn't think of his team projects as philanthropy. "Philo," he pointed out, means "loving." Hence philanthropy means loving humanity. That's not his dish. He is willing to be known as being involved in "philecology," which he says "looks at the entirety of life."

Besides, he said, he can consider the projects as recreation, "the opportunity to travel and working with and in other cultures" (presumably as a business expense).

No, he has no boats, private planes, or swell cars.

Could this near-billionaire live on a mere $1 million a year?

"I could live on the *interest* on a million and have money left over. I don't have time to consume a lot."

CHAPTER 16

DEMONSTRATING

SOCIAL

RESPONSIBILITY

How Benevolent Are They,

Really?

"A man who dies rich dies disgraced."

— ANDREW CARNEGIE

Just before Christmas in 1986 *Town & Country,* which covers activities of the rich, carried a glowing article on "The Most Generous Living Americans."[1] Only in America, it said, do you find such a philanthropic tradition. As evidence, it reported research showing that 186 living Americans had each given more than $5 million during their lifetimes.

A few of the examples were indeed inspiring but the overall picture was simply astonishing. During the same year that *Forbes* announced finding twenty-seven billion-aires, these researchers found only eight living Americans who had given away as much as $100 million, and only three of these were billionaires. I have reason to believe the *Town & Country* writer did not fully uncover total giving in certain areas; but consider some of the examples he cited. The benefactors' lifetime givings were listed by categories of "Over $5 million," "Over $10 million," "Over $20 million," "Over $50 million," et cetera. The comparative net worth figures I use are from *Forbes*.

Over $5 Million

Sam Walton of Bentonville, Arkansas. Net worth: $4.5 billion then. It would seem that his lifetime giving could be as little as one-thousandth of his net worth.

Trammell Crow, the big Dallas developer. Net worth: $600 million. Here it would appear that his lifetime giving could be as little as 1 percent of his assets.

Over $20 Million

Four billionaires — Marvin Davis of Denver, Harry Helmsley of New York, and Jay and Robert Pritzker (taken together) of Chicago — were cited in this category. Their lifetime giving could be as little as 2 percent of their net worth. (And it was noted that in the case of the Pritzkers their now-deceased father had been included in the computation.)

The researchers found only twenty-one philanthropists who had given $50 million or more during their lifetime in a land that has, by my estimate, close to a thousand people worth more than $100 million.

A study on the charitable giving plans of wealthy people was made for the Council on Foundations and a Yale project dealing with nonprofit organizations. One analysis of the findings reported that top holders of wealth tend to give away only a tiny percent of their wealth while they are still alive.[2]

A lot of very rich people feel good about themselves and feel they are demonstrating their social concern if they spend $250 to $2,000 for tickets to a charity ball. A year of ball-going can add up to tens of thousands of tax-deductible dollars in giving. A *New York Times* society writer reported that in Palm Beach sponsors have little trouble selling the tickets because people like to go out and the women like to dress up. In Dallas, where rich socialites go ball-crazy in the fall, they not only stage extravaganzas at benefits such as the Crystal Charity Ball, where there may be carousels with live horses, but they may have a "big gifts" party afterward for big givers.

The eminent New York investment banker Felix Rohatyn and his wife Elizabeth have been prominent ball-goers and sponsors for years. In 1986 he said they were fed up. Not only were the opulent balls becoming an embarrassment in being an end in themselves, but they were tending to focus the wealth of the city's richest citizens on a few prestigious hospitals, museums, and libraries having little to do with the social problems of the city's poor. He told a reporter that "people in our world are swimming in money but in order to get the city's rich to give a lousy thousand dollars to the poor who are drowning in front of their eyes you have to . . . give them party favors." He urged rich New Yorkers to get involved in less prestigious causes such as shelters for the homeless, community houses, programs for unwed mothers, and adopting neighborhood associations.[3]

All of this is not meant to suggest that there are not, out there among today's immensely rich, some extraordinary individuals who are concerned about putting much of their wealth into promoting the well-being and enhancement of our society. And some are willing to do it while they are still alive. For example:

- The most spectacular contributors to philanthropy while still alive have been William Hewlett and David

Packard of the Hewlett-Packard Company. Classmates at Stanford, they set up their electronics company in a garage with about $500 in 1939. Hewlett mainly handled the engineering, Packard the business. As their company exploded in growth, they each held on to more than 10 percent of the company stock; with Packard holding somewhat more than Hewlett. Both became extremely rich. Hewlett led off the big giving. By 1983 his family foundation had more than a half billion dollars in assets. It was believed to be the largest foundation ever created by a living American. This did not leave him broke. By 1987 he burst into the billionaire ranks. In 1988 partner David Packard took the title of greatest living philanthropist away from him with a really dramatic flourish. He announced that over the next few years he would put about two billion dollars in his family foundation, or virtually all of his wealth that was still in company stock.

- The Texas billionaire Ross Perot has gotten himself deeply involved in trying to improve the quality of education in Texas, and has said that although he has four children he has no plan to weaken them with a load of inherited wealth. His wealth instead, he hopes, will go to benefit society.
- An Wang, founder of Wang Laboratories, net worth $725 million in 1987, has been called the Boston area's top benefactor. A shy, thoughtful man, he has made a wide array of expenditures to improve the quality of life in eastern Massachusetts, particularly in run-down inner city areas.
- Arnold Beckman, founder of Smith Kline Beckman, has never shown up on any *Forbes* 400 list, but in 1985 alone he gave $75 million to nonprofit organizations concerned with scientific research.
- Louisiana's elderly oilman C. B. Pennington gave $125 million to the Louisiana State University to set up a nutrition and preventive medicine center in 1983 when he was not even on the *Forbes* 400 list. Its minimum for entry that year was also $125 million so it would

seem that Mr. Pennington gave away his last nickel. That, however, turned out not to be the case. He apparently was a zillionaire who had not yet been fully appreciated by the magazine's sleuths because in 1986 he was listed as having $400 million.

As for the thirty extremely wealthy people I visited, there was, as indicated, some small skewing toward the socially concerned. For example I had sought out one individual, Edwin Whitehead, specifically because he had made a remarkable gift. Still, the idea of sharing wealth in any major way had not seemed to infect the thinking of the large majority of the people I visited. Some would cite as evidence of philanthropy a gift that could not have cost more than $30,000. Fewer than ten seemed to be planning to put a significant part of their wealth into philanthropic causes while they were alive. A few more planned to be major givers after death.

In the 1985 edition of *The Foundation Directory,* which tries to cover all private foundations that have a minimum of $1 million in assets, I could find only half a dozen of the people I visited listed as donors. Others were listed as "directors" of foundations created by their parents or grandparents. Given that the people I visited have been credited with having, in total, close to $10 billion in net worth, their commitment to foundations appears to be about one-third of 1 percent. Others had, of course, been doing their giving outside the foundation format, as for example Edwin Whitehead, whom we will meet directly. But I would be astonished if all giving by the thirty exceeded a few percent of their total net worth.

Edwin Whitehead's Super Bequest

The father of Edwin Whitehead developed, in a Bronx loft, a machine called the Autotechnicon. It cut the time required to analyze body tissue after an operation from four

days to one, and hence was soon in great demand. Young
Edwin had dropped out of college to become the first employee of his father's new company at $10 a week. The com-
pany, Technicon, did exceedingly well, and took on other
innovative medical devices.

Edwin eventually became the sole owner and a centimillionaire. In 1982 *Forbes* pegged him at $200 million.

Meanwhile, he had become restless. Friends were advis-
ing that he ought to get a bodyguard, which he thought was
an awful way to live. A triple-bypass operation had stimulated his long-term thinking. And he was getting bored with
running a vast company. "When your company gets to be an
institution with 5,000 people involved, then, you know, you
have rampant politics, and things like health plans and
parking become terribly important. It's crazy and I hated it,"
he has recalled.[4]

When I saw him he was happy again. He was about to
disappear from the *Forbes* list. He was hopping about the
country in a ten-passenger plane as head of Whitehead Associates, giving management advice to a flock of innovative
small companies that had advanced to about where his
Technicon in its early stages was. He had arranged a neat
way for his children to have a say in an ongoing institution
he had created. And he had, whether intended or not, built
a spectacular monument with his name on it.

What he did was sell his company and dedicate at least
$135 million to the nonprofit Whitehead Institute for
Biomedical Research. This newly created institute has a
close association with MIT and his creation of it involved the
largest gift ever made to a scientific facility. The whole focus
of the institute is to push forward the horizon of knowledge
about molecular biology, in the hope of uncovering secrets
of nature that will permit dramatic advances in medical
treatment.

Mr. Whitehead proved to be a chunky, bald man with big
black-rimmed glasses and a sardonic sense of humor. He
met me in shirtsleeves. He was living in a large Mediterranean-type mansion on a dramatic point of land jutting out

from Fairfield County, Connecticut, into the Long Island Sound, obviously a multimillion-dollar place. There was a tennis court and boat basin. A small twenty-two-foot sailboat was attached to the dock.

I remarked on the smallness and wondered why he didn't have an eighty-foot boat more appropriate for a man of his economic background. Yeah, he said, "that would be fashionable but I like sailing." He explained that the smaller the boat, the more you are really involved in sailing. "It's more fun. I'm an active sportsman, not a passive one."

As he led me into the mansion, he decided the library was too hot to talk in and took me out to a grand circular salon overlooking the sea. Because the Whiteheads had recently had a party there, the sofas had all been pushed back. He asked me to help him push two heavy sofas into a conversational grouping even though a servant was in sight. And he mentioned that he was thinking about getting a smaller house.

His fourth wife, a lovely young woman of Chinese ancestry, joined us and at one point brought us Diet Pepsi. She had been educational director of a medical foundation and an old friend of his third wife, who died a few years ago. The other two marriages had been dissolved by divorce. Altogether he had three children of his own and felt responsible for six more stepchildren. Of his three natural children, one son has been serving as an executive at Technicon. The second son was an architect. And the daughter was an assistant district attorney in Brooklyn. They have been provided with what he called small trusts.

The Whiteheads go out to dinner a couple of times a week but it is a problem because he is on a strict no-fat, low-salt diet. When he eats meat, his favorite is goat.

Mrs. Whitehead commented that he was incredibly active despite the bypass and a coronary. In addition to his sailing and tennis, she explained, he rode his stationary bicycle twenty miles every morning and was a superb skier. They maintain an apartment on the slopes of Vail, Colorado, and he skis to music via earphones.

The Whiteheads said that they live on less than a million dollars a year, and obviously very nicely. Money, he explained, is simply a "medal of success" in business. "But, you know, a million or ten million or fifty million dollars really doesn't make an awful lot of difference."

Setting up the Whitehead Institute turned out to be more complicated and time-consuming than he had assumed, because he had not fully thought out what he wanted to create or how. It took several years and he concluded it is easier to make a million than to give it away (if you try it his way).

He explained he could have set up a foundation to take charge of the matter, but that seemed too impersonal. A foundation, he said, is primarily a conduit. Or he could have given the money to a university, "which it would very much appreciate," and let it do the job (as Mr. Pennington did in Louisiana). But he finally decided on the most difficult course, a hands-on, do-it-yourself creation. "I think it the most rewarding because we can be guardians of our own destiny and have an independent board of trustees."

Since he was thinking of making a medical contribution of some sort he bought up a chunk of land near Duke University's fine medical center and then brought a group of scientists together to decide what the mission should be. What disease to tackle? The experts couldn't agree. He now admits he was dumb and had it backward. He should have decided on his mission before picking a site. So he made a Nobel Prize–winning biologist director of the institute-to-be. The biologist finally suggested that the real area of challenge was not medical but a more basic one of exploring molecular biology. So the project was shifted to MIT, one of the world's great centers of biological research. (Whitehead still granted several million to Duke.)

At MIT, Whitehead would have prestige and access to leading biological researchers, but still he wanted to keep his institute independent. A number of MIT faculty members were distinctly unfriendly. They thought he would be getting control over who got hired by MIT in biology. Finally an agreement was made that left everyone happy. MIT could veto any scientists appointed to the institute's staff.

Mr. Whitehead committed about $35 million to get the institute launched in 1984 and promised the other $100 million in endowments within a specific time.[5]

One of the best things about the arrangement for Mr. Whitehead is a nice sense of perpetuity. His three children will be among the institute's thirteen trustees.

Leslie Wexner's Thoughts about Sharing His Wealth

Mr. Wexner of Columbus, readers will recall, had become a billionaire while still in his forties through his Limited chain of specialized women's apparel stores. He told me that his thinking about what to do with his money had been affected by a nasty episode. A few years ago he was stranded by a summer snowstorm while skiing on a Colorado peak. He stressed that he probably was not in real peril but while stranded he was stimulated to wonder, "What if I die? What will they say?" Hot merchant? Was that enough? He groped in the following months toward arriving at a life philosophy he could feel comfortable with. Although he is a bachelor, he doesn't think his conclusions would be a bit different if he had a family.

"I think that a lot of people fantasize about their own obituary or the speech that's given at their own funeral, their own eulogy. I thought about it. I'll just write my own eulogy ... kind of a whimsical idea and then I wondered what people think about me. Bullshit. What do you think about yourself? I would not postpone career decisions until I'm fifty or sixty. Why do I postpone community responsibility decisions?

"Giving away your wealth when you're living is acknowledging in a concrete way your own mortality and it's like giving away a little bit of your blood. It's much easier to say as long as I hoard my wealth and I make these legal provisions, then ... that horizon of eternity keeps staying farther away. . . .

"I've asked people who are in their seventies, 'Why don't

you give it away? Why have you hoarded all this money?'
And some don't know why. Some perceive themselves as
being philanthropic when they're really not. Some say that
when you give away your wealth, even if you're accumulating it faster than you're giving it away, it's like giving away
your power. I'm not power-oriented so it's easier for me. . . .
[Many] people who create great wealth spend [a lot of] time
with their attorneys and accountants figuring out their
trusts and how to avoid taxes at their deaths so that they can
keep their wealth intact."

Others, he said, spend immense amounts of time "planning for somebody else to give your money away when
you're dead. That is really dumb. . . . I think that people who
accumulate wealth and don't give it away in their lifetimes
have subconsciously decided to hoard money and I think
that's very unhealthy."

Mr. Wexner indicated he had already committed more
than $50 million into foundation-funding but considered
that just a beginning. And he wants to put some of his own
well-established creativeness into setting the foundations
up to handle interesting problems. He has done considerable research on foundations and has concluded that simply
turning the management over to lawyers and accountants is
wrong for him. He wants his foundations led in a humanistic
and spiritual way; so he hired a rabbi to oversee his giving
through foundations. Accountants and lawyers, he said, can
handle the technical management.

Another innovation is that he is not thinking of just one
monumental foundation in his name. "I think maybe setting
up a lot of foundations and letting them compete while you
can watch the competition and see who does the best job in
supporting different things" is better. He said he wants to
get more horses into the race.

While Mr. Wexner has plunged into supporting programs to ameliorate and enhance life in once-dull Columbus, he has spurned being a one-man band just because he's
the city's richest citizen. He believes urban life has more vi-
tality if most of its well-to-do citizens actively support community projects.

He was approached, for example, to pledge $100,000 to support research at a children's hospital. Instead, his preference was to spend the $100,000 to support an endowment director whose goal would be to raise $1 million a year for research.

And he was asked to give $1 million to support the Columbus Symphony. No, he said. Instead, he would guarantee to bring in every year world-class guest artists such as Placido Domingo and Luciano Pavarotti to perform with the symphony if the symphony's board members would personally guarantee to raise $1 million a year by ticket-selling and fund-raising. Wexner explained: "When you feed the bears they quit looking for food. I think there's some charitable giving by very well-meaning people that's counterproductive because it takes the vibrancy, the energy out of the organization. It's so well funded that no one has to think hard."

He says that after his reflections on the mountaintop he made a deal with himself. If he was going to give money then he was also going to give his time to things that were important. Hence he not only undertook to head the Capitol Committee of business leaders that meets regularly with the city council but has headed Ohio State University's endowment drive. To start the ball rolling he guaranteed $10 million for a visual arts center.

As a result of all the thinking that started on the mountaintop, he says, "I am much happier about myself, I feel more balanced. It has enabled me to meet a lot of interesting people that I otherwise wouldn't have met. I guess maybe philosophically I've come to the conclusion that God helps those that help," he says. "I was telling this to a rabbi and he said, 'That's Aristotle.'" Mr. Wexner grinned and added, "I thought I was inventing it."

The Ewing Kauffmans on
Benevolence to One's Children

We left Mr. and Mrs. Kauffman, dressed in bathrobes, in their gold-gilded mansion outside Kansas City. They created the drug company Marion Laboratories. Their net worth then, they said, was $340 million and growing every week.

What on earth were they going to do with it all? Would their children inherit it?

Mr. Kauffman: "Nothing to the kids. They have all they need. They don't need but four or five million each and the grandchildren will get part of that and that's all they need. The grandchildren are probably worth a quarter of a million each. We've given stock to them and in another five years they'll be worth a million, maybe. And that's enough. It just spoils them."

Mrs. Kauffman: "Our oldest granddaughter is going to the University of Southern California and we're making her pay her way."

Mr. Kauffman: "When you have to pay your own way through school you do a better job of studying."

It turns out that, when either of the Kauffmans dies, that partner's share of their wealth goes to the Kauffman Foundation, already a thriving institution with specific educational goals.

As baseball club owners the Kauffmans felt distress when four players were convicted on drug charges. The present major goal of the Kauffman Foundation is to teach youths to stay away from alcohol and drugs.

Mr. Kauffman: "It's the greatest program, the biggest, most complex program in the world. There's nothing like it. We're blazing a trail for other cities to follow. This is in Greater Kansas City [now]. Every year we teach 16,000 sixth- and seventh-graders the principle of self-management and the skills to resist the temptation of alcohol and drugs. You won't believe it but at the sixth-grade level 30 percent of them have had alcohol in the last thirty days. We're going to interview 24,000 this year. The schools are wild about it. . . . The kids like it. It will be the greatest thing we've ever done.

"I don't want any buildings named after me."

Through the foundation, they were also launching a program — still small — to help pay the costs of college educations for children of all "associates" (employees) of Marion Laboratories. The students will pay back 10 percent. If it costs $20,000 they will pay back $2,000. They also expect to get into programs to educate nurses and pharmacists with a 25 percent payback expected, and medical doctors with a 50 percent payback expected.

How big would the foundation become?

Mr. Kauffman: "They [at the foundation] get half of everything I own. She [Mrs. K.] gets the other half. She's younger than I am — I'll probably go first. . . . I expect it will be worth $500 million if I live five more years."

Mrs. Kauffman: "And with them paying back an amount [loans], it will go on forever."

Mr. Kauffman: "Anybody who makes money and doesn't utilize it for the betterment of other people is making a mistake because he doesn't realize how to enjoy it. You can only eat one steak at a time, you can only drink one bottle of champagne. But when you take your money and use it where you do good for other people it just means so much more to you. And this is the nice thing about Mrs. K. — she doesn't mind spending this money in any way, shape, or form."

The Man Who Refused
to Be a Centimillionaire

Stewart Mott's father, a founder of General Motors, was a crusty gentleman who went around turning off lights and was sixty-two years old when Stewart was born. He sat on the GM board for fifty-eight years. At one point, Stewart estimates, the family was worth about $1 billion. The father created a foundation mostly to benefit his home city of Flint, Michigan, that is still worth about half a billion. His surviving fourth wife and five offspring from two different wives are together worth several hundred million dollars.

Stewart Mott, now in his late forties, was considered a maverick, and seemed to rub his father the wrong way. He refused to guard and nurture his inheritance properly so that it would grow each year. If he had simply put all his money with sound managers he would be a centimillionaire now, or would be within a modest number of years.

Instead, he chose to be a professional philanthropist, supporting causes he felt were important to the future of our society. To accomplish this, he in effect put a cap on his net worth at around $20 million. Everything else, after taxes, goes to his causes. He says, "It reassures me that I am not a leech on society."[6] Counting what he has given plus what he has raised as a full-time fund-raiser over a quarter century, he has made available many tens of millions of dollars for such causes as prevention of nuclear war, family planning and world population control, honesty in government, civil liberties, and women's rights.

Because he has rejected centimillionaire status I do not count him among the thirty immensely rich people being looked at as a group in this book. However, I was curious to see him and we did have a long visit. Here are some highlights.

A handsome, buoyant man, I found him in his two-and-a-half story penthouse on Fifth Avenue overlooking Central Park. He was wearing denim shorts, denim shirt, and moccasins. His lovely, slender wife, Kappy, a dozen years younger, was wearing blue jeans. Before they met he had been for a decade known as Manhattan's most eligible bachelor. She is a professional sculptor and when they met she was living in tiny quarters.

Almost the entire top floor of his penthouse was taken up by an open area with room divisions indicated simply by furnishings that were mostly casual. The room was dominated by a sculptured head Kappy did of her husband's hero Roger Baldwin, founder of the American Civil Liberties Union. Mr. Mott had been attracted to this particular condo penthouse with its large open sweep because it would be great for fund-raising parties. He therefore was partly frustrated when house rules for the building were passed curtailing large parties. There could only be four parties a year where there were from thirty to a hundred guests, and only one party where there would be more than one hundred people.

Several of the other rooms of the apartment were used as work areas occupied by several young, casually dressed staff members who help him handle his philanthropic activities. Outside to the rear was one of Manhattan's larger vegetable gardens. Mr. Mott has loved working with the soil since boyhood months spent on the family farm.

Mr. Mott does most of his traveling within the city on his moped. If he wants to pop out to the country, he scoots across the park on his moped to a parking area where he picks up his Volkswagen.

He said his only other home is a twenty-one-room mini-mansion in Washington next to the Supreme Court building. It is mostly rented out at bargain rates to organizations he supports such as Fund for Peace and the Fund for Constitutional Government, which sues government agencies it finds are not doing their duties. He explained of his own quarters there: "It's a working office really. I just have a bed at the side of my office."

He has said his career has been skewed by all his money. "It's a hell of a dilemma, but I'm glad that I've chosen the role I have."

In the middle of his college years he spent one whole year bumming his way around the world by hitchhiking and traveling in ailing cars. His family was frantic about him at times. Total year's cost: $1,500. After college he spent a year teaching English at Eastern Michigan University, thought about studying law, worked as an executive trainee in one of his father's companies, but as he finally started coming into his own money, largely through trusts, he got interested in working for causes he favored. High on his list was Planned Parenthood. He decided to set up a branch in his home city of Flint, and got himself a small apartment in an integrated area of Flint several blocks from the family estate. He distributed thousands of fliers about the availability of free contraceptives, set up a trailer in a low-income area, and from this trailer began passing them out.

Meanwhile, he was seeking in vain to be appointed to the staff of his father's vast foundation. The father wanted no part of his wild-eyed ideas about improving the world. So young Stewart drifted to New York City and plunged into philanthropic work there. Another source of friction with his father was Stewart's assertion of financial independence. He explained that his father "was initially pissed because I took my account away from Flint where he was supervisor of all accounts." When his father died and there was a family opening on the board of the father's foundation, he again sought the seat. But he was blackballed from the grave. Instructions had been left.

He showed me a 3,000-word letter he had sent his mother in France seeking to interest her in letting him distribute some of the funds from her foundation of about $50 million. He started out with a clear description of his philanthropic priorities, then under the heading "Personality" he sought to reassure her about the colorful personality he had been developing:

"If a philanthropist doesn't have an outgoing, extroverted personality then he/she might stay home, shielded by a Board of Directors . . . not getting involved in any hands-on manner. . . . Mother, let me remind you that twenty-five years ago I had never given a public speech, I was not extroverted, I was a very mixed-up and unhappy young man. I was not a leader. I was a loner. . . . Gradually I learned to overcome my hesitant inhibitions and to acquire leadership and public-speaking talents."

Another piece of literature he gave me was a fine profile, "The Triumph of a Prodigal Son," written by Dan Rottenberg in *Town & Country*,[7] while Stewart was still a sought-after bachelor. It indicated how well he had overcome "hesitant inhibitions" in another area. A Washington newspaper had implied he had slept with forty women over an eight-month period. Mott was annoyed mainly, Rottenberg wrote, because the paper had gotten the numbers wrong. He quoted Mott as explaining: "The fact is, within the last year I've spent an evening or more with sixty women and about twenty of them I've been in bed with."

When I saw him Stewart Mott guessed that his income

then was running somewhere around $1.5 million a year and that the bulk of it (after taxes) was going to charitable causes or supporting his fund-raising efforts. He is flooded with appeals, which his staff screens in terms of his interests. At the moment, he said, he was contributing to about 300 charitable causes. For about twenty of his favorite causes the contributions ran into the tens of thousands.

His big challenge at the moment was to raise $3 million for Planned Parenthood. And he was planning shortly to make a trip to Silicon Valley, California, where a flock of instant zillionaires had been created by the computer revolution.

"With a few introductions in hand I'm going to see if I can get to some of the newly rich who, you know, . . . haven't quite grasped the sense of what their $200 million could do for the society in which they live."

Speaking more broadly, he explained: "You know a lot of people feel very insecure about giving money away when they can't see and touch and feel what it did. [My father] could walk down the streets of Flint and everybody would pat him on the back and say, 'Oh, Mr. Mott it's wonderful what you're doing.' He got feedback all the time. I don't get much feedback. People don't come up to me on the street and say, 'Thank you for preventing nuclear war today.' And I don't see the women in the clinics in Bangladesh who are getting sterilization thanks to family planning. So I'm working in an entirely different fashion."

Despite all his commitment to benevolence he seems as loath as any super-millionaire to supporting our national government through payment of taxes. In some years in the past he has been so thorough in arranging deductions that he has paid little or nothing to the federal government.[8] In his letter to his mother seeking her support in his philanthropies he said that his financial advisers had done "a splendid job in . . . minimizing taxes."

C.

Ways
Family Dynamics
Shape Treatment
of Wealth

CHAPTER 17

THE YEARNING FOR
—AND PROBLEMS OF—
FAMILY DYNASTIES

"My life has been as close to the American Dream as anybody I can ever imagine. My children work with me, my wife too."

— WILLIAM MILLARD, whose net worth rose from minus zero to $600 million in eight years, then abruptly dropped back a few hundred million

Like the family farm, the family business is cherished in our folklore. It can offer at least a glimpse of personal immortality. It reinforces our sense of the importance of both the individual and the family. The family that is proud of an ongoing business also tends to feel committed to maintaining a certain high quality in its product or service. And some families may feel loyalty to the larger manifestation of the family they see in their employees.

There are families that are still firmly at the helm after

three or more generations of enterprises now doing business up in the hundreds of millions of dollars. They include, for example, the Busch family of St. Louis, the Sulzberger, Newhouse, and LeFrak families of New York City, the Bechtel family of San Francisco, the Mars family of Virginia. All have individual members in the *Forbes* 400.

On the other hand there are famous old families with one or more representatives on the 400 list that have little to do with the enterprise on which the fortune was built except to own shares, and perhaps serve as directors. Names that come to mind are Mellon, Ford, du Pont, Rockefeller, and Heinz. And there are a lot of famous old families whose names symbolize American enterprise that are so dispersed that they have no individual members who loom either as major entrepreneurs or great fortune-holders. Examples would be Carnegie, Chrysler, Guggenheim, McCormick, and Biddle.

Of the 150 individuals at the top of the 1986 *Forbes* list of wealthiest Americans, sixty-two were descendants of founders of thirty-six family dynasties that were at least well into the third generation. Of these thirty-six "dynasties," only fifteen were true dynasties in the sense that they were continuing to provide active top management to an ongoing financial empire.

It is perhaps of interest that of these fifteen, five were publishers. Family-controlled "houses" have a long tradition in publishing. In 1987 *Forbes* cited studies indicating that 70 percent of family businesses fail to survive their founder.

As for the very wealthy people with children whom I visited, about half clearly had a strong orientation — some even an obsession — toward establishing or maintaining a dynasty. But only two of these represented one of the eight families interviewed with existing fortunes that had been passed on through two or more generations. These two reasonably true dynasties that were still providing active management and looking toward continuing this in succeeding generations involved Samuel LeFrak of New York (who is a fourth-generation builder), and Sigfried Weis, who with his cousin operates a supermarket chain in central Pennsylvania founded by their grandfather. A third dynasty, involving the family which owns the Waggoner ranch in Texas, has been an off-and-on thing in terms of active management. The ranch was largely ignored by the second generation. The husband of a third-generation person (Electra II) finally took over management. Presently it is under professional management with a young fourth-generation in-law working along with the professionals.

A number of others I visited were proud that their children had achieved success in totally different fields such as science or medicine. And some, as we saw, were in flight from any close identification with a dynastic situation.

Ewing Kauffman, founder of Marion Laboratories, considered it a big plus for his company that none of the Kauffman children or six grandchildren worked in the family business. As noted, he is famed for his success in motivating employees. He said flatly:

"We won't hire relatives. I don't believe in it. It's not good for the company. We get better executives because they know they don't have to fight any [nepotism]. Everybody has got their job because they are good, because they produce, because they've proven themselves."

A number of articles in the *Harvard Business Review* have made the point that the very strengths of family ownership of a small business can turn into liabilities once a company becomes large.[1] You may get conflicts between goals of the company and the family. These can involve capital shortages, misguided financial secrecy, ingrown company policies, lack of a profit discipline, nepotism. And all these can be aggravated by conflicts within the family itself over who is to run the company, how it is to be run, how much of profits are to be taken, and how said profits are divided among family members. Among the ultra rich you can get relatives fighting over money when none of them has any plausible need for it; there is simply rivalry for a "fair" share.

And now there is a relatively new problem arising from the growth of raiders. If a substantial part of the company is held by family trusts and a raider appears, the trustees managing the trusts have a fiduciary duty under law to vote in favor of enriching the beneficiaries.[2] Hence the company may be an easier target for take-over buccaneers.

Here we will visit with a man whose dream of keeping control of his empire within the family might be viewed by some as an obsession.

William Millard: Father, Daughter, and a Mess of Trouble

Our recent folklore has celebrated the tinkering whiz kids who built great fortunes in the personal computer revolution: youngsters such as Steven Jobs of Apple Computer, William Gates of Microsoft, and Mitchell Kapor of Lotus. William Millard of Oakland, California, was not exactly a whiz kid.

In fact he was notably slow in getting started in any kind of entrepreneurial activity. But he built the biggest fortune of all in personal computers — by selling them. He created ComputerLand, the world's largest retailer of personal computers. In 1985, while he was still in charge, he had 820 stores in twenty-five countries, including China. Only a year before that his net worth had been put at $600 million.

Even when ComputerLand, with its whirlwind growth, was close to being a $2 billion business, William Millard was trying to keep control, as far as possible, within the family. He rejected repeated proposals to go public. Mr. Millard has been called autocratic. He told me: "One of the great joys for me is the extent to which my family has chosen to work in the business and participate."

His wife was made a director of the corporation. All three of their daughters (Barbara, Ann, and Elizabeth) had skipped college to go directly to work for the company. He made the oldest daughter, Barbara, president and chief operating officer at the age of twenty-six. She is an attractive, tall, cheerful blonde with high school acting and singing experience. In doing this he bypassed four division presidents who had risen to their positions presumably because of high competence and who presumably thought they had a shot at the presidency. Barbara's husband, also age twenty-six, was made vice-president of the whole U.S. division.

One authority on corporate function, Peter Davis, director of the Wharton Applied Research Center at the University of Pennsylvania, has been quoted as commenting that the main questions were whether the offspring — male or female — could "handle the responsibilities and be independent, rather than just being an appendage" of a strong father.[3] In this report in the *New York Times* doubt was expressed that Mr. Millard was looking for independence in his closest associates. On the other hand, his daughter, in her twenties, appeared to be very much in tune with him. A few years earlier he and she had spent weekends together in the intense psychological EST training programs for maximizing control over thought and emotion. The report cited additional unnamed sources as questioning whether she had the experience or independence from her father to be an effective chief operating officer of so large an enterprise.

When I met him his empire was in turmoil. His franchise dealers were up in arms. And he had just been hit by a staggering legal verdict of mismanagement unique in legal annals.

His house in Piedmont on the hills behind Oakland was a towering plaster structure with exquisitely groomed shrubbery. It was virtually on the street, not set back, and commanded a striking view of the San Francisco Bay. A locked gate guarded the steps.

An aide led me to a study and in a moment Mr. Millard, a lean, beaming, handsome man in his early fifties, strode into the room as if nothing in the world was bothering him. He was dressed in coordinated shirt and trousers. His voice was warm, and sounded very sincere. The words tended to be bland, lyrical. I mentioned I had just learned of his legal horror story. He said:

"Can you imagine the travesty. I founded that company, built the company, the whole thing; and they're after this incredible, valuable star, if you will, and then claiming mismanagement." I gathered he was referring to himself as the incredible star.

He had been reared in a working-class family down the hill in Oakland. His father was a clerk for Southern Pacific Railroad. He was the oldest of six children. All the rest were girls.

For three years after high school he worked as a railway switchman and an assembly-line worker. In one phase he was "shoveling gravel, digging ditches, driving a truck and ended up a welder's helper." Hardly a portrait of a rarin'-to-go entrepreneur or electronic whiz kid. "We didn't have a lot of money and money was a real issue."

After the three years he did get to the University of San Francisco for three semesters, learned he had a gift for numbers, dropped out, and worked for a finance company. Had he tried any entrepreneurial experiments in making money?

"Not really. . . . I tended to immerse myself totally in the job. I did then the same as I do now, which is to work sixty or seventy hours a week, and that's one of the reasons that I was promoted. I went through all the chairs up to branch manager in about twenty-four months." Meanwhile, he was reading "religiously" journals such as *Scientific American* and so got in on the dinosaur age of computers. He rose from programmer trainee in the county government offices to computing supervisor and got a job installing a computer system for the county.

So it was that in his late thirties he set up a little company to custom-tailor computer installations and software for businesses that used certain IBM computers. He got into financial trouble with that, and with the help of bankers launched a software consulting firm called Information Management Science Associates, Inc. or IMS. Also he began tinkering with the new microprocessor chips starting to become available. And in the tinkering with them and with circuit boards he came up with one of the first personal computers, to which he gave the imposing name IMSAI 8080. A writer for *Fortune* has related:[4]

"Millard, his wife and their three young daughters would

gather around a kitchen table covered with muffin tins filled with parts. They would hand-sort parts out of the tins into plastic bags which went off with instruction sheets to hobbyists [on how] to solder them together. Beginning in 1976 as the personal computer market suddenly sprang from the hobbyists' magazines and into the storefronts IMS tried to manufacture the 8080 [through a manufacturing subsidiary]. For a time the IMSAI 8080 was at the leading edge of the PC revolution. But Millard had no experience with manufacturing operations or financial controls and his furious drive to get the product out the door led to serious quality problems. The IMSAI manufacturing subsidiary ... went bankrupt in 1979. . . . Among the debts was a $250,000 promissory note due to the Marriner venture capital group." It was supposed to be paid off by May 1981.

Meanwhile, even before his manufacturing subsidiary collapsed, Millard decided the real opportunity was in opening stores to sell other people's computers. With $10,000 he set up a chain using local franchisees. First he called his chain Computer Shack. When Radio Shack's owner strenuously objected, he switched the name of his chain to ComputerLand. It was an almost instant success, adding first dozens and then hundreds of new outlets each year in malls across America. Within a few years he became incredibly rich.

It perhaps should be noted that of the eighteen enormously rich entrepreneurs who had created brand-new fortunes that I visited, seven did it with chains. Chains, as indicated, seem to offer a vastly more efficient method for rapid growth than is available in a manufacturing industry, which requires the building of complicated plants, numerous layers of management, numerous specialized departments. Fast growth with good chains is possible especially if the stores are owned by franchisees rather than the home company.

Millard pointed out to me that by letting the local businessmen own each of ComputerLand's 800-odd outlets he was getting the push of extra commitment from 800 people. These 800 people, he felt, would provide extra entrepreneurial drive, and a lot less headache at the home office. He explained why franchising was superior, for him at least, to trying to set up a company-owned chain:

"It eliminates a whole layer of management. We have subsidiary organizations in only five places in the world, and that's it. If we had [owned] all those stores, for every six to ten stores we'd have a district manager, and then we'd have to have so many district managers that we would have to have a regional manager ... so many regional managers we'd have to have an area manager ... and so many area managers we'd have a country manager, then have a hemisphere manager. Right? And they'd all have cars, offices, secretaries, expenses, and problems. Right? Just even imagine trying to administer salaries in twenty-five countries with different rates of money going up and down and benefit packages and those things that do not lend themselves to economy of scale.

"Now what does lend itself to economy of scale is worldwide purchasing."

What Millard was offering his 800-odd franchisees was really quite simple: a nice copyrighted name, Computer-Land; the cut-rate advantage of mass purchasing; prompt delivery; and national advertising (which the franchisee was required to help pay for).

Things went marvelously for a few years as his net worth exploded. Then two things went wrong. Probably both all along could have been averted or eased by a less autocratic, more adroit chief executive guided by some competent professional managers. President Barbara Millard was his chief management associate during all or most of the crises.

First, franchisees came under pressure from the general overbuilding of computer stores and started taking a sharper look at what they were paying Mr. Millard. He told me that one of his big problems had been loss of his privacy and anonymity. The *Forbes* estimate that he was worth $600 million, he acknowledged, didn't sit well with a lot of his franchisees, and they threatened legal action. Until then, he said, "I could go anywhere and do anything and be entirely anonymous."

The situation was that he (ComputerLand) was taking 8 percent of each franchisee's gross sales. That was okay when things were going crazy but came under scrutiny when the pinch started. Also, he was taking 1 percent for national advertising. So he had a revolt on his hands when I saw him.

The second, bigger thing that went wrong was a lawsuit so remarkable that *The American Lawyer* gave it about 11,000 words of fascinated attention.

And it was all over that $250,000 promissory note he had signed on behalf of his manufacturing subsidiary back when he was hurting for cash in the late seventies.

Since wildly different claims were made, I will confine my brief account to facts stated in *The American Lawyer* report (October 1985).

The promissory note held by Marriner & Co. had a clause stating that the holder had the option to convert the note into a 20 percent share of the unrestricted voting stock of IMS, holding company for Millard's manufacturing subsidiary. A few months after he signed the note, an argument had developed over Millard's alleged plan to restructure his companies in Panama for tax purposes. The note was rewritten to include, apparently, Millard's brand-new company, ComputerLand, in the conversion option.

In 1981, a month before the note was to mature, Millard got a letter from a firm he had never heard of, Micro-Vest, informing him it had bought the note from Marriner and was invoking the conversion clause. Millard was dumbfounded and outraged. He claimed he had a clear verbal agreement with Marriner that the inclusion of ComputerLand was just temporary and that the note could not be assigned without his consent. It turned out that Micro-Vest was a shell company formed by a couple of disgruntled former associates who knew of the conversion clause.

Annual sales of ComputerLand were now up to $150 million, on which he was getting the 8 percent. Micro-Vest seemed in the mood to settle on its claim of a 20 percent stake and he might have settled for a few million dollars. Instead, he resolved to fight. The case dragged on and didn't get before a jury until 1985, by which time Computer-Land's sales had increased another tenfold. To help finance the court fight, Micro-Vest had taken on fifty-five more investors.

The trial itself dragged on for months and the jurors were getting mad because they were getting $10 a day and because Millard's lawyers didn't seem able to prove what they had said at the outset they would prove. The plaintiffs were still eager to settle out of court, but Mr. Millard was adamant. The plaintiffs' lawyer kept referring to Millard as a "billionaire" (not quite correct) and in his peroration called on the jurors to "put this sucker down." After four hours of deliberation, the jury granted the plaintiffs 20 percent of everything Millard owned, including even his house and dude ranch in Oregon. Certainly the total would come to more than $100 million.

But that was not all. The plaintiffs' lawyer, working on contingency, went after punitive damages because Millard was, he claimed, an evil man trying to manipulate the system. This took the jurors by surprise. They thought it was just an argument over a contract.

Apparently they did not fully understand the judge's instructions on awarding punitive damages if any. The judge made it clear that if they felt Mr. Millard should be punished, it should be enough to make him hurt. But they apparently didn't all hear his further instruction that any punitive damages must bear a reasonable relation to the actual damages.

So at $10 a day the jurors wrestled with the problem of punitive damages. One young woman in the jury reportedly proposed: "Why don't we just give them five thousand dollars." But others were afraid that if they did that the judge would say it was "not enough to hurt" and send them back. So they wrestled with trying to comprehend big wealth when they had no clear information on how many hundreds of millions of dollars Mr. Millard had. They talked in hundreds of thousands of dollars' worth of hurt, then millions and tens of millions. In the end the jury hit Mr. Millard with $115 million in punitive damages and added another

$10 million punishment for ComputerLand. The decision was appealed.

A few days after the trial Mr. Millard assured me that his family had always lived on less than $1 million a year. And referring to the whole thing as a "nightmare" he insisted: "The facts from my personal knowledge would result in that outfit not being given anything."

The 1985 *Forbes* list came out a couple of months after the court decision, cited his misfortunes, and cut his net worth to no more than $480 million. By the next year, however, Mr. Millard and daughter Barbara had quit their jobs as chairman and president to quell the growing franchisee revolt. Later, the whole family got off the board as a part of a settlement with their Micro-Vest enemies. The 1986 *Forbes* list had put Millard's remaining stake in ComputerLand at $200 million. He sought to sell most of his interest in 1987 and 1988 but some of the family's ComputerLand stock remained in a trust pending full settlement of his continuing battle over the Micro-Vest claim. Mr. Millard had settled in faraway Saipan, which had a very attractive tax code as a U.S. protectorate. Legislative actions, however, have been taken to lower the tax attraction.

Millard had big plans to supply power to the Mariana islands, but ran into some annoying problems. The natives, he claimed, wanted him to share his wealth by making payoffs. It was, alas, not a paradise, at least for him.[5]

When I talked with him he scorned any idea of retiring. This man who fought like a tiger to maintain total control of his corporate creation, whether for money or principle, claimed to me it didn't take much to make him really happy. He said that if he has a pencil and pad or is talking to someone "I can be happy as hell under a tree sitting on a log."

Family Feuding
over Really Big Fortunes

Another threat to family dynasties, as indicated, is the bad feeling that often develops among the heirs. They may feel that they are not getting their fair share, or their fair say in the family business. Some of the kin may want top dollar now, whereas others put preserving the family's financial dynasty above immediate reward.

There has been an element of fighting over money in eight of the thirty family situations I examined. But most of the bad feeling was of the simmering type. Only one turned into a spectacle. (We'll get to it.) Among the ultra rich in general there have been several spectacular battles among kin, where either hundreds of millions of dollars were involved or family empires were on the line. I'll mention just one of each sort.

The Cullen Family's Italian Kinfolk

The biggest estate case in American history occurred in a Houston, Texas, courtroom in 1984 as two grandsons of Hugh Roy Cullen claimed they had for years been euchred out of their "rightful share" of the Cullen fortune. They wanted about $2 billion. More than forty lawyers were in the courtroom. Mr. Cullen had been known as "King of the Wildcatters."

Mr. Cullen had four daughters. Three of them had grown up to be, with their husbands, quiet pillars of Houston society. The fourth daughter, Lillie, was strange. She ran off and married a bit actor in Hollywood, Paolo di Portanova, who called himself a baron. His claim to a noble Italian title was difficult to trace.[6] After giving birth to two boys, Lillie got a divorce, left the children with their father, and took up residence in a seedy Times Square, New York, hotel. She wandered the streets with a big bag, bought junky clothes and replaced buttons with safety pins. Gradually, she bloated herself up to 400 pounds on a diet of soft drinks and cream.

One of the two boys grew up mentally disturbed. The other, Enrico, grew up dashingly handsome. He developed a mustache appropriate for a baron, a title he also used. When he went to Italy, he tried acting and being a jeweler. Then in his mid-twenties he came back to America and tried to get his allowance increased.

The elder Mr. Cullen accepted him as a grandson but remained tight on allowance and urged him to get a job doing something useful.

In 1957 Mr. Cullen died and there was apparently some ambiguity in what he intended in the will. Then in 1964 Lillie's three sisters sold off a controlling interest in a major family company to their husbands and nephews for an allegedly modest price.[7]

Enrico began crying foul through lawyers. Meanwhile, he married a couple of times. He played the baron title and his Cullen connection to the hilt socially. And he arranged to have himself appointed guardian to his brother. By the early eighties, as the Cullen dynasty grew financially, the good fortunes of him and his brother also grew. Their trusts from mother and grandfather were, for the two of them, spilling out each year a total estimated at between $10 million and $25 million a year. Enrico's share was serious money, and would have piled up quickly if he hadn't tried so hard to spend each year's pay-out. Still he kept suing, and claiming he had been given a raw deal.

He, possibly more than anyone on the U.S. landscape, was leading the life-style that we fantasize for all very rich people: gold and diamond studs on his dress shirt, caviar or champagne in one hand, a Cuban cigar in the other, a beautiful lady on his arm. He had thrown parties for people such as Henry and Nancy Kissinger and Frank Sinatra, and in turn had had parties thrown for him by Brooke Astor, perhaps the top New York hostess.[8] There was usually a bodyguard in the background. His "taxi" for nation-hopping was a Learjet. The newspapers usually called him Baron.

And his numerous mansions or apartments in Houston, Acapulco, Rome, Monte Carlo, London were strictly out of fairyland. The colossal $10 million Houston place featured nude statues and green marble columns. It was just a few blocks from the proper southern mansions of his Cullen kin. He thought the air of Houston a bit warm and humid so he covered much of his backyard with an air-conditioned 75-ton glass structure.

His main Acapulco house, with about twenty-eight

bedrooms and twenty-six baths, and several indoor water-falls, was built in three tiers on a cliff overlooking the bay. At night the twinkling lights of the city and boats could be seen through a host of fountains.

In 1984 a probate judge in Houston dismissed the claim of the di Portanova brothers that they were entitled to more from their relatives. He felt they had undercut any claims they had by making a deal in 1968 that gave them greater control over their trusts.[9]

The Dismantling of an Empire

For three generations the Bingham family has pretty much dominated the newspaper world of Louisville, Kentucky. As indicated, the newspaper industry has an above-average share of situations involving family dynasties. During all or much of this century some of the nation's finest newspapers — the *New York Times* and the *Washington Post* to cite just two — have been maintained by family dynasties. On the other hand, some of the nation's most conspicuous right-wing bully sheets, over the decades, have been family run. The Bingham's *Louisville Courier-Journal* and *Louisville Times* have been conspicuous examples of the former. They have won high repute for their excellence and progressive spirit. They are powerful influences in their region.

In recent years the voting stock had been set up to make the company invulnerable to outside raiders. The arrangement was that Barry Bingham, Sr., son of the founder, and his wife, Mary, controlled a voting trust that represented a majority of the company's stock. But in 1985 the raiding, in effect, started from inside the family.[10] (The family empire had grown to include a broadcasting company and a printing company.)

The editor and publisher of the newspapers was Barry Bingham, Jr. Two of his sisters, Sallie and Eleanor, along with two other female members of the family, were on the board and Sallie in particular kept expressing dissatisfaction with the way Barry Jr. was running things. Barry Jr. finally responded by replacing all family females on the board and created what he called a professional board with only himself and his father representing the family.

Sallie responded by putting her 15 percent of the family media empire up for sale. Few members of the family were speaking with each other. Finally father Barry Bingham, Sr., threw up his hands and put the entire family enterprise up for sale. He said there were not only the interests of his three children to consider but those of nine grandchildren. Some were already adults.

Barry Jr. quit and issued a statement saying his father's action had been "both irrational and ill advised" and was "a betrayal of the traditions and principles which I have sought to perpetuate." The family enterprises were sold off for a total of $434 million."[11]

A *New York Times* writer, revisiting Louisville about a year later, reported a lingering bitterness. Father and son were living in next-door houses on the family estate overlooking the Ohio River but were rarely crossing the strip of lawn to visit. An in-law said: "It's like the green line in Beirut separating the Christians and the Moslems."[12]

And sister Sallie Bingham was making public appearances deploring the "sexist treatment" she had received.

CHAPTER 18

THE FRAGMENTING
EFFECT OF
MODERN FAMILY
FORMS

"Oh my! I don't know why that happens
so often. We're all such nice people."

— Secretary to the twice-divorced Marshall Field III upon hearing that one
of his offspring was into a second
divorce

While it is often difficult for
natural siblings to try to take over the running of a huge
business enterprise amicably, the situation becomes substantially more challenging when marital disruption intro-
duces half brothers and stepsisters. Until the past forty years
divorce was difficult to obtain and once obtained was typically considered a serious family embarrassment. Today
roughly half of all families have at least one adult member
with at least one ex-spouse. As suggested above, one effect
of this change has been to introduce in America a disrupting

factor in the otherwise more orderly passage of power and purse through family dynasties based on a financial empire.

Of the individuals in the *Forbes* 400 who have ever married, about 30 percent have married at least twice. The extremely wealthy people I visited turned out to have had an even higher percentage of turnover of mates than the *Forbes* group. Of those who had ever married, a majority did so at least twice and had children from a previous marriage. In the case of wealthy males, their first set of children commonly had remained primarily in the custody of the former spouse. Several of my interviewees who had remarried had inherited existing children of the new spouse. Two of the people visited have had four marriage partners, one has had five, and one has had seven.

In two cases family fragmentation contributed to corporate upheaval. In one, a faction of offspring ousted the father from his pinnacle of corporate power.

First we will visit Marshall Field V, the ostensible head of a great dynasty that has been overloaded with tenuous family ties. His net worth in 1986 was around $375 million.

What Divorce Did to the Field Dynasty

The Marshall Field family has long been a First Family of Chicago. And the Field dynasty is apparently unique among prominent American families in the number of generations carrying the name of the founder: six.

Marshall Field I and Marshall Field II developed what was for a while the world's largest department store. Marshall III, a New Deal liberal, sold the store to obtain funds to establish a liberal newspaper, the *Chicago Sun-Times*. Under Marshall IV the publishing empire expanded and became more middle-of-the-road. He died when Marshall V was barely out of college. After a crash training program, Marshall V was rushed into the job of publisher at age twenty-eight.

The only other immediate male blood relative from the

Field line was a sixteen-year-old half brother, Ted. Marshall V and Ted barely knew each other, but when Ted reached age twenty-five, the trust arrangement changed. He and Marshall V found themselves locked into holding equal shares of more than 40 percent of the ownership of Field Enterprises, with sisters holding nonvoting interests.[1] The organization had in past years expanded into television, syndication, real estate. Meanwhile, Marshall Field VI had been born.

Marshall V, whom we will meet, was conscientious about trying to maintain the family dynasty. Ted, more unconventional, had become an avid racing car enthusiast. He thought there were faster ways to make money than running media, especially newspapers, and wanted to take his chances on movie-making and commodities. There was tension between the two men. The upshot was that in the early 1980s the two began dismantling the empire piece by piece, and as one of the final acts sold the *Sun-Times* to Rupert Murdoch, long the publisher of sensation-seeking newspapers, the highest bidder. Chicago's initial reaction was one of shock. Many Chicagoans felt betrayed. But the dissolution of the Field empire was just symptomatic of a more general dispersion of the Field dynasty.

Marshall V is a slim, cheerful, frank, handsome man in his late forties. As we discussed the ramifications of the family tree he generously arranged for me to see a copy.

It is an incredible maze of double lines (main dynasty line connecting the six Marshall Fields), single lines to blood-related kin, and dotted lines to kin related only through marriage or remarriage.

The main source of the complexity is that Marshall Field III had three wives, Marshall Field IV had three wives, and Marshall Field V has had two wives. Way off in right field, for example, there is a Count Louis de Flers. It seems that Marshall Field III's third wife had a daughter named Phyllis and her third husband was the count.

Marshall Field V has a sister, a half brother, and two half sisters through his father, and a half brother through his mother. His only son, Marshall VI, was born of his first marriage, which lasted five years. At this writing he has three daughters born in his second marriage.

Between marriages Marshall Field V occasionally had custody of youngster Marshall VI and had him brought west from Pennsylvania where he was living with his mother. In order to get in as many hours with his son as he could, Marshall V occasionally brought Marshall VI to the *Sun-Times* office. During one meeting of executives in the boardroom, young Marshall VI was playing under the table and father, deciding he was making too much noise, directed him to please leave. Young Marshall VI complied but flipped off the light switch as he left. The executives were in darkness. Father Marshall V announced: "Will the vice-president closest to retirement please go out and kick his ass." Marshall VI has now entered his twenties, and Marshall V reported him as still not fully decided about a possible career.

Marshall V himself as a youngster was rarely in Chicago, the family home base. He was six years old when his mother and Marshall Field IV were divorced. She took him back to New Hampshire, then married a CIA official and moved to McLean, Virginia. Marshall V studied fine arts at Harvard, but for a career he wanted to go into marketing. He liked selling and even though he had an inheritance did door-to-door selling of books for experience and selling suits at a New York department store, which he said he loved.[2] He confessed to me that he had little interest in, or aptitude for, newspaper work:

"I never saw Chicago. I would come out and see my father maybe for a month in the summer on his farm and I didn't know where State Street was when I finally came out here" (to be groomed for presiding over the media empire).

He professed to feel that being geographically removed from the family seat of power was an advantage. "It took a lot of the pressure off. I think there is something terrible about being brought up on a big place or right in the seat of power."

His half brother, Ted, too had been removed from the

seat of power. His mother, Katherine, was the second of Marshall Field IV's three wives. After she went through divorce she set out to be a newspaper woman and moved, with young son Ted, to Anchorage, Alaska, where she and a subsequent husband bought a newspaper. She went on as Katherine Fanning to become one of America's most eminent editors, at the *Christian Science Monitor*.

When Marshall V and Ted sought to free themselves of their forced embrace by converting Field Enterprises into cash (which is more easily divided), Marshall V stalled on selling the family's *Chicago Sun-Times*. He was resisting the interest being shown by chain-owner Murdoch, whose newspapers tended to carry such banners as HEADLESS BODY IN TOPLESS BAR (*New York Post*). Executives of the paper scrambled to patch together a counteroffer but came up a few million short. Ted pushed to accept the Murdoch bid. He has said he was not obsessed with carrying the family torch. Marshall V was quoted as saying, "Had this decision been mine alone I probably would not have taken this action."[3] But the sale went through and the breaking up of their jointly controlled empire was soon complete.

The outcome for the *Chicago Sun-Times* was not as bad as feared. Murdoch started shifting it to being a more lurid journal. Dozens of staff members quit. Readership fell, perhaps partly out of resentment. Meanwhile, Murdoch had gotten interested in other kinds of media, so his interest shifted. In any case, the paper gradually regained respect from the community.

As for Marshall V, the dismembering helped him gain all the family's interest in Cabot, Cabot & Forbes, a nationwide realty firm specializing in commercial space. He also owns something called the Old Mountain Corporation, which he explained is for odds and ends.

In the four years after the split-up *Forbes* estimated that Ted's fortune had moved from $250 million to $400 million while Marshall V's had moved from $250 million to $450 million.

Most days Marshall V leaves his twenty-room neo-

Georgian brick home in Lake Forest on the North Shore and takes the commuter train to his office high above downtown Chicago. (He says: "I'm a prisoner of the train station.") His office quarters are truly the kind that would please a movie director. There is a vast, dramatic area about 100 feet long leading to his very handsomely modern office. From his desk in the corner he has two views: one of downtown Chicago, the other of Lake Michigan.

He explained that since he has very good people under him at the real estate firm he can spend about 30 percent of his time out working on public enrichment–type projects such as being a fund-raiser for the Chicago Art Institute and the great Field Museum, which was set up by his forefathers. Regarding his philanthropic interests he said: "You can give them [institutions] some money but you've got to want to spend some time trying to help them if you think you can and if you are really interested. When I'm not fund-raising I am sitting down and planning meetings, interviewing people to help hire a new director or something." Thus, deliberately or not, the Field image is to some degree being refurbished among Chicagoans.

I think there are responsibilities as well as pleasures if you are wealthy," he said. "I think, though, that there is a world of difference between inheriting wealth — even if you make something from it — and making it all yourself. I think that with inherited wealth there has been time to teach the children that they are going to get money. (And how to treat it responsibly.) With people who are self-made it's very unusual to see those qualities in the first generation. So I don't expect from ... new money what I expect from second- or third-generation [money]. I'm talking about things like charity."

He and his wife have a second home on Jupiter Island, Florida, where they go with the kids during school vacations. He has a fifty-foot powerboat and used to take a gang tuna fishing. That has become too rough for him now and he favors salmon fishing in Iceland or Canada.

Mr. Field is one of the few people I interviewed who said

his living costs run over a million a year. "When you are running two big places . . . and let's say a staff of two in each one . . . and you're paying real estate and income taxes . . . and school for four kids . . . it has to be two million." And he didn't mention alimony. He has set up trusts for his children of both marriages.

His comment about people with inherited wealth seems solid but only as a general tendency. I think he would agree that he and his half brother Ted were not equally dedicated to the concept that the Field family should demonstrate responsibility.

In my inspection of thirty very wealthy people about 40 percent of those who had started adulthood with substantial inherited wealth were, in my view, quite strong in demonstrating public responsibility. Among the self-made, about a third were quite strong in demonstrating such responsibility. In short, the difference was not as great as people of inherited wealth like to pretend.

Mr. Field made the point that while he feels a responsibility to preserve the family tradition he has insisted that everyone in the family should feel free to do his own thing. At the time the financial empire was being dismantled he was quoted as having said: "The only real tradition is that each succeeding generation shouldn't blow it. If you can leave the family fortune a little bigger than you found it, that's what counts."[4]

Centimillionaire with
a Shoeful of Restless Children

Leonard Samuel Shoen is one of the more extraordinary persons I encountered in my exploration of the extraordinarily wealthy. As founder of U-Haul, he pioneered techniques that made trailer rental into a nationwide industry for mobile Americans. The family wealth he controlled in 1986 was put at $300 million.

He has at least five distinctions that set him apart from the average super-millionaire.

- Although he was the richest man in his state (Arizona) when I saw him and had a big, handsome contemporary home on the edge of an exclusive country club, I was told by a member that he probably would be excluded from membership in the club if he applied. The club is in greater Phoenix.
- When he and his lovely bride, who is a third of a century younger than he is, sit down to dine at night, the main course is a baked potato. Sometimes they supplement it with a vegetable or piece of fish or chicken. When they go out to dine their favorite restaurant is Wendy's because it features baked potatoes. They go out to someone else's house about once a month.
- He has more years of higher education, probably, than anyone else in the *Forbes* 400, certainly more than any of the other super-rich I encountered. And now, at around seventy years of age, he was still taking classes. He said he had been in college the equivalent of eleven years. One of his major disappointments in life is that he did not persist in his effort to become a doctor. That's what he would most like to be. But he did, at the age of thirty-nine, get a law degree by going to school nights. He was the head of his class at Northwestern College of Law in Portland, Oregon.
- He has more children than anyone in the *Forbes* 400, a full dozen, borne by three of his five wives. He loves them but they have definitely complicated his life and business.
- Some of these offspring undertook to unseat him at the large company he had created.

The reason he probably couldn't get into the country club, the member explained to me, was that first of all he was not socially prominent. His area of Phoenix had its old rich and its flashy new rich and he was neither. (Mr. Shoen mentioned to me that he had on occasion been in the social whirl of his area, but he didn't "get any kick out of it. I think it is a pain in the ass.")

Also, he had all those wives which might lead to the conclusion, probably erroneous, that he was not a person of constraint.

Finally, I was told, his name was Jewish, which might sway some on the membership committee. That's a ground for exclusion that would undoubtedly surprise, and perhaps amuse, Mr. Shoen. He is a lifelong Catholic, with scars to prove it. An autobiography written years ago[5] describes his boyhood on a farm near McGrath, Minnesota. His mother was French-Swiss. His father was Scotch-English. Both came from farming backgrounds. In explaining his own large family to me he said:

"I was born a Catholic and my first wife was Catholic. She died at the age of thirty-four and left me with six children. The next girl I married was a Catholic too, and she tried to keep up with the first one in terms of children, and that's about the only terms. That didn't work out so well. . . . I've tried to maintain the Catholic deal but it all went to hell when I got a divorce from my second wife after about eighteen years and five children. It was a real incompatible personality situation, but in the Catholic faith you stay with the woman you marry, you know." The Church gave him a sampling of holy hell. He recalled, "I went through a very traumatic time when I got a divorce."

Another of his ex-wives had even made it difficult for him to see their son. Then, on top of the twelve children, there is the matter of inherited children. His current wife, for example, brought to the marriage a pre-teen youngster of her own who has been living with them.

Mr. Shoen was also unique in being the only super-rich male I visited who talked wistfully about retiring. He had a specific place at a beach community in Puerto Rico where he planned to retire. The main thing he would take with him there would be a lot of books. He loves to read. He might also do some writing. His son Sam, he felt, was almost ready to take over management of the company. He had been handling the international end. Mr. Shoen explained the long breaking-in of his son by saying, "Usable knowledge is usually only learned by experience."

Fifteen years ago, he said, he almost retired. He had a chance to sell out and receive for the family a cash sum in the hundreds of millions, clear. He emphatically didn't want such a spilling out of cash. Under the structure he had set up — presumably at least partly for tax reasons — his children by various marriages were given title to more than 90 percent of the shares of the company. That was all right as long as the money was tied up in the company and they couldn't get their hands on it. But if the company was converted to cash, they could reasonably expect a gusher of money pouring out to them. Some might spend it carelessly. Money can just disappear. Definitely he did not want them wallowing in money. He had tried to raise them on the work ethic, and to be frugal. Money was just something that helped make an organization function. He said:

"I saw my family just getting the money and I saw that it wouldn't do them any good. An organization such as this is about the best place to store wealth for a family if it's going to do them any good. I wouldn't like to see this organization disappear. I tried to set it up in such a way that it will last into the future a long ways. I organized it, and organized where the stock will go, all that sort of thing." He expressed admiration for Japanese companies he did business with that go back 400 years.

"All my children are working pretty damn hard or going to school. They're not consuming a hell of a lot. I'm not either." He said he had tried to keep his kids "at a level of income so they work for a living and are out trying to do something that's useful and not trying to spend money to have a good time."

I arranged to meet him at his office, where I could meet son Sam, then age forty. And later his wife would be driving by to pick him up to go out to the university at Tempe where they were both enrolled in a psychology class. They could drop me off at my hotel.

Our conversation began in his boardroom. He was attired in open shirt, jacket, and jogging shoes. He probably wore them because of a bad back. Once dapper, he was now somewhat rumpled, bald, and paunchy as he slumped in his

chair and talked much of the time with the eyes of his
broad face closed. At one point an aide brought in his lunch
in a plastic container: salad and an apple. He didn't eat
the apple.

"I never wanted to be in business to begin with. I only
used it as a way to make a living" while going to school, he
began. His father had moved West to seek opportunity in a
farming venture in Oregon, which failed badly; young
"Sam" Shoen had spent much of five years working as a
farm laborer in this venture. At college while taking pre-
med courses, he made money cutting hair in his room. By
the time he got to medical school he was known as "Slick"
because he was having a good time with his own convertible
and cabin cruiser while running a chain of barbershops and
beauty parlors and getting good grades. He was jolted by a
suspension at medical school; he was suspended mainly because he had answered in class for his lab partners.

Meanwhile he had gotten married. He obtained acceptance in a navy program during World War II, but came
down with rheumatic fever. During the months in bed he
pondered the fact that so many million Americans on the
move because of the war were trying to haul their possessions about in makeshift trailers, often using axles and
wheels from junker cars. He came out of the hospital with a
fully developed scheme to build, around service stations, a
chain of outlets for sturdy trailers that could be left off in
some other city. And he had invented the name U-Haul.

He learned welding and started building trailers at his
father-in-law's ranch. His trailers were painted bright orange with the name U-Haul printed large on sides and back
so that each trailer would be a big advertisement, whether
on the road or parked at a service station. His first one-way
rental service was between Seattle and Portland for $5.

And he had been growing ever since. He learned every
facet of running a business by reading books and attending
night school. The fact that he had an enormous thrust of
energy greatly aided him in his empire-building. Much of
that energy was spent visiting service stations as he ex-

panded across the country. Within a decade he had 10,000 trailers on the road. Still, in his travels he slept in the back of a car at a service station and washed up in the morning at the station's toilet. The parent company that he created for U-Haul is AMERCO, a Nevada corporation with most of its executive offices in Arizona.

Along with his empire, his children from his first two marriages were growing. "You get into all this mixing of families and you get into a big . . . well, that's a long story in itself," he said with a chuckle. "In truth they get along pretty good among themselves." He had greatly enjoyed the children when they were young but as they got older they were less of an enjoyment. And as for his children's children he said: "I have not really enjoyed my grandchildren though I have about twelve of them, I think, or so."

His offspring, particularly his sons of the first two marriages, I gathered, had become a real problem for him in connection with the business. "Brothers kill off brothers through history. . . . That's the problem. So you've gotta have it set up in such a way that you have a clear succession and there is no doubt about who the hell it is so they won't kill each other." That's why, he explained, he had in a letter set up a clear succession. He had designated that son Sam from the first marriage succeed him and that son Jim from the second marriage succeed Sam.

He said he got more support from the younger offspring from the second family than he did from sons of the first family. Five out of the six children from his first marriage were boys. "These boys were all aggressive and you know it is real difficult to sit back and not be aggressive. . . ." The combination of this aggressiveness and family mixing had created a problem.

He said he had no desire for money and only kept 2 percent of it in his name, presumably largely for tax reasons. As noted, at least 90 percent of the stock was in the names of his children. They, therefore, theoretically controlled the board of directors. But, he added, "Nobody has sold any stock and nobody's in a position to sell the stock. It is [held] in such a way that they can't sell it." He added that he had set up a situation so that corporate stock must go to great grandchildren. Clearly preservation of the institution he had created meant more to him than money.

In the months before my visit his children had become an even more acute pain to him in connection with the business. He showed me two long, typed letters he had recently addressed to "Sons and Daughters of L. S. Shoen." They were signed "Much love," but the letters were tough, the second tougher than the first because he had attempted to be diplomatic in the first. In the first he had stressed the many opportunities open to them outside the world of AMERCO and that being on the company's board of directors was "not a worthwhile objective" for them and that they needed to be "free" of him. And that financially it made no difference whether they were on the board or not. He needed a board of directors that could act fast and knowledgeably. The present system wasn't working (with him legally having to consult with his kids on the board before taking any major action).

He wanted his twelve working vice-presidents on that board instead.

The second, more recent letter was more brief, clear, and urgent. He wanted their signed proxies taking themselves off the board and authorizing a new board dominated by working vice-presidents. The way it was he and his top executives were "hamstrung" when they met and made strategic decisions because they then had to get them ratified by offspring on the board who were not knowledgeable. He concluded: "The way I have tried to make my sons and daughters as the board of directors fit into the management" simply was not working and was uncomfortable for the outside lenders and inside executives. "I hope you can see the wisdom of this change." Apparently, per their ensuing actions, which we will get to, they did not.

He confessed he had not been much into civic activities except "what I've done, you know, as a Catholic for a lot of my life. I did my share." And he had no foundation.

His one splurge in terms of recreation was to obtain a Chinese junk with the idea of sailing it, with his family, from Houston to Miami. He recalls: "It was such a disaster for the whole damn family that I wouldn't talk about it for two years. The trip took a couple months or so and taught me a lot about sailing."

Regarding money he observed: "As you've probably learned, you can't take money and go out and have a good time. Money won't buy you joy. It won't buy you fun. It won't buy you satisfaction. Satisfaction is a thing that goes on in your mind. The thing that buys you the sort of mental attitude that is called happiness is when you make a difference — when your efforts in this world make a difference for your fellow man. If you are a productive person, you can make a difference. I tell you truthfully I could have remained a barber and been happy because for one thing I was doing it myself and I was making a contribution and doing something to make people happier." He said that once he retired he could be very happy with $50,000 a year.

The man whom Mr. Shoen had chosen to take over when he retired, son Sam, came in. He was handsome, bearded, about forty, obviously from some of his remarks a well-organized person. I said I had just heard that his father was thinking of "dumping this whole thing on you." He expressed mock horror. And he announced that his stepmother, who, he explained cheerfully, was younger than he was, would be arriving shortly.

Father Shoen said that after the divorce from his second wife, "I went through three or four women. You know how that goes. You try and you think that [a new wife] is going to help your life work. My present wife does help my life work. She damn well is a benefit to me and a very important benefit. Her dad was an anthropologist. She's just an ordinary girl, a wonderful person. She's very sociable, a typical girl of her age. She tries this and she tries that."

Mrs. Shoen number five, a poised, very handsome, friendly young woman, entered. We chatted while Mr. Shoen explained some final details to son Sam.

She confirmed their unconventional dining habits. "Shredded wheat and skimmed milk for breakfast. Salad for lunch. And a baked potato for dinner. Many times that's all or maybe he'll have two baked potatoes. That's the whole thing. That's it, usually. My daughter now eats baked potatoes too. Once in a while we'll have scrambled eggs or fish or something. I love potatoes. And they're a good food to have if you want to lose weight or keep your weight down because they fill you up."

The three of us went down to her car. On the way he showed me proudly, outside his building, two statues of lions he had picked up in mainland China on a trip. The car was a small cream-colored Continental. He lets her drive because of his bad back. Still, politely, he insisted on climbing into the back seat so that I could be in front with her.

As she expertly whipped through traffic she told how they had met. They were both enrolled in an EST program for enhancing human potential, in Phoenix. They had signed up for a two-weekend course. She said that "afterward they have these follow-up seminars. You sign up for a series of ten. When we signed up for the series we did not know each other.

"They divided the group of 300 up into pods of six. We were in the same pod. And then you pick a sharing partner to call every week. He picked me." And they were soon happily married.

After my visit Mr. Shoen's problems with the offspring of his several marriages increased. As indicated, he had designated that Sam from his first marriage would succeed him and that Jim from his second marriage would succeed Sam.

About a year after my visit, there was an uprising by his offspring, who had, despite his letters, retained their control of the board. Both father Leonard and son Sam were ousted from their jobs. Sons Sam and Jim, at last report, were permitted to remain on the board.

Sons Joe, Paul, and Mark of the first marriage, whom their father had referred to in our talk as "aggressive," took over the top three jobs. *Newsweek,* in reporting on the upheaval and the new regime, said that the U-Haul company had lost momentum largely because of the battling and was starting to face serious competition from the Ryder System. It cited a report that one meeting of two brothers ended up in a fistfight.[6]

In late 1988 *Business Week* reported that the feuding of the twelve brothers and sisters was entering a new phase and might lead to the dismantling of a business worth almost a billion dollars. A group of five offspring who had achieved control and called themselves key employees with special rights were trying time-tested strategies to maintain control. Father, Sam, and six other offspring were taking the control group to court to try to balk such moves. Family members of the two groups were speaking to each other only through lawyers.

Meanwhile, Leonard Shoen had considerably more time to enjoy his passion for reading books.

D.

How
They Protect
Their Wealth

CHAPTER 19

PROTECTIVE

STRATEGIES

WHILE

STILL ALIVE

"My clients decide what they want to pay the government and we work at it that way."

— Tax attorney with long experience in helping wealthy clients in Washington, D.C. area

A friend who works at a New York law firm that handles the affairs of many very wealthy people commented: "Most of the really wealthy people I know pay less taxes than I do. Some don't pay anything. Some with hundreds of millions pay less taxes than I do."

Very wealthy people can be very conscientious, straightforward taxpayers. We will meet one. But for many people of great wealth, figuring out ways to protect their wealth from tax collectors seems to contribute excitement to the game, or problem, of being rich. And thousands of tax attorneys and estate planners are eager, for fees, to press ideas upon them. The changes made every couple of years in the extremely complex federal tax code add to the prosperity of the advisers.

Changes made in the code in 1986 were hailed as revolutionary in producing fairness, but they did not cause panic in the ranks of the very rich. Rich people continued, for example, to be as interested in setting up trusts as ever. The *Boston Globe* in an analysis carried the headline: "Under New Tax Bill, the Really Well-to-do Will Do Better Than the Merely Well-to-do."

People of great wealth typically are either entrepreneurs, inheritors, or landowners. Hence, ordinary earned income typically accounts for only a small amount of their wealth, and the income tax on it is a minor worry. Even the 1986 change specifying the treatment of capital gains from investments as ordinary income was not regarded as catastrophic because taxes on the highest brackets of income were lowered, so that the change amounted to a few percent. An estate planner told me: "I've just told my clients to turn down the faucet in taking profits."

In general, the ingenuity of the tax planners is focused more on easing taxes on the transfer of wealth, via gifts and bequests at death, than on easing income taxes.

Thus, changes produced by the 1986 laws which most caught the attention of the really rich, or their advisers, involved trusts and limited partnerships. In the second case, if for example the wealthy person's role in the limited partnership was just that of a "passive" investor and not an active partner, it has become more difficult to take paper losses.

Of the dozens of types of trusts, a few were affected in some noteworthy way. One was the so-called Clifford trust, which involves the wealthy person's putting some of his millions in the names of his children under age fourteen, who of course are in a lower tax bracket. The lawyers think they can handle the new tightening simply by putting the money in tax-exempt zero-coupon bonds that will not pay off interest until the child is past fourteen. Generation-skipping trusts were made somewhat less attractive, as we'll see.[1]

My sources of information on the strategies often used for protecting wealth included a few of the wealthy people I visited. More important in offering detailed insights, however, were three former commissioners of the U.S. Internal Revenue Service (Mortimer Caplin, Don Alexander, and Sheldon S. Cohen) and a number of lawyers specializing in estate planning, including two who are nationally known from their writings, Jonathan G. Blattmachr of New York and Jerry McCoy of Washington, D.C.

One of the major objectives in high-level tax planning is to put assets where it is hard for the tax man to get at them. For examples:

Place money in municipal bonds. They pay less interest than corporate bonds but the interest is free of tax to the IRS. There has been an explosion in purchase of such bonds, from $14 billion in 1971 to $198 billion in 1986.[2]

It is no coincidence that most of the bonds are bought by wealthy people with incomes in the top ½ percent. A host of pseudo-municipals were invented purely to provide protection for investors seeking to escape taxes. There were, for example, bonds for the Oregon Department of Veteran Affairs and for the Arizona Student Loan Finance Corporation. The 1986 Tax Act made the game harder to play for promoters and purchasers of bonds that do not directly cover government obligations or government-owned facilities.

Put the money in overseas corporate holdings. There are, for example, foreign-based trusts in countries such as Lichtenstein, the British Virgin Islands, and the Netherland Antilles, where taxes on trusts are negligible. The U.S. Treasury has been seeking ways to lower the appeal of the Antilles. Former IRS Commissioner Caplin mentioned that people may build large foreign business empires not subject to U.S. tax. For example, if an American owns a part of a company that is operating in France and selling most of its products in France, he is not subject to U.S. tax on that holding.

Sink the money into the ground or other forms of real

estate. This is very popular. A large proportion of centimillionaires include "land," "real estate," or drilling and mining rights to land among their major holdings. Pet supplier Leonard Stern moved massively into New Jersey real estate. Jeno Paulucci (as we'll recall) got his start in the chow mein and pizza businesses but now is mainly absorbed with owning and developing real estate. *Forbes* said of its own centimillionaire publisher Malcolm S. Forbes that he "owns vast real estate."

Raw land in a good location is, of course, ideal since it just sits there appreciating in value while not producing a penny in federal taxable income. One ex-commissioner of the IRS said of rich people seeking a low tax situation: "A super-rich person would be heavily into income producing real estate. This would provide deductions [from depreciation] and would lead to virtually no tax paid on the property. He or she would also be involved in . . . oil and gas." (You can still deduct from taxes a lot of "intangible" drilling costs, such as preliminary preparation costs.)

Former IRS Commissioner Caplin referred to real estate as "one of the greatest games of them all." He pointed out that if you want to buy a $10 million residential building in a good location you might put up $1 million and borrow $9 million from the bank. A lot of good things usually then happen. Even though the building is growing in value instead of depreciating, you can, under the depreciation tables, get tax reductions against your rental income for the whole $10 million over twenty-seven years because you are the legal owner.

Mortgaging yourself up to the hilt even though you are rich can often be attractive. If you borrow $4 million to buy a $5 million house, you not only can deduct from federal taxes the local real estate taxes you pay but also the interest you pay on the mortgage. Billionaire Leslie Wexner mentioned that he still had a mortgage on his Columbus-area house.

The same deductability applies to debt in general. Debt is great as long as assets are greater. Clayton Williams, Jr., the oil man, banker, realtor, professor, and communications man from Midland, Texas, emphasized the nice aspects of debt in our talk.

"I paid $22 million worth of interest in one three-month period — so I haven't had to pay a lot of income tax. Our income structure is such that you don't pay taxes till you are ready to quit. Then when you've got the real money, you pay taxes. I've always had assets and I've been building. As long as you're building on a debt base you don't pay a lot of tax." (The 1986 Tax Act put some limits on the deduction of certain types of interest payment.)

Another major objective of the tax planning experts is to find ways to transfer assets so that they will not be included as taxable assets of the wealthy client while leaving him or her with substantial control over them while still alive. The game is to minimize any tax bite on the transfer. For example:

When giving to the kids, see that they get the part of your assets most likely to grow. If you have a growing $30 million family-owned business, the strategy is to restructure it so that Dad and Mom own $29 million worth of the company in preferred stock, which pays dividends but does not grow in value. (The arrangement can be handled so that they retain voting control.) Give the kids the remaining million dollars' worth of the company in the form of a million shares of common stock worth a dollar a share. As the company grows in fifteen years from being a $30 million company to being a $100 million company, the kids have acquired $70 million worth of assets tax free.

In the giving of gifts make sure the tax consequence is favorable to the donor. For example, if a person is giving noncash gifts to charity on which he can claim tax deductions (such as paintings or raw land), the donor may want the highest conceivable valuation placed on his gift. On the other hand, if he or she is giving the same gifts to his own children he may maneuver to assure that a very low value is placed on the gift in order to minimize transfer taxes.

Consider the valuations placed on noncash gifts to charities, gifts with unique characteristics such as paintings, sculpture, gemstones, manuscripts, rare books. Ex-Commissioner Caplin pointed out that a lot of charities such as museums have started playing games to aid in the boosting of valuations as the number of museums in the country grows and they compete for desired items to display.

In 1983 the *Washington Post* explored in depth the way one official of the government's own Smithsonian Institution had sought to build up its gem collection by cooperating with a tax-shelter outfit in Florida. The report stated that this official actively solicited gems by "touting" the tax benefits. He even supplied the tax-shelter firm with a promotional tool: a brochure on "The Lure of Gems." For a while gems were pouring into the Smithsonian faster than they could be processed.

The donors commonly had been provided with appraisals, provided by obliging appraisers, amounting to five times what the gems had cost only a year or so before. Donations shrank when the IRS installed new penalties for excessive overevaluations it uncovered.

Obtaining a valuation on a piece of art has in any case become a guessing-type situation at best, particularly since a Japanese business firm paid a bafflingly high $39 million for a Van Gogh *Sunflower.* And at least one higher price for a Van Gogh has since been paid ($53 million for *Irises*). (What would a Titian three centuries older bring!)

The gift of a work of art, Caplin pointed out, has enormous tax-shelter potential unaffected by the IRS's using a panel of appraisers to try to spot valuation abuses. A Degas may have a fair market value today of $1 million. The donor can get a tax deduction for that amount even though he picked it up for one-hundredth of that amount a mere decade ago.

On the other hand, if you want to convey to your children a share of your business you may fix things so that the share will appear to have quite limited value. The general strategy is called "estate freezing." A setup is devised that will almost automatically insure that the children will be getting their piece of the business at a very big discount. As tax specialist Jerry McCoy put it, you "create legal tangles" around shares of a closely held company. A claim may be made that a 30 percent minority interest in a company controlled by someone like Dad who has the other 70 percent isn't worth 30 percent of fair market value. The reasoning is that you as a minority owner have no control. But why couldn't the same argument be made if Dad gave you a few million dollars' worth of shares in a beautifully performing public company where management has firm control of voting rights? The *Washington Post* had such a stock throughout most of the 1980s. McCoy said: "The IRS is unhappy with the concept that the sum of the parts can equal a lot less than the whole."

An ex-IRS commissioner pointed out that a closely held business may also set up a "buy-sell agreement," which greatly restricts the value of shares in the company for a specified time. If Dad is able to sell his shares only to other members of the family, such as offspring, he is not going to get from prospective buyers within the family the same price that his shares would command on the open market. Thus the shares are passed to the kids at a bargain. Another approach has been to make, with some winking, a regular sale to children but to do it on the installment plan. At Dad's death, or sooner, the unpaid installments are forgiven.

Of course, the wealthy can simply start giving their children fairly substantial sums of money — and thus reduce their own estate somewhat. A father and mother, for example, can each give up to $10,000 a year to each of their children and each of their grandchildren, and if desired to nephews, sisters, et cetera. Thus if we are talking about a situation where there are three children and eight grandchildren, Mom and Dad in concert could make twenty-two gifts of $10,000 each. This would move about a quarter-million dollars out of their estate each year — or in ten years $2.25 million — with no need even to report the actions to tax authorities.

When direct giving gets above $10,000 a year per person

by a parent, the unified tax credit takes over. Gifts above the $10,000 allowance must be reported. To handle these amounts gift and estate taxes are now lumped together as a unit. In 1987 a person could give up to about $600,000 in reportable gifts and bequests in his or her lifetime before there were tax consequences. Or a husband and wife could give $1.2 million in their lifetime over and above the annual $10,000 nonreported individual gifts they might be giving to family members.

However, if there are only a couple of children and no grandchildren or if a person's assets are up in the $25 million to $2 billion range, then more serious measures are needed for the wealthy couple that resents paying taxes. The top tax rate on reported gifts and bequests above $600,000 in 1987 was around 55 percent.

The favorite instrument for trimming down the size of one's taxable assets while transferring them to others is the trust. As readers may have noted, a number of the very wealthy people I talked with mentioned trusts for children as being in their picture. Melvin Simon, the Indiana shopping center magnate, offered the surprising comment: "Obviously they all have their own trusts, you know, which I like to borrow from all the time."

Attorneys for the rich have invented a bewildering variety of trusts, and sometimes they use different names for the same type vehicle for moving money. Here we will stick to a few of the basic preferred forms. A trust is just a legal entity that holds assets contributed by a grantor for the benefit of one or more beneficiaries. Trustees supervise it. "Living trusts," which go into effect while the grantor is still alive, have the advantage of not being a part of the grantor's will at death and hence escaping estate treatment.

If they are irrevocable living trusts they can also have the major advantage of instantly reducing the size of the grantor's taxable assets. He or she has technically given up control over them. (We'll get to the trusts which typically go into effect after death in the next chapter.) Here are two examples of irrevocable living trusts that are widely used by wealthy Americans:

A trust that can pay you income while holding your money for the ultimate benefit of others. This is commonly called GRIT, or a "Grantor Retained Income Trust." Say Dad as a grantor is age forty and he wants to move $40 million out of his estate in such a way that it will eventually go to son Joe Jr., now age fourteen, with most of it not subject to estate taxation. He may arrange that the trust holds the money for, say, twenty-two years before turning it over to young Joe. Here we get into the weird arithmetic of "valuation discounting," that some call a shell game. Under the present regulations which the IRS must follow, it estimates the interest-earning capacity of money over the twenty-two-year period.

After consulting its current valuation tables the IRS may put a "present value" on this eventual gift to Joe Jr. at only perhaps $8 million. The only tax, which Dad will pay in setting up the trust, will be on that $8 million of "present value" — or about $4 million in taxes. The rationale is that $8 million invested today should be worth $40 million in twenty-two years if it earns an average of somewhere around 9 percent a year. Meanwhile Dad, the grantor, may be giving himself a "retained income" over the twenty-two years of whatever income the money is earning, say, $3 or $4 million a year. Furthermore, he can be the trustee and decide how the money will be invested, and even give himself a trustee's fee.[3] After twenty-two years, the money goes tax free to Joe Jr., now a sensible thirty-six-year-old adult. Dad by then would be sixty-two. And meanwhile during the same twenty-odd years he may have had similar money-moving vehicles going for daughters Nancy and Denise. If so, $120 million might be passed to the children at a total transfer tax cost of perhaps $12 million. And meanwhile in the twenty-odd years Dad would have gotten more than $100 million in income from the three trusts.

One big hazard in this, however, is that if Dad happens to die before the trust terms expire, the value of the principal or corpus of the trusts will be included in his taxable estate.

A trust where charity begins at home. There are a variety

of ways to create charitable trusts that are very attractive tax-reducing devices for the wealthy. One basic form is the "Charitable Remainder Trust." You give, say, $20 million to a favorite charity with a specification that all the income on the $20 million comes back to you while alive or, after you die, to your surviving spouse. That could be, say, $1.6 million a year. Only after both spouses die does the charity receive spendable money. Typically the charities are glad to wait. The nice part is that in addition to the annual income that you receive, you can also receive a charitable deduction on your income taxes for the value of the remainder that is going to charity.

In one variation you receive a stated sum annually for life from the money involved in the gift. In another variant you and spouse can receive a fixed percentage, say 5 percent, of the fair value of the gift each year.

Any of the variations assures you of plenty of pocket money plus a substantial reduction in taxes.

CHAPTER 20

STRATEGIES

FOR THE

HEREAFTER

"There are about 100 different post-death planning things which a lawyer can consider."

— JONATHAN BLATTMACHR, attorney specializing in estate planning

In 1982, a U.S. Congressional Research Service report stated that the nation had a relatively comprehensive system for taxing the generational transfer of wealth.[1] It stated that there were not only estate and gift taxes but taxes on any efforts to pass money directly to grandchildren or great-great-grandchildren. The goals of these taxes, it said, were "to raise revenue and to avoid the indefinite perpetuation of very large estates."

Any success in achieving each goal has in fact been on the comical side, but never more so than since the laws favoring the rich, made under the Reagan administration, began having their effect.

In the three years between 1982 and 1985 the proportion of the total money collected by the Internal Revenue Service contributed by estate and gift taxes dropped from a slight 1.3 percent to an even more slight .8 percent.[2]

As for socking vast estates, the inheritance of the five children of William du Pont, Jr. offers a case in point. In recent decades they came into a total of a half-billion dollars. Estate and gift taxes taken out during two generations of transferring this particular du Pont fortune had amounted to 5 percent per generation of the amount that the five "children" inherited.[3] During some of the decades involved, estate tax rates were officially more than 70 percent.

The explanation, of course, is careful planning. Taxable estate money that remains to be dispensed at the time the will of a very wealthy person is read has been referred to as the tip of an iceberg. Only family servants may be left in suspense. Important inheritors have typically been briefed by family lawyers on the situation, often well in advance. Where old money is concerned it is not uncommon that an individual inheritor may be the beneficiary, from various family sources, of a dozen trusts already in place.

In the eight years ending in 1982, the number of what the IRS calls "complex trusts" that went on record in America grew by more than 179,000 — a 47 percent jump.[4] These are the trusts that best preserve wealth for inheritance.

Some of the simple, noncomplex trusts are created primarily for management. A grantor may want to specify when trustees may release money to children and how much. As one ex–IRS commissioner explained: "Grantors don't want their children to get enormous amounts of money at eighteen or twenty-one or twenty-five. The typical plan is to have it held until they feel the child has reached sufficient maturity: thirty or forty years of age or whatever. And generally they have it paid out not all at one time but by fourths or thirds or halves."

One of the tax changes produced in the early 1980s was to permit unlimited passage of wealth to a surviving spouse without taxation. But with the recent fragmentation of families, a grantor may feel uneasy about unlimited passage of wealth to his or her spouse. The grantor may wonder whether the surviving spouse may pass unreasonably large sums to children of some previous marriage — or to the children of some person the spouse may subsequently marry after the grantor's death — or to a subsequent spouse!

Lawyers have now invented a trust that not only eases such management anxieties but also can reduce taxes paid on the passing of money by deferring the passage. As one tax attorney explained it, "A lot of people go by the adage a tax dollar delayed may never be paid." This trust is known as the Q-TIP ("Qualified Terminable Interest Property"). Through wording of the trust, the grantor typically specifies how the money is to be distributed upon the death of the spouse, including something perhaps for the college the donor attended or any other recipient of his choice.

Another essentially managerial trust is known as the spendthrift trust. The grantor suspects that a particular offspring may be a damned fool about handling big money; so safeguards are built into the trust specifying how the money is to be doled out, and perhaps supervised.

A very wealthy person's thoughts are much more likely to turn to major charitable giving when confronting death than at any other time of life. As indicated earlier, a study comparing estate tax returns with income tax returns of the same individuals in the years just prior to death revealed that top wealthholders tended to give away only a very small percentage of their wealth during their lifetime.[5] Perhaps in preparing for death they are devoting more thought to the public image they hope to perpetuate ... or making up for previous slight attention to public responsibilities such as philanthropy ... or thinking more about their standing with their Maker.

Perhaps also they are thinking more urgently about their final confrontation with the federal tax man who wants about half of whatever is permitted to remain in the taxable estate of a very wealthy person.

Such thoughts lead some top wealthholders to become

genuinely charitable. And such thoughts lead other top wealthholders to think of charity as one last ploy to transfer their wealth to descendants.

If the latter is the situation — or there is a combination of charitable and dynastic thinking — then an attractive so-called complex vehicle available is the charitable lead trust. (This is not to be confused with the charitable remainder trust described earlier. In that, the charity did eventually get all the money in the trust.) I cite the charitable lead trust here in discussing the Hereafter because while the grantor may still be alive when the trust is set up, he or she typically is no longer alive when the money involved finally passes to the children or other survivors.

There are variations, but essentially this trust typically lets the charity have a fixed percentage or fixed income from the assets in the trust for X number of years. Gifts to charity are deductible and so not subject to the gift tax. At the end of those X number of years, the untouched body of the fortune — called the remainder or corpus — may pass totally free of taxes. Furthermore, the children can serve as trustees during the years that the income is being given to favorite charities. And as one estate manager advised me: "They [the children] are controlling it. They're getting the community recognition and the fun and stroking that comes from doling out large amounts of money to charities that you're interested in."

If any taxes at all are paid on such a transfer of, say, $100 million of wealth to a daughter, they would be paid up front by the grantor. If the charitable phase is less than fifteen years, the grantor might have to pay, say, a 10 or 15 percent estate tax — instead of the roughly 55 percent on a direct transfer of money.

The tax planners, however, usually seek to assure their client that the whole transfer will occur totally tax free. To achieve that goal of zero dollars to the IRS, they plan "back-ward," as one tax lawyer put it. They ask: "How many years will the income from $100 million need to go to charity in order to achieve the goal of a totally tax-free transfer of the money to the kin? The number of years largely depends on the assumption the IRS is making, in the year the trust is created, about the growth potential of the invested money. How much annual yield can be assumed? Six percent? Seven and a half percent? Ten percent?

The IRS builds its "valuation tables" around its current assumption. (These valuation tables that list the "present value" of money which is to be gifted over a number of years are, as indicated, at the heart of much tax planning.) Recently the IRS has been assuming a 10 percent yield. Hence since X dollars today at 10 percent would be worth $100 million in fifteen years, taxes would only have to be paid on X dollars. A wealthy person could pass $100 million to heirs while paying transfer taxes on only a small portion of that amount by using a charitable lead trust.[6]

A realistic alternative when the yield assumed by the IRS is high is simply to set aside $100 million to be gifted to the daughter. The IRS will take say $50 million and the other $50 million goes to the daughter. Prudently invested, the $50 million will normally grow to at least $150 million in around fifteen years even after income taxes. But a lot of wealthy people can't stand the idea of giving that much of their own money to Uncle Sam.

Another approach is to use the charitable lead trust format, but instead of gifting money, to give the daughter $100 million worth of commercial buildings. Charity gets the rent on the buildings for X years. Then the daughter will have not only ownership but income. No tax is paid. And quite probably the buildings will have doubled in value to $200 million, and be producing double the income they did at the time of the gift. Yet another approach using the charitable lead trust and essentially the same strategy is to give charity the income from a sound portfolio of securities for X years before the portfolio, presumably greatly enhanced, goes to the daughter.

Lots of times, though, as tax planner Jerry McCoy pointed out, the children are already well taken care of by gifts. "You don't need to just pile more money on the estates of the children. You skip this generation and let the money go to the grandchildren."

Until recent years you could get away with various kinds of generation-skipping gifting with relatively little tax. You could, for example, let your children have the income on trusts that would pay out to grandchildren. When a tax was enacted to discourage such tactics, the planners began gifting wealth directly to grandchildren. Now there are taxes on both kinds of generation-skipping; but the planners still have ways to get results fairly gratifying to the grantor, and even advise making gifts to great-grandchildren. In 1987 *Trusts & Estates* carried a report that concluded: "The generation-skipping transfer tax has become a major component of and a challenge in estate planning."

Heavy lobbying by Ernest and Julio Gallo, the wine-makers of California, has been credited with getting an important exception written into the law effective at least until 1990. The Gallos were concerned because they had twenty grandchildren and about $700 million in net assets. Changes in the tax law in 1986 happily for them contained a provision that there would be an exemption from the generation-skipping tax of up to $2 million for each transferor to each grandchild. If there are two grandparents, this could come to $4 million per grandchild. For a family like the Gallos, it could amount to around $80 million. If the $2 million exemption is not extended in 1990, then the exemption will become $1 million per grandchild from the generation-skipping tax.

Because of the complications there is confusion among government officials regarding the generation-skipping tax and in actual fact there has been relatively little enforcement.

Tax planners McCoy and Blattmachr both pointed out that the generation-skipping tax is no real obstacle if you have a large sum you want to move to grandchildren. A centimillionaire in his or her senior years may find he has already passed on to his children more money than they could conceivably need and has, say, $100 million he would like to move to a ten-year-old grandson. All he needs to do is set up a charitable lead trust that is to run, say, twenty-five years. That should not cost anyone a nickel in taxes. And the corpus of the trust (at least $100 million) will be going to the grandson when he has reached a mature thirty-five years of age and presumably by then has gotten well over Fool's Hill.

Then there is insurance on one's life that can be used to pass fairly large amounts to one's heirs tax free or tax favored, if certain precautions are taken. It is relatively cumbersome to attempt on a large scale, though, and so has limited appeal to the tax planners of the super-rich.

There is no point in a wealthy person taking out life insurance on him or herself because at death it will simply go into his taxable estate. Someone else must take out the insurance. He can give annual payments of, say, $100,000 to spouse or children and let them take out the insurance, but this is hampered by the amount that can be transferred to them before the transfer tax applies. One's closely held company can take out the insurance, but that will just be tax favored, not tax free. A third approach is to set up an irrevocable trust and let the trustee take out the insurance. If certain rules are met, the amount is not included in one's estate. One requirement which may make one pause is that the insured person must remain alive three years after the trust is set up for the arrangement to take effect.

I presented estate planner Jerry McCoy and his partner with a seemingly hypothetical case of a man named John Walters who had by the age of fifty-two made a fast $500 million in the computer business. He had three children. All the details cited actually fit those of the finances of William Millard, whom we have met, before a jury hit him for a contract violation.

They mused over the problem. First of all, they said, Mr. Walters should have started making protective moves well before his fortune got up to a big fat half-billion. (Quite probably our subject had.)

At any rate, they started figuring out ways to "whittle"

down the $500 million estate in Mr. Walter's name and get more of it "downstream" to second and third generations. Altogether they came up with eight ideas. A few were esoteric but most have been mentioned in these past two chapters. Naturally there would be a GRIT (Grantor Retained Income Trust) and some sort of a charitable trust. There would be a restructuring of the company to freeze Mr. Walter's holdings in preferred stock and let the growth go to the kids. There would be annual gifts, installment sales, and second-to-die life insurance for the married couple (which significantly cuts the life insurance cost).

All these means cited by the tax advisers to help very wealthy people to reduce taxes before or after death are only the more common strategies. Tax advisers told me of situations they knew about where multimillion-dollar yachts or planes were registered offshore so that they wouldn't trigger a tax when sold . . . where assets were kept in living blind trusts whose beneficiaries were not disclosed on the public record and whose names could be changed at will. One told of an arrangement where a mother kept her grown son on an allowance that amounted to hundreds of thousands of dollars.

But timing is perhaps most important of all. Tax attorney Joseph Cressy of Boston and Edgartown, Massachusetts, who has worked with many wealthy clients, offered a viewpoint shared by many tax attorneys. He said:

"It is correct structuring at the very beginning that really counts. Once the successful person has attained, say, $10–$15 million with the reasonable expectation that success and therefore wealth will continue to accumulate, that person should not transfer anything outright. From then on everything should be sheltered, held in trusts (family beneficiaries or the like), owned offshore, et cetera.

"If success doesn't continue, it can be reversed if necessary. But once you've got something in your own name it is harder to hide it later or diffuse it without triggering a taxable experience or an IRS audit, et cetera. Own nothing directly and therefore, from the beginning, avoid income, gains, and estate taxes."

When you are working with a really big fortune it can in some ways be less challenging to protect than a small fortune. Jerry McCoy explained: "You reach a point where an estate can be so large that almost nothing matters. I mean, no matter how poorly it's handled or whatever . . . it's going to be large when it gets over to the other side, wherever that may be. The smaller the estate, the less room for error on whatever there is."

Are all these ingenious efforts to pass the bulk of one's fortune to offspring even beneficial to the offspring (not to mention society)? Ex-commissioner Caplin said he had seen many young people partly undermined in their personality and motivation by being recipients of extremely large trusts. They lose the ability to understand the value of many things in life, including money. Some have gotten into cults and all sorts of exotic relationships. He suggested that parents should bear such factors in mind before saying, "I can save money this way, that way, on my estate."

Another of the ex–IRS commissioners consulted said, "I've supported the idea of having a more effective estate and gift tax because I just don't think it's a good idea to preserve family fortunes in America for a hundred years."

To sum up, the current tax code does not prevent extremely wealthy people from transferring the bulk of their wealth to the next generation.

CHAPTER 21

A TYCOON
WHO WOULD
CRACK DOWN ON
THE SUPER-RICH

"I know people who are worth five times as much as I am who brag that they never pay any taxes."

— SOL PRICE, centimillionaire

Mr. Price had a net worth of about $200 million when he made that remark to me.

At the time of our meeting I knew less about Sol Price than I did about almost anyone I visited. I knew he was a San Diego merchandiser who had pioneered a new way to move lots of goods. He was very rich. He was a very private person. That was about all I knew. I did not know he had some very provocative ideas about coping with the explosion of great fortunes, and coping with the strategies used to protect those fortunes. I did not know he was financing a study at the University of Oregon on how it might best be done.

Mr. Price believes that a much greater proportion of large fortunes should be returned to the public through charitable contributions or taxes to enrich our society.

When I called him to firm up our appointment the following day, his voice seemed abrupt. Any interest he may have had in seeing me had diminished. He indicated that his home in La Jolla was out as a meeting place. Finally he said that he would pick me up at my hotel and we might walk the beach somewhere.

And so he arrived at the agreed hour wearing a sports shirt and driving a small BMW. He was a lean man with a rather solemn face. We started out in his car, I assumed for a beach. At first he challenged just about every observation I made, then said it was just a habit of his to be challenging. He had spent seventeen years practicing law. Finally he asked:

"Well, what is it that interests you about people who have been lucky enough to get rich?"

I picked up on the reference to luck. Very few of the others I had visited had mentioned anything about luck.

He explained that he had quit being a lawyer to set up Fed-Mart Corporation, a prospering mass-merchandising firm. It was reasonably successful. He sold shares to a German, who somehow became a majority shareholder. Shortly thereafter Price was fired. Infuriated, he brought legal charges of violation of security laws but was unsuccessful in his case.[1] So thus it was that in the late 1970s he started fresh with a completely novel idea for a supermarket chain. He would set up Price Clubs so appealing that customers would pay for the privilege of shopping there!

His new concept took off in a spectacular way. As he was shooting up toward centimillionaire status he took his company public. Mr. Price is chairman, but said he was taking no salary, a novelty in itself. Meanwhile the old Fed-Mart where he had been fired was fizzling.[2] He explained:

"When I say luck, you know, had these [German] people

played out their hand [and kept me on as president] I would have finished my career in five more years and had a modest amount of money. So [instead] I came up with this crazy idea. No, no, as we go through life, almost every day there's a fork in the road." Sometimes, he added, the choice brings good luck.

He told of a dinner party he and his wife attended where a number of prominent business leaders and their wives, along with some leading political figures, were present. The wife of one executive was carrying on about how people get to the top by Horatio Alger–type virtues of diligence and so on. She contended that everything one achieves one has earned and so one deserves appropriate rewards.

Mr. Price inquired if luck did not sometimes play a role. Absolutely not. Soon the area around him was in an uproar of argument, most of the people strongly siding with the lady. The discussion became so heated that one wife had to be assisted from the room.

Mr. Price firmly believed in capitalism as the most effective way to get things produced but was not totally enchanted with the reward system that went with it at the upper end. Capitalism, he said, was a tremendous incentive. But he suggested that people would drive just as hard even if the monumental jackpots were not as big as they have recently grown.

"I'm a little bit of a radical," he said, finally smiling. He explained that maybe it came from his background. His father had helped organize the International Ladies Garment Workers Union, then had himself become a manufacturer and helped organize the manufacturing association.

We got to talking about his "crazy idea" for a new kind of discount chain. Each super-outlet was set up as a club. He inquired if I would like to see one. Sure. "Let's take a ride," he said.

En route he explained that he had twenty-one of them, mostly in the West, but was starting up a few in the East, and was starting to be copied. One of the major copiers, I learned later, was America's richest billionaire, Sam Walton of Wal-Mart.

So shortly we pulled into his original club. It was in San Diego proper in a warehouse-type building that was actually an abandoned World War II airplane plant. There was a vast parking lot. Hundreds of club members were pushing giant metal carts, almost three times the size of ordinary grocery carts, toward their cars. The carts were loaded down with radios, groceries, books, lamps, toasters, cartons of light bulbs, and so forth. Mr. Price explained that club members that day would probably haul away about $400,000 worth of goods from that store alone. He added that he was going to have to tear down the present building in order to get more parking space and would move the "store" into other buildings farther back in the complex.

Soon we were in the building full of milling club members loading their carts. Mr. Price explained that he does absolutely no advertising. And not just anyone can walk in and become a member. You have to be a member of a group permitted to belong. Groups can consist of credit union members, bank employees, government employees, and so on. A bank, for example, may take out a $25 annual membership in order to offer employees purchasing rights at the club as a morale-boosting privilege. Everything is cash only and costs nearly 50 percent less than ordinary retail.

Other members are small businessmen. It is for example a real pain for a restaurant owner to try to order 500 candles from a supplier because of the bookkeeping and delays involved. So he just sends a boy to Price Club to pick up the candles at about 7.5 percent above cost to Price.

Fifteen minutes later we were back in the car headed toward La Jolla, which is on a vast stretch of hillside overlooking the Pacific and has as residents, as indicated, a number of very rich people. I assumed we were headed for a beach. Mr. Price explained that La Jolla goes to elaborate lengths to pretend it is a separate city but it is actually a part of San Diego. From research I knew his address and inquired what general part of La Jolla it was in.

Now more congenial, he said, "Would you like to see it?" I said it would save me a trip. It turned out to be a low, very wide, narrow structure with its back to the road. It faced out

over a golf course to the Pacific. He said it had three bedrooms. Nearby there were much more imposing houses.

It was his only house. And he owned no yacht.

Could he live on $1 million a year?

"It's hard to spend a million dollars a year unless you
have something like a plane. I'm the only idiot I know that
pays his own expenses [for plane and travel] and doesn't
charge them off or anything like that."

He does a lot of traveling for both business and personal
reasons. His plane is transcontinental and takes nine people
comfortably. Whatever the purpose of the trip, he pays for it
all out of his pocket. He and his wife dine out three or four
nights a week at some local restaurant. Mr. Price usually has
chicken, but sometimes tries fish. At my request he gave me
the name of a favorite restaurant. That night I dined there.
It was small, quiet, and excellent. My bill, including drinks,
came to $43.

Now we were swinging down into the business area of
La Jolla. He pulled into a parking space next to Harry's, a
coffee shop. The waitress who seated us and brought us
beverages was obviously an old acquaintance of Mr. Price's.
Clearly, I gathered, we were not going to walk any beach.

We got to talking about what he was doing, and going to
do, about his hundreds of millions of dollars. First of all he
said, "I have no tax shelters. The only tax deduction I have
is the deduction for charity that I give. I have no other thing
and I don't worry about it. In the first place, I can't spend all
the income I have. I just don't know how to spend seven
million dollars a year." (Or whatever.)

He had created no trusts for his two sons. The older son,
who was his chief executive officer, he said, was already
well fixed and lived modestly. The younger son "is well off
too. I'll leave him something if he is a good boy," he added
with a laugh.

He had set up trusts for his five grandchildren but clearly
the trusts were designed more as holding instruments than
tax-avoidance schemes because only a modest amount of
money was involved in each. He stated a flat figure that
would go to each grandchild, startlingly low considering his

net worth. Later he asked me not to reveal the specific figure but just to say that more than 90 percent of all his assets
was going to charity.

The process of shifting his assets to charity has already
started at the rate of more than a million dollars a year.
Some of the bequests go to causes he believes are good for
the country such as the American Civil Liberties Union and
the Nader consumer protection organization (even though
he occasionally disagrees with positions both take). He explained that he had also already put a "substantial" amount
of his fortune into a charitable trust.

"My wife and I will have income as long as we live. . . .
And when we pass out of the picture the substantial bulk of
our estate will go into charity."

He said he enjoyed the fact that "I can give money away
and can buy what I want and travel where I want." But he
didn't like the fact that "somehow people think more of you
because you're rich than because you're a wonderful man
or a bright man. I'm not entitled to be worth, say, $157 mil-
lion. It's just not fair."

And he was considerably annoyed that so many rich people were mad at the government and tried to pay as small
an amount of taxes as possible. "I would say what the hell is
wrong with paying money to the government. It's a nice government and it takes pretty good care of us." Who in the hell,
he asked, is going to pay for all the things people want like
clean air, safe roads, safe skies, munitions, health care, and
social security? "Everybody should give part of their net
wealth every year just for nothing else than for the police
protection." (Note that he said "net wealth," not "income.")

"I can't understand these people — they must be very
shallow — who spend their lives with this horrible antago-
nism toward the government and say, 'I'm not going to give
it to the government.'

"To me it is much more exciting to make money and to
do something useful with the money than it is to be constantly needing the damned lawyers and tax men trying to
figure out how to gyp the government out of some bucks."

Mr. Price had some specific ideas for revising the tax

laws to get a larger contribution from wealthy people. These were of particular interest to me because in my examination of the rich I had already been inspired to assemble a substantial body of research on the topic.

He thought that President Reagan's tax-simplification program, then in the process of being enacted, was a joke. Under the new tax law he, a centimillionaire, would end up paying a half-million dollars less per year. What was fair about that!

Regarding his ideas he said:

"Number one. I think there really ought to be a limit on inherited wealth."

And number two, he thought that the tax system should be shifted so that the emphasis would be on taxing a person's overall wealth rather than just his annual income. "If you are talking about collecting money from people [based] on their ability to pay, wealth is a hell of a lot better [way to approach it] than income.

"I would eliminate the corporate income tax. I would eliminate the estate tax. I'd put in a value-added tax. [A tax on the value added to a product, for example, at each step of its production. It has substantial support in Europe.] *And I would put in a 4 percent annual wealth tax.* [Italics added.]

"Let's say I'm worth a hundred million dollars and the government says to me, 'Look, Price, make as much as you want. You owe us four million dollars at the end of the year. That's going to move my money into productive things instead of defensive things like . . . sheltered income. I'm now going to start saying, 'How can I make 16 percent a year' . . . instead of 7 percent tax free."

The taxing on wealth might start at, say, a half-million dollars to eliminate the detailing of such odds and ends as automobiles and home furnishings.

We talked about the constitutional problems of a wealth tax (which I'll take up later). He said that the study he was sponsoring at the University of Oregon under Professor Richard Lindholm was looking into that. Lindholm was concluding that the problems were surmountable.

One of the extra bonuses of a wealth tax he said was that it not only would catch the people who have their money sunk in tax exempts or land but "you would get at a lot of these people whose income never surfaces, what they call the underground economy which is estimated at about 20 percent of the whole annual net production. Big money."

Mr. Price also suggested as a possibility a taxing system that might combine the regular income tax with a wealth tax. It would assure that the annual tax bill of the humblest centimillionaire would at least be in the millions, and a billionaire's in the tens of millions. He explained: "Okay, we use the present income tax law, but the tax has to come to at least 2 percent of your net wealth. If 2 percent of your net wealth is greater than the way you compute your income tax, then that would get all these sons of bitches that have all their money tied up in tax exempts and never file a return!"

With that he paid our $1.20 check and, much more cheerful, drove me back to my hotel.

CONCLUSIONS

How Should Today's Society Treat Vast Accumulations of Private Wealth?

CHAPTER 22

THE LOWERING RATIONALITY AND INCREASING CONSEQUENCES OF GREAT PRIVATE FORTUNES

"Your standard of living doesn't change after the first million."

— LAURENCE TISCH, in 1983, when his net worth was put at $400 million[1]

M ost of the thirty ultra-rich people we have visited, I think readers will agree, did not conform to common perceptions of how such people live, think, and function. There were some vivid, extraordinary, and admirable personalities. But they did not present an overall picture of an elite leadership group sufficiently important to our society that they — and people like them — should be nurtured in their further accumulation of wealth and encouraged by society to preserve their vast fortunes through succeeding generations. That, at least, was my feeling.

Some that I visited seemed to agree. Sol Price made the offhand comment that "I don't like people who try to convince themselves that there is something different about them because somebody left them some money."

Most of the very rich whom I saw were not using their enormous fortunes even to try to maintain a life-style proportionate to their wealth. Only eight of the thirty might be called big spenders. Few maintained grand manors with large staffs. Only one in ten had a room high-ceilinged enough to be appropriate for a decent ball. One in six had a gatehouse. At least a third had no live-in help. Only a few were people who would warrant such adjectives as glamorous, elegant, aristocratic, austere, or commanding in their presence. And only a small minority were socialites.

Almost all the self-made centimillionaires I encountered were high-energy people with a high level of thrust. In contrast, most of the people who had started their careers with substantial inheritances, while often hard workers, were not high-thrust people. Many of the people I met succeeded to some extent because they happened to find themselves in the right place at the right time to flourish fantastically. Of the eighteen self-made entrepreneurs, fourteen were helped to success by the fact that they were in or near the forefront of some new trend in American life.

And most of these trends were peripheral to what has

traditionally been considered the heart of American enterprise: the invention and manufacture of needed or desired products. Of the eighteen self-made entrepreneurs, only five were involved in new product creation. The rest had been highly successful in merchandising or financial services or running real estate operations or drilling oil.

A number of leading economists are now contending that we have been oversold on the concept that America has been moving happily into a "post-industrial economy" in which we will thrive on services, "information," and so on. They contend that our future still depends very heavily on having a competitive, creative manufacturing industry.[2]

By my grading, somewhat more than half of the thirty people I visited would score low on sense of social responsibility. Their contributions of money and effort were nominal or negligible when you considered their assets. I would give high grades to about a third of them as being either serious philanthropists or seriously committed to public service. Only seven seemed to be community leaders.

And while we assume that all people of great wealth are eager to create a family dynasty of some sort, my findings provide only partial support for this concept. Of the twenty-six who had children and were engaged in business, twelve — or almost half — showed no real inclination to think in dynastic terms. A half-dozen families that were dynastically oriented had grounds for disappointment with the way things were working out. Several, as indicated, were proud that their children were succeeding in completely different fields such as science, medicine, or the arts.

The sons of Allen Paulson of Savannah present a typical picture of the mixed responses of offspring. As noted, one son was in management of his father's company, another son was a sheriff in California, and a third son had his own small business.

Family fragmentation created by divorce may have played a role in inhibiting dynastic aspirations in some families. Of the twenty-seven people visited who had ever married, sixteen had experienced divorce at least once.

One common theory is that people accumulate fortunes far beyond conceivable family needs because of a desire for power over others: economic power or political power or both. The great extent to which the very rich were acting as malefactors of wealth and robber barons got plenty of justified publicity in the early part of this century. And within the last few decades we have read descriptions of rich people forming power networks or using their fortunes to exercise power abusively in such books as *The Power Elite* by C. Wright Mills, *The Rich and the Superrich* by Ferdinand Lundberg, and *The Powers That Be: Processes of Ruling-Class Domination in America* by G. William Domhoff.

Certainly we still have rich elites and money barons who play hardball, as for example some of the strip-mining barons of Appalachia who have splintered their mining into small "front" organizations to get away with despoiling the landscape and not having to restore the areas damaged. A glance down the pages of the *Forbes* 400 reveals the names of quite a few other centimillionaires who have played rough with their money.

In my visiting I encountered many who seemed to relish the personal power that their money gave them. About half were powerful figures in their areas. But at least five of these seem to be using their power benignly. Several families involved in my visiting had come under criticism for using their financial power to get their way. Witt Stephens of Little Rock had a clear history of using his wealth to get his way in terms of favorable legislation for his power companies. Jack Simplot, the potato baron of Boise, obviously had used his financial clout to try to control the potato market. Jeno Paulucci was charged with using political contributions to bring about changes helpful to his real estate empire in central Florida. The Bass brothers of Fort Worth had at times used their great wealth to greenmail companies into buying them out at immense profit to the Basses in possible takeover situations. Edward Bass, whom I visited, had attended strategy meetings on how to invest the brothers' wealth. June Hunt of Dallas was not herself involved in the

Hunt family's use of its great financial power, but her half brothers had sought to make an immense killing by cornering the world's silver market.

So, to generalize, the possession of great wealth provides the potential for power-wielding but does not automatically make a wealth-possessor a power-wielder. A few tried to ignore their wealth. A few others seemed to be not the least bit interested in being powerful movers and shakers in their area. However a larger number — especially among the self-made males — clearly were enjoying being powerful figures in their areas.

I got the impression that many of these ultra-rich people I encountered viewed their money not so much as a source of power but as a means for providing them with continuing proof of potency. And quite a few seemed caught up in the joy of unending accumulation just as a few slashing bluefish in a sea of smaller fish will keep on killing and eating until their bellies can bloat no further. Rational need has almost nothing to do with it. Nor does standard economic theory, which holds that people accumulate money solely to assure themselves and their children a desired level of consumption.[3]

The Lowered Relevance
of Great Personal Wealth

The vast markets available in the world today for goods and services that happen to be in demand — from pizzas to teddy bears — offer occasional opportunities for individuals to drive their net worth into the stratosphere. Quickly made fortunes of $50 million, $300 million, or a billion dollars are becoming common. Rather suddenly thousands of people have that kind of hard-to-comprehend money.

If the average wealthy person I visited (average net worth around $330 million at the time) decided to get his or her net worth down to some sensible figure such as $10 million within the next ten years, it would take some doing. It would mean spending about $32 million a year, or about $600,000 a week. (Actually, the spending would have to be somewhat higher because earned income from interest would more than equal income taxes.)

One noteworthy fortune-holder who seemed resolved to spend herself into poverty through consumption was Barbara Hutton, once regarded as the world's richest woman. She came into a five-and-ten-cent-store fortune of $50 million in 1933 when she was twenty-one. That would be worth about ten times more today. C. David Heymann detailed her strenuous efforts in *Poor Little Rich Girl.*

She went through a flock of husbands and typically gave millions in dowries at the outset and/or alimonies at the end. In one phase she was spending more than a million dollars a year on jewelry. One of the husbands charged to her sixty suits and fifty pairs of silk pajamas. She had one of the world's biggest yachts and several vast houses, each usually staffed with about thirty people. When she met a stranger who seemed interesting, she gave him or her a Rolls-Royce or a sable coat. At hotels she liked she gave every employee a nice present, such as a sable stole or a diamond ring or a prize watch. If she went to a resort, she took over the place. She gave a $400,000 diamond to the brother of a friend. By the age of sixty she was haggard. By death a few years later she had succeeded in getting her savings and checking account balances down to $3,500. Success! But the managers of her estate found odds and ends of rare snuff boxes, jewels, rugs, and desks that were worth more than $1 million.

Today, even more than a half century ago, great fortunes are losing their function except for really power-hungry or dynasty-craving people. People of great wealth mostly don't want the bother of coping with grand manors or an elaborately elegant life-style. Centimillionaire heiress Alice Francis du Pont Mills living on super-elite Jupiter Island answers her own telephone.

Large household staffs in America have largely been made superfluous by pool services, cleaning services, grounds maintenance services, catering services. In the rich enclave of Scottsdale, Arizona, there are about forty catering services and eighty more nearby.

Opulent display through six-course banquets that open with caviar mousse with lobster sauce and end with soufflés in cream have lost much of their popularity because the rich too have become diet conscious. Their doctors scold them about cholesterol and calories. Of the thirty wealthy people I visited, eleven mentioned eating patterns that were Spartan or plebian.

The world is running out of exotic places that only the rich can reach by expensive expeditions. For less than $8,000 a person can get on a tour that will include an African safari or a journey up the Nile or a visit to the extremely remote Seychelles islands or a walk on the Great Wall of China. At home a plumber and the nearest centimillionaire may be spending several nights a week watching the same great movies on the same brand VCR sets.

With the growing anonymity of urban living there is, as indicated, less chance for conspicuous display. Most large-city newspapers devote less coverage to Society. You may have a $4 million condo on the Chicago North Shore, but the only people who know about it are delivery boys, friends, and people whom you invite. Even the very rich may lose track of who lives where. I was surprised, as indicated, to find that centimillionaire Robert Guccione did not know that centimillionaire Sam LeFrak lived just up the street from him in Manhattan.

Much of the recent desire by many of the very rich to "live quietly" springs from dread of robbers, blackmailers, kidnappers, IRS investigators, or charity fund-raisers. Even those with stretch limousines typically ride behind darkened glass windows. This is quite different from riding in grand carriages drawn by four horses or in the glorious Cadillacs of the 1950s.

The most compelling evidence I uncovered of the lack of any significant relationship between wealth and consumption patterns came when I asked the thirty people I visited about their annual living costs. These were people, remember, who had an average net worth of about $330 million. A substantial majority, after reflecting, said that they lived on less than a million dollars a year. Twenty-one of them, to be precise. Several lived on less than $200,000 a year.

The last of the thirty very wealthy persons I visited was Sigfried Weis of Lewisburg, Pennsylvania. (I have mentioned his civic activities.) His net worth when I saw him was around $350 million. By 1987 it had soared to $600 million (and despite the crash showed a good gain for the year). He and his cousin run a highly successful grocery chain they inherited from their parents. They thrive by keeping their profit margin about 4½ times the industry average, which they are able to do partly because they stay out of debt and own the land under their stores.

Sigfried Weis, a lean, grave, formal man, lives with his wife in a French chalet–type house on a hillside, down from the road, outside Lewisburg. The house is large for the area but certainly not spectacular. Behind the house is a golf green and spreading out from it at various directions and distances are five golf tees. He in effect can play five holes from one green. His wife does needlepoint and volunteer work. He is very active in local philanthropy. They have no other house, and no boat or private plane. Their main splurging is that they take a month off every year to visit some area of the world they haven't seen (and they shun resorts). They have no live-in help and she does some of the cooking. That night they were going to have pork chops.

They said they definitely lived on less than a million dollars a year. In a small town, they said, that was a lot of money. And they got to talking about the values of money (beyond the possibility of using some of it to help others). He commented:

"As my wife has said many times, one of the advantages of having money is that you don't have to think about it, you don't have to talk about it." In short, you don't have the bother of worrying about paying bills. You don't have to put up with someone giving you a hard time because of your shortage of money. You don't have to worry about losing a job you may not even like because of the financial bind the loss might create. You don't have to worry about being a burden when you get old.

But you don't need hundreds of millions of dollars — or even one million — to have that kind of peace of mind.

As I was about to leave, he went to the closet to get my hat. It was a tan cloth hat with a maroon and blue band. I had bought it only a few days before. The hat he handed me met that description but seemed to have had quite a bit of wear. I asked if he was sure he had given me the right hat. He looked again and brought out another hat, this time mine. It seems that I and the man with $350 million had identical $16 hats.

The Serious Consequences
of Great Private Fortunes

In assessing possible consequences for our society of this explosion in the number of extraordinarily wealthy individuals several general propositions seem relevant. My thoughts on this derive from both my interviewing and broader research.

Any kind of wealth that is used to generate legal economic activity has some value to the general economy. So we should not denigrate the great wealth of one particular individual solely because it is grossly excessive for meeting the consumptive yearnings of that individual's family in the world of today and tomorrow. Any society that is to thrive needs a surplus of wealth after its citizens meet necessary living costs for investment in economic growth.

When, however, you have thousands of people accumulating fortunes grossly excessive for meeting consumption costs, questions of social utility do arise.

Some forms of accumulated wealth are more beneficial to society than others. Wealth that is put to work creatively is more valuable to an economy than static wealth or wealth spent in perpetuating existing patterns of activity. Some individual wealth is long-term functional, some is short-term functional and some is virtually nonfunctional. The creation of new or expanding industries or the opening of new frontiers is long-term functional and greatly stimulates the environment for the long run. Money spent to create a better and less costly mobile telephone or to build a new factory is far more valuable to an economy than money spent in short-term functional ways, such as using it to purchase antiques or to stage $400,000 wedding parties or to buy $600,000 necklaces of diamonds cut abroad or to invest in apartment houses built in 1950. And wealth put into land or gold bars is virtually nonfunctional. There are exceptions, but inherited wealth is commonly managed much more conservatively than new wealth. The professional managers tend to put major emphasis on preservation of capital. Wealth so managed tends to be of relatively low utility in stimulating the economy.

At any rate, only about a third of the people I visited were using their wealth in what I would consider long-term functional ways — contributing to economic growth by genuine innovation.

After one has accumulated personal wealth that far exceeds that needed to meet personal desires in living standards, the goal of accumulation typically undergoes change. The *process* of accumulation itself may create more happiness than the hard-to-comprehend fortunes that are achieved. Ross Perot, net worth $2.5 billion in 1987, recalls, "I am no more happy and no less happy than when my wife and I first drove into Dallas with everything we owned in the back of our car."[4] Ivan Boesky, the financial manipulator who pushed his worth up from $150 million to $200 million in one year before he was charged with illegalities, explained his zeal for accumulation in these words: "It's a sickness I have in the face of which I am helpless."[5]

The prospect of achieving wealth — either for use or for the mere process — is a powerful and much-needed motivator to induce individuals to undertake bold endeavors of the kind that advance an economy. A part of the economic woes of the state-controlled system in Russia, theoretically based on communism, is due to the fact that economic leaders there have had until recently little incentive to be bold (except in awarding themselves perks).

Still, it was not the possibility of gaining hundreds of millions or billions of dollars in assets that motivated some of our recent notable innovators such as Steven Jobs, David Packard, Ross Perot, Leonard Shoen, Ewing Kauffman, or Jack Simplot to set forth on their journeys of enterprise. Their financial goals typically were at most in the tens of millions of dollars range. They would have striven at least as hard if after a sizable fortune was achieved the rules of the game made it harder instead of easier to add additional tens of millions of dollars to their private wealth.

Great accumulations of money offer more gratification and inspiration to the initial accumulators than to the heirs to whom the money is passed. That is particularly true if the heirs are not actively involved in seeking to build upon the family business.

A half-dozen of the very wealthy people I chatted with expressed concern about the way their offspring were growing up. Some felt sorry their kids were missing the challenge they had experienced. Two of the younger people with inherited wealth that we visited had had a substantial amount of psychiatric therapy.

Lewis H. Lapham, author of *Money and Class in America,* and himself a descendant of wealth, made a preliminary study of about fifty families of wealth at the turn of the century and followed the descendants for sixty years. He reports: "I noticed that with notable but relatively few exceptions ... the lives of the heirs were marked by alcoholism, suicide, drug-addiction, insanity and despair." He also observed, "New money is more fun to be around. . . . Old money is niggardly and defensive."

Billionaire Warren Buffett of Omaha does not believe it is wise to bequeath great wealth to children, including his own three grown offspring.[6] In fact he thinks it can be "harmful" to them and is an "antisocial act." In 1986 he said his feeling was that giving each of his offspring a few hundred thousand dollars seemed about right. That would be enough to make them feel they could do anything. The bulk of his wealth, he said, was going to a charitable foundation.

Individuals with enormous wealth have an inherent capacity to create more havoc in the marketplace for corporate control than do corporate boards. The individual alone, or the individual acting as head of a small band of very wealthy partners, can act more quickly and secretively with little or no concern about the impact of an action on a company's personnel or on the company itself. Hence it is no coincidence that the great rise in corporate raiding and greenmailing of targeted companies has occurred in the few years since there has been a great increase in numbers of extremely rich individuals with tens or hundreds of millions of dollars (and access to billions, often in junk bonds) that can be used for quick plunging.

In 1986 alone there were 4,000 corporate takeovers, mergers, or leveraged buyouts.[7] Very wealthy individuals have commonly been the principal actors. In one year recently New York's young super-realtor Donald Trump, more or less as a hobby, began using some of his hundreds of millions in cash or credit to take strong positions in the stock of three companies. This almost predictably caused the prices of the stocks to jump. *Newsweek* reported in late 1987 that within a year he had made $122 million in profit on these maneuvers.

The argument that such wealthy prowlers are theoretically producing leaner, more efficient corporations may have some small basis of truth, but any such resulting value would seem to be overwhelmed in both social and economic terms by the devastation and turmoil being caused in our economy.

The negative impact of all the raiding shows up in the low morale of company personnel created by the persistent appearance and reappearance of possible raiders (often seen as jackals, since assets of raided companies are often stripped and widespread layoffs are frequently made). It shows up in the substantial increase, typically, in a targeted company's debt regardless of whether the targeted company succeeds in beating off the raider or succumbs to the raider. It shows up in the increasing inability of companies to make long-term plans such as doing the research and development to launch new products. The main preoccupation of the company's executives must be with the company's next quarterly statement and with defensive strategies for coping with the raiders. Entire industries are in some instances apparently being wounded. Overall the ratio of corporate debt to equity has recently been soaring.[8] In economic terms the rich raiders frequently are not creating anything but profits for themselves and a whirlwind of paper shuffling by troops of lawyers, accountants and experts in making or faking raids.

In a very real sense these wealthy raiders and greenmailers are becoming the new robber barons of our society. If they are willing to throw their weight around in the financial markets, we must assume that they soon will be throwing their weight around politically to maintain sets of rules that favor their operations.

The presence of large numbers of individuals with vast wealth certainly is contributing to the already existent gulf between the percent of our country's wealth held by the top 1 percent of the population and the wealth held by "Everybody Else" in the bottom 99 percent of the population. The drop in living standards occurring in the general population during much of the 1980s, which at least has coincided with increased concentration of wealth at the top, tends to increase the inefficiency of the national economy.

If we are prudent we should bear in mind the view of some economists that extremes in concentration of private wealth can lead to economic malfunction. Southern Methodist economist Ravi Batra, as indicated, is one of several economic forecasters who argue from history that the greater the concentration the greater the hazard of poor economic functioning. Batra, in comparing the high concentration in the 1980s with that at the onset of the Crash of

1929, warned: "Extreme inequality has generated some of the worst economic disasters in history."[9] If the assets available to the common man decline because of the concentration at the top, debts rise. Batra's reading is not shared by all economists. But the economic tremors in October 1987 suggested that the 1929 parallel was worth noting.

At the least the presence of vast accumulations of private wealth when economic well-being for "Everybody Else" is not rising seems bound to aggravate class tensions and add to other disquieting economic developments.

In America today a lot of working-class people are feeling a pinch for reasons not associated with concentration of wealth at the top. More Americans are finding themselves working in service industries where incomes tend to be significantly less than in industries involved in production. Many people in manufacturing are feeling a squeeze from third world competition, which is facilitated by third world wage scales. And many farmers are feeling pinched by a worldwide surge in agricultural production.

Still, many respected economists feel that when you get a significant share of the nation's private capital concentrated at the top, hazards do arise for the whole economy.

The reasoning goes that people with few assets, with considerable encouragement from credit card companies and lenders, increase their borrowing. Bankers competing for their business find themselves with a lot of shaky loans. An obvious result, an increase in bank failures, can cause a general flight to safety by investors. Business and employment thereupon decline.

Add to this the monumental hazard posed by the unprecedented U.S. national debt — much of it owed to foreigners — and we have a very reasonable cause for concern for rich and nonrich alike.

MIT dean and economist Lester Thurow has offered a picturesque parallel relating a balanced distribution of wealth to the delicate balance between wolves and caribou. If the wolves ate all the caribou, the wolves would also vanish. He feels that a concentration of wealth in the hands of a few should trouble anyone who is already concerned about the possible effects of the accumulation of economic power in the hands of a relatively few people.

There can be an element of indecency in having so much of the national wealth tied up in a few hands when the nation has so many urgent economic problems, along with a huge national debt.

The net assets of the 400 richest people listed in *Forbes* not only greatly exceeded the federal deficit in 1987 but exceeded all dollars spent by the federal government to ease the problems of the nation's tens of millions of underprivileged people (if you exempt Social Security).

And the problems keep mounting: hundreds of thousands of homeless people, scandalous functional illiteracy, threatened devastating epidemics, the prospect of an energy crisis returning within a few years, widespread drug addiction, mounting hazards from chemical wastes, et cetera, et cetera.

Finally, we must wonder what is happening to the value system of ambitious young businessmen today. Have they accepted the concept that success requires them to acquire tens of millions of dollars beyond conceivable family need?

To sum up, individual accumulation and investment of capital is essential for our capitalistic (or free enterprise) system to function.

The accumulation is most efficient, economically and socially, if it is widely dispersed in the population and hence creates both wide potential markets and a general sense of well-being. It is most inefficient as the very wealthy increase their share of the total pie of national individual wealth.

Both the growing irrelevance of large fortunes and the negative consequences for society in permitting them to proliferate raise important questions about their continued existence.

There is a clear need for a national policy which puts the concentration and perpetuation of vast accumulations of private wealth under closer social control.

CHAPTER 23

ON CURBING
A MONEYED
ARISTOCRACY

"We tax income but don't really tax
wealth in America to the degree that we
should."

— Former Congressman
CHARLES A. VANIK of Ohio

The fact that free enterprise
still remains the most successful method of stimulating economic growth does not mean it requires a reward system
that creates and sustains increasingly grotesque accumulations of family wealth. The accumulations are starting to
have a negative influence on the efficient operation of our
economy. They have the potential of being hazardous politically. And in a democratic society they are becoming inex-
cusable socially.

In 1987, several dozen Americans increased their assets

by more than $50 million in a single year. Dr. Carl S. Shoup, author of *Public Finance* and former consultant to the U.S. Treasury for tax policy, warned Congress some years ago that "There are dangers in allowing the accumulation of vast sums in the hands of family dynasties. . . ."[1] This was before the recent great surge in accumulations of wealth. He said that social and philosophical implications were high among his concerns.

The current situation, I believe, requires that our society reexamine its priorities and search for tools to regulate the fortune-building which is occurring at extremely high levels.

Our tax system is in the forefront of potential sources of useful tools. During most of this century, until the 1980s, this taxing system has had a strong built-in assumption that great accumulations of individual wealth should not only provide a good source of government revenue but ought in any case to be curbed in a democratic society by applying progressively higher rates at higher levels of wealth. President Reagan's distaste for our progressive income tax was indicated in 1982 when his primary counselor on policy, Edwin Meese III, said, "The progressive income tax is immoral."[2] As of the late 1980s, thanks to an overhaul of the tax system, the rates on the income of the billionaire and the policeman became much closer to being equal than they had been. And the billionaire usually has a staff of experts that works to limit the exposure of his overall fortune to taxation.

But there is a larger, inherent problem in our system. Overwhelmingly, taxes collected from individual Americans are based on their annual income. (The income can come from paychecks, fees, dividends, or profits from sale of assets.) The policeman's income via paycheck may account for 95 percent of his wealth. In contrast, the billionaire's annual income may be less than 1 percent of his wealth. If he has expert estate planners, his income may be just enough to pay his bills. He may take no salary or only a nominal one. He may place his wealth in land (perhaps oil-rich land) or stocks with negligible yields, perhaps stock in his own company. Land and nondividend stocks simply grow and grow. There need be no federal tax reckoning whatsoever until he sells these assets or until he dies. And by death his lawyers have usually dispersed much or most of his taxable assets through trusts and other strategies. (His advisers may shun bonds because bonds pay income in the form of dividends.)

Presently the U.S. government collects about sixty times as much from income taxes on the general populace as it does from the estate and gift taxes it imposes when huge assets are transferred by rich people to their heirs.

So a logical question arises: Since we are witnessing a great leap in accumulation of large fortunes at a time when real assets of the average person are declining, why do we not put a direct tax on wealth? It could be a supplement to the income tax.

This is not a revolutionary proposal. About sixteen countries include among their taxes of citizens a direct tax on wealth (or net worth). Most are advanced European democracies. West Germany and France have been trying such a tax and so have a few countries in the Asian subcontinent.

In almost all the countries, however, these wealth taxes are seen mainly as fair revenue measures and as measures to stimulate affluent people to invest idle money. Most are not structured to curb great fortunes — perhaps because most advanced democracies don't have a conspicuous pattern of increases in vast private wealth comparable to the American explosion. The taxes often amount to less than 1 percent of net worth. In some Scandinavian countries, which offer extensive free public services, the tax is 2 percent of net worth or more.

For simplification, household and personal effects are usually excluded in valuing one's wealth. Typically the taxes affect only people with above-average net worth. The French, in experimenting with the tax, confined it to quite rich people. They set their tax up in 1982 to apply only to people with a *"grande fortune"* of at least three million francs.[3]

In the United States a number of economic and legal journals have discussed the wisdom and problems of instituting a wealth tax in this country.[4] It has been suggested that even a 3 percent wealth tax on the people financially in the top 1 percent of the U.S. population would raise tens of billions of dollars.

The major arguments for a wealth tax in the United States have placed the main emphasis either on the fact that such a tax would inspire the very rich to put more of their money to work productively in bold ventures, or on the fact that it would counter the current trend toward concentration of great wealth in a few hands. An acceleration of this concentration was occurring while income sources of the general populace were dropping. In the first seven years of the 1980s, real wages of U.S. workers dropped 3.5 percent. A labor economist in California said: "It amounts to a reversal of the American dream."[5] Lester C. Thurow long ago suggested that a net-worth tax should play a part in our national taxing system. And he advises me he still feels "it should play an important role in a democracy." He feels that the main idea of a wealth tax is not to collect government revenue but to force a deconcentration of wealth to offset the concentration of wealth automatically brought about by the market.

Some years ago former U.S. Attorney General Ramsey Clark proposed an annual 3 percent wealth tax on all millionaires. He was running for the Senate and contended that economic justice required some leveling at the top of our economic structure.

Economist Richard W. Lindholm of the University of Oregon, who, as indicated, has had the enthusiastic support of centimillionaire Sol Price, would put a modest 2 percent tax on net wealth above $500,000. He contended that even a 2 percent wealth tax would "chip away at concentration of wealth while also stimulating holders of wealth to use their wealth more productively."[6]

What about a wealth tax that would have the effect of putting a cap on great private wealth that can be accumulated? The thought has occurred to me frequently in the course of my research. A former investment banker, Michael M. Thomas, has advanced the idea of a cap of $50 million per person, which is a lot of money. He proposed: "Every five years an alphabetical segment of the rich, beginning with A through E in Year One, would be required to slim down to not more than $50 million per person. Disposition of the excess wealth would be entirely in the hands of the disposer." He added brightly that "Unless something like this is put in place, folks may get restive about the way wealth is accumulated in this country and start eating millionaires."[7]

Conservatives, especially wealthy ones, may recoil at the idea of a cap, but the general idea of using governmental caps to control money flow is not exactly a radical one. President Reagan in 1986, horrified at the growth of huge subsidy payments going out to some farm operators, proposed a $50,000 cap on annual payments to individual farmers.

The main reason that a tax of some sort on net wealth has gotten relatively little attention in America is constitutional.

A straight annual wealth tax would at present probably be ruled unconstitutional because of a vague phrase which the Founding Fathers, in one of their less glorious moments, wrote into the Constitution. Article 1, section 2, clause 3 says that "Representatives and direct taxes shall be apportioned among the several States ... according to their respective numbers." This has been interpreted to mean in effect that there can be a direct tax only if, for example, the people of Mississippi (with low average incomes) are taxed at a vastly higher rate than the relatively rich people of Connecticut, so as to get the same required tax per capita from both states.[8] That is, of course, a preposterous requirement.

Sentiment for some curb on direct taxation partially arose from a general yearning to curb any federal taxes on the people of a state and a yearning somehow to relate taxes to representation. After all, the Revolution had been fought largely on the issues of outside taxation and lack of representation.

But more specifically, the phrasing of the weird require-
ments for any "direct tax" somehow got inserted into the
Constitution as a sop to persuade slave states to accept representation in the House of Representatives based on the
three-fifths rule. Under the three-fifths formula, a slave
would count as three-fifths of a person in the enumeration
of a state's population.[9]

Whatever contributed most to the institution of this curb
on "direct tax," there was considerable confusion even
among the Founding Fathers about what they were enacting. At the Constitutional Convention, Rufus King of Massachusetts demanded to know what was meant by a "direct
tax." In his notes of the convention James Madison wrote:
"No one answered."[10] And in fact the Constitution never did
supply an answer.

The elimination of slave states after the Civil War eliminated any possible specific interest of southern states in the
clause. But it still stands.

In 1913 the Sixteenth Amendment, containing just one
brief sentence, was passed in order to give clear legal back-
ing to an income tax. The amendment specified that the tax
could be instituted "without apportionment among the several States."

Lawyers and courts still wrestle with the meaning of a
"direct tax." It is reasoned that a tax on our real estate property is not a direct tax on us. It is a tax on the property. The
$200,000 value of our house is what is being taxed even
though we may have a $190,000 mortgage on it. There is
also agreement that taxes on estates at death and on huge
gifts are not "direct taxes." Rather they are seen as excise
taxes on the transfer of property.

Some tax authorities such as Richard W. Lindholm in his
recent book *A New Federal Tax System* argue that we could
still legally enact nonapportioned direct taxes if they are
"sufficiently restrictive." Lindholm suggested that we could
get by with a tax on net worth if it is restricted enough in its
application not to be viewed as a general tax. Possibly con-
fining it to people with net worths of more than $10 million
might do it. But certainly lawyers of the rich would cry

"unconstitutional!" Unfortunately, the concept of "direct tax" is still fraught with uncertainty.[11]

A one-sentence amendment to the Constitution paralleling the wording of the Sixteenth Amendment would settle two hundred years of confusion. The new amendment would empower Congress, if it wishes, to collect taxes on a person's total net wealth, without apportionment "among the several States."

Amendments take time. Four years elapsed between the time Congress proposed the Sixteenth Amendment and the day the necessary number of states ratified it.

I believe that as a long-term goal we might reasonably work toward phasing in a tax structure that includes a progressive annual tax on that part of the net worth of an individual which exceeds a certain very high base. I suggest that that base for starting the annual taxing of net worth be 100 times the annual salary of the president of the United States. In 1987 his salary was $250,000, so taxing of total net worth would start at $25 million. I suggest that a multiple of the president's salary be used as a base because his salary presumably would be adjusted in future years to reflect changes in the cost of living. It also seems useful as a reminder of the absurdities of our present reward system. (Readers will recall that Dr. Laszlo Tauber found the president's salary a convenient guideline for setting the maximum his children could receive from inheritance in any one year.)

The taxing of net worth above, say, $25 million might start at 8 percent and increase progressively to 25 percent a year for those having two or more billions of net worth above the $25 million ceiling. Within about a dozen years after enactment this taxing should eliminate billionaires and most centimillionaires from the landscape of our democracy. And it would make semi-centimillionaires considerably less common.

This arrangement should accomplish several important results beyond shrinking the biggest accumulations of private wealth: It should encourage the rich to invest more venturously ... it should produce tens of billions of much-needed revenue for the federal government ... and it would reenforce the underpinnings of our democracy.

Those self-made centimillionaires we encountered who kept adding tens of millions a year to their net worth, for reasons relating to a passion for accumulation or a need to keep score or to keep busy, could readily find other ways to keep score. For example they could keep score in their enterprise's revenues before taxes ... or corporate net worth ... or profits shared with employees ... or profits plowed back into the enterprise ... or in the tens of millions given to promote social well-being. And there is another possible means we could use to give them pride. We might start publishing a new kind of elite 400 list — an annual list of the 400 individuals who have expended the most to support the activities of their national government.

All this however is for the future. In the meantime there is no reason why our society cannot act immediately to curb the worst manifestation of wealth accumulation. That worst manifestation is the passing of the vast accumulations of private wealth on to heirs generation after generation.

Tax laws on the transfer of wealth in estates at death or by gifts while alive are available for use right now.[12] They simply have to be enacted in a tough form, with safeguards to minimize evasion.

The Congress, I believe, should set as an immediate goal the establishment of a ceiling on the transfer of personal wealth by will, trust, or outright gift. (An alternative, if too many opponents cry that any kind of flat ceiling constitutes "confiscation," would be to impose a 95 percent tax on any transfers beyond a certain high level.)

Some tax reformers would set the ceiling on the amount transferred at the receiving end through an accessions or inheritance tax on individual heirs receiving the assets. No heir, for example, could receive in total in his or her lifetime more than, say, $10 million in 1988 dollars. Proponents of placing such a tax on the receiving end say it would have the advantage of promoting equal treatment of heirs and might be easier to administer. Such an approach certainly might be explored.

I feel however that the more prudent course would be to set the ceiling on the donor. The advantage of taxing the donor rather than the beneficiaries (typically heirs) would be, of course, that it fixes a more firm ceiling on the amount of wealth transferred. If the limit was only on what each beneficiary could receive, there could be gifts of, say, $10 million each to each of fifty relatives and friends, and hence at least a half-billion could be passed.

No wealthholder should be allowed to transfer to other individuals more than $25 million in 1988 dollars, after taxes.

This ceiling would apply to all transfers by will, trust, or outright gift. Transfers to spouse would, of course, as under present law, be excluded; but transfers by any spouse would be included in the same $25 million ceiling.

Until that ceiling is reached, the current taxes on transfers would prevail. When total giving (or transfers) gets above $2.5 million, the tax to be paid equals about 50 percent of the amounts transferred.[13] After the ceiling of $25 million in 1988 dollars is reached, further transfers to heirs should be banned, except for people who already have provable assets of more than $100 million. In fairness, they probably should be allowed some additional transfers during the first seven years of phasing in the new ceiling.

Those who establish that their worth is between $100 million and $500 million could be permitted to transfer, after taxes, an additional $1 million for every $10 million they have in assets above $100 million. Those worth between $500 million and a billion dollars could transfer an additional $1 million for every $20 million they have above $500 million. Thus the billionaire could transfer an additional $25 million for a grand total of $90 million. This would be the absolute ceiling for transfers. There would be no extra allowance for multibillionaires. And these extra allowances would end in seven years.

A ceiling on the amount a wealthholder can pass on to his offspring or others would not require a dismantling of the family enterprise in the vast majority of situations where great family fortunes are involved. There are plenty of ways for the family, if it wishes, to maintain a controlling interest in the enterprise.

The simplest way is to issue two kinds of stock, A and B. Only class B stock has any voting rights — or it has much more voting power. That is kept in the family, or among family and friends. One of the people we visited, Chris Bancroft, the Dow-Jones heir living in a small southwestern city, has been involved in such a situation. He and about thirty other Bancroft heirs have owned 56 percent of Dow-Jones, which publishes the *Wall Street Journal* and *Barrons* magazine. There was concern that with so many heirs at large a takeover prowler might easily lure away some of this stock and attempt a coup. So a class B stock was created in 1984 for family members or family trusts only. The owner of a class B share has ten times the voting power of the owner of an ordinary class A share of common stock. Family control was assured.[14]

And what follows demonstrates that the issue of who controls a company is not a major concern of most investors (unless a takeover has occurred or there are severe management problems). The Dow-Jones company's common stock dropped briefly after the announcement of the plan but showed a 65 percent increase in the three years following the announcement.

Dozens of companies — particularly media companies where family control has been a strong tradition — now have two classes of stock. Such two-class stocks are traded on the American Exchange and over-the-counter and on a number of foreign exchanges. And at this writing the New York Stock Exchange has been under pressure to accept such stocks. The class B stock typically has the same value as common stock but typically there are restrictions on selling it outside the family. It is not unusual in such an arrangement that heirs with $25 million can maintain control of a $500 million company, if they want to do so.

Some who are wary of any move to curb family fortunes still argue that the family company would suffer. They say important assets of the company might have to be sold off to pay tax bills. That would not have to happen if the company has gone public. About three-quarters of the entrepreneurs I visited were running private companies, but among the most sparkling performers, at least until the 1987 crash, were the few that had gone public (examples: Ewing Kauffman's Marion Laboratories, Leslie Wexner's The Limited, Sol Price's The Price Company, Sigfried Weis's Weis Markets). The stocks of all were eagerly sought by investors, which provided loads of money for expansion. Jack Simplot's explanation for keeping his potato operation private was that he was a "loner." Many operators of large private companies tend to be secretive. Arthur Jones of Nautilus was an example.

I believe that all companies with revenues of more than $100 million a year should be required to be public companies. Such companies have by that point become major segments of our economy and so deserve the public scrutiny that goes with being a public company.

If a company is public, there is no need to worry about being forced to sell off essential assets to pay taxes. The wealthholder being taxed simply sells some of his shares on the open market.

Also I believe that any individual with a net worth of $25 million or more should be required to file an annual statement of assets and liabilities, including the details of all trusts in which the individual is either a donor or beneficiary. This is in the public interest. It would give the Internal Revenue Service a comprehensive source of information for analyzing strategies being used by individuals of great wealth to minimize their payments of income and transfer taxes. It would discourage dubious tactics, and it would give Congress a clear picture of where the tax laws need to be strengthened. Also such a requirement would provide aid in prosecuting very rich people engaged in illegal activities such as drug-running. Failure to file a correct statement would in itself be an indictable offense.

If a law is passed to put a ceiling on the transfer of great wealth to others, there must be implementation that involves laws and regulations to curb strategies to minimize taxable transfers. As it stands, gaping holes are available for transferring wealth to heirs at greatly reduced valuations for tax purposes. We reviewed these in two earlier chapters. Some are easier to close than others. Strategies commonly used to lower the value, for tax purposes, of assets to be transferred deserve scrutiny.

A ceiling on the amount a donor can transfer to heirs should greatly reduce the popularity of the host of trusts described earlier designed to transfer fortunes with a minimum of transfer taxes. Still in an equitable society the Congress should review all forms of trusts, and curb those that have a clear tax-avoidance effect. This would include for example the GRIT-type trust, the charitable lead trust, and the charitable remainder trust. George Cooper, the well-known professor on taxation, long at Columbia Law School, has stated: "Trusts were originally developed as tax avoidance devices and they survive in large part as tax avoidance devices."[15] And Professor Cooper says of the existing common procedure for discounting the value of money being transferred by trusts by delaying the transfer to get a big discount based on the IRS tables setting assumptions about earning power: "The valuation discount situation is such a shell game that even an unsympathetic judiciary might be convinced to cut back on it."[16]

The fact that some of these trusts purport to have a charitable purpose should not obscure the fact that they may well be essentially tax gimmicks that need to be overhauled. And let us not forget that the trusts are used for tax avoidance by many wealthy people with less than $25 million net worth.

When our society has in place a ceiling on the amount of wealth that rich individuals can transfer to heirs, we'll have a new situation. Charitable causes will have no need to be dependent for support upon tax gimmicks designed for the rich. With ceilings on transferable wealth in place there will almost certainly be a great upsurge in genuine charitable interest.

CHAPTER 24

ON ENCOURAGING THE WEALTHY TO SHIFT PRIORITIES

"A government cannot have too much of the kind of activity which ... aids and stimulates individual exertion and development."

— JOHN STUART MILL, *Essay on Liberty*

Without disturbing the concept of America as a land of opportunity, I have shown, I believe, that we can make corrections in a reward system that is getting seriously out of hand at the uppermost level. The processes of correction can in fact win for these mostly unknown people of great wealth a good deal of public admiration while not affecting their life-styles in any significant way.

There are several socially attractive possibilities that will arise if a ceiling is placed on the transfer of assets by major wealthholders to heirs or other individuals.

1. With a ceiling on transfers, the wealthholder might become much more interested in becoming an honored patron of his or her national government. Even a very wealthy person can usually find many laudable programs insufficiently funded by the existing federal budget. As a patron, he might be happy to give a large gift for a specific program of the federal government that he or she favors. Such a donor could specify that the funds go to such existing programs as saving the bald eagle, building a stealth bomber, saving the seashores of the Carolinas, or building refuges for our mounting number of homeless families. Granted, Uncle Sam is so unused to receiving large gifts that such gifts presently would simply have to go into the general fund. However if it became clear that hundreds of millions of new dollars might come pouring in if some designation was permitted, the Congress would almost certainly hasten to modify the present law (31 USC, Section 4841) to permit some designation for gifts in the millions of dollars. The Treasury might even be happy to publicize an annual list of big donors.

2. Arrangements could be made to exempt from the ceiling on transfer of wealth all profits made on investments that met two criteria important to the general welfare. First, such investments would have to be in enterprises that required venture capital to succeed. Second, these enterprises would have to be either aimed at helping to solve important national or international problems or aimed at opening up new fields that could be extraordinarily productive by generating socially useful economic activity. By solving important problems, I refer to such projects as developing new sources of energy for the time, a few years hence, when the oil crunch returns ... developing new products or services to cope with AIDS ... coping in new ways with pollution ... launching new enterprises in friendly third world countries ... working to reverse the growth of illiteracy in this country ... providing work projects that mothers of young

children could do at home. A staff of experts at the IRS could not only maintain guidelines on the criteria but advise on the eligibility of specific projects.

3. If faced with a ceiling on transfers to heirs, wealthy businessmen might well shift from being self-centeredly focused on accumulating wealth to having a broader-minded focus on growth by sharing. Specifically, they might assign some of their wealth to setting up profit sharing plans or stock ownership plans for employees.

In chapter 10 we met Ewing Kauffman of Marion Laboratories (Kansas City), who is widely regarded as a genius at motivating his business "associates." For many years he has had both a profit-sharing plan and a stock-option plan because, he says, "You should treat your associates [your employees] the way you would want to be treated if you were an employee." His associates now own nearly half of the company, more than he and his wife own. Mr. Kauffman said, "That's the way it should be. They're still going to vote me in."

At the time we talked, he said the two plans for sharing had created eighty-three millionaires (and there are a lot more now because the stock continued to soar). The company's stock, he said, had split forty-eight times in twenty years. He asserted that Marion Labs was number one in sales per employee in its industry. Typically, if Marion advertises that it wants to add ten salesmen, it will get 5,000 applications. Marion Laboratories is near the top of the 100 best U.S. companies to work for.[1]

About a quarter century ago I met a man in San Francisco, Louis Kelso, who had a pretty radical idea when you consider that he was an investment banker. We have kept in touch over the years.

He thought capitalism was becoming sluggish because capital for producing goods and services was becoming too concentrated. A plutocratic 5 percent of the populace controlled almost all investment capital. Two centuries ago, he pointed out, most Americans were capitalists. They had their own farm or shop. As we have become, through advancing technology, overwhelmingly a nation of employees, he felt enterprises and our society would perform better if employees could earn money not only as "labor workers" but also as "capital workers." They would have an investment stake in the success of their company.

Out of this conviction that capitalism should be democratized came his concept of ESOP (employee stock ownership plan). His main contribution was to figure out a way to create a credit mechanism. This makes capital credit available to employees to enable them to buy stock in the company. (With a benevolent owner faced with an overabundance of wealth, there could be less dependence on credit mechanisms.) In any case, all employees have a chance to become shareholders without having deductions taken from their paychecks. Congress has cooperated in making the concept popular with employers by enacting more than a dozen tax incentives to facilitate the financing.[2]

By 1985 *Business Week* was reporting that "a remarkable force" was "sweeping American business.... Suddenly the concept of worker as owner is spreading.... Millions of employees are gaining direct ownership of stock in their own companies — thus getting a foot in the door that has historically been shut to all but the wealthy few." About 7,000 companies with nearly 10 million employees, it reported, were already involved and it was estimated that in a dozen years perhaps a fourth of all U.S. workers would be shareholders in their own companies. It cited Kelso as the ESOP pioneer and described a study of 360 high-technology companies which concluded that the companies in the sample that had plans for employees to share in ownership were growing two to four times as fast as those where employees did not own stock.[3] The degree of voting rights that go with shares obtained in one's company varies with each plan.

Kelso recently advised me he saw the ESOP movement as helping to offset "the current ruthless increase in the already over-concentrated ownership of capital" that is being fostered by the rampant surge of mergers and takeovers.

At any rate, an employer overblessed with assets that

greatly exceed what he can transfer to heirs when a ceiling is in place could find substantial rewards in some kind of sharing program with employees. There would at least be the psychological rewards coming from the increased loyalty and dedication of his employees.

4. The placing of a ceiling on the amount of assets that a great wealthholder could transfer to heirs would produce a sustained explosion of benevolence. Wealthholders would certainly correct the current situation in which significant philanthropy does not begin until death, and even then occurs only on an average scale that is not noteworthy. We would see an enormous increase in genuinely charitable thinking. And we would see the wealthholders getting much more recognition as public benefactors (if they don't mind the recognition).

With a ceiling on transfers to heirs in place there would be individuals in virtually every state in the Union who would have in excess of $100 million available for some kind of public service or direct philanthropy. This last option offers a grand array of opportunities. The choice might be to focus on enriching life in their region, as by funding neighborhood renovation, underwriting local symphonies, funding drug education programs in the schools, building better libraries, or guaranteeing that all children of promise in a given low-income school system will receive a college education.

Another area of choice might be to focus on national problems such as illiteracy in high-crime areas, desecration, pollution, building community centers in areas of high-mobility, underwriting large-scale scholarship programs, or building badly needed research centers.

And still another area of choice might be to work for a better world by focusing on projects such as the battle against overpopulation, student exchange programs, attempts to remedy malnutrition, or the teaching of bootstrap skills in nations handicapped by lack of knowledge of skills needed for industrial development.

A person with hundreds of millions (or billions) might have fun sampling projects in all three areas.

The big wealthholders might choose to handle philanthropy on a project-to-project basis, or they might set up one or more foundations to handle their areas of enthusiasm. They and their heirs could be on the board. One advantage in addition to convenience to using foundations is that they give the wealthholder an opportunity to pass the buck when importuned by fund-seekers.

The creation of foundations has been pretty much out of vogue with the really rich since Congress, a couple of decades ago, destroyed the value of foundations as self-serving tax gimmicks. At least 5 percent of a foundation's funds must now be distributed to philanthropic causes each year. There are only a few people alive who have created one or more of the nation's top fifty foundations. But when we have a ceiling on what a donor can transfer to heirs, foundations should come roaring back in popularity.

Donors wishing to use a foundation not only for benevolent purposes but as a way for their family to maintain a controlling interest in a company can do so. The funds of the foundation they create to support philanthropic activities can consist — up to 20 percent — of stock in the family company. And the foundation's board can consist of family and friends. Hence the 20 percent of the company's stock held by the foundation can be voted, if desired, to help the family's viewpoint prevail. If 20 percent of a foundation that has been created doesn't give the family the control it desires, it can create more or bigger foundations.

No one named Pew has ever been on the *Forbes* 400 but members of the Pew family control at least a quarter of the $10 billion Sun Company (founded by a Pew) through a series of family charitable trusts.[4]

There are also no Astors in the *Forbes* 400 list, but the noted New York socialite Brooke Astor has made a career of philanthropy. Over a quarter century she has supervised bequests totaling more than $136 million to help young people, museums, libraries, and projects for parks, health, and housing in New York. The *New York Times* in a lead editorial commenting on this in 1985 stressed the fact that she seemed to have "so much fun giving it away."

The time is certainly ripe for our society vigorously to encourage, in schools and elsewhere, an ethic of public responsibility.

The proposals I have advanced in these final chapters will not affect in any negative way the productivity, profitability, or job-creating potential of any company in America. The odds are strong, in fact, that such goals will be enhanced.

And the reasonable goals of any rising entrepreneur will not be affected by the proposal made for a ceiling on the number of millions of dollars they can transfer to heirs or other individuals. Extraordinarily successful entrepreneurs should in fact finish their careers feeling much better about themselves if they have used some of their funds to demonstrate social responsibility.

Most important, we will end up with a more rational, enriched, and dynamic society.

REFERENCE NOTES

Opening Quotation

1. Robert D. McFadden, "America's New Super-Rich Men: Fortunes Founded on the Prosaic," *The New York Times,* August 27, 1978.

1. Our Dreams and Apprehensions about Big Wealth

1. "The Billionaires: The World's Richest People," *Fortune,* October 12, 1987, pp. 120–129.
2. From John Tebbel, historian, author of *Presidents and the Press.*
3. *The Papers of Thomas Jefferson,* ed. Julian P. Boyd, vol. VIII (Princeton: Princeton University Press, 1953), pp. 681–683.
4. *The Works of John Adams,* ed. Charles Francis Adams, vol. IX (Freeport, N.Y.: Books for Libraries Press, 1969), pp. 376–377.
5. C. Wright Mills, *The Power Elite* (New York: Oxford University Press, 1956), p. 272.
6. Gustavus Myers, *The Ending of Hereditary American Fortunes* (New York: Julian Messner, 1939), citing *The Congressional Record* 59th Congress, Second Session, pp. 27–28.
7. Ibid. *The Congressional Record,* 63d Congress, First Session, Pt. 4, p. 382.
8. Jacqueline Thompson, *Future Rich* (New York: William Morrow, 1985), p. 38.

2. The Explosion of Personal Fortunes

1. "In Search of 'Instabucks,'" *Newsweek,* December 2, 1985.
2. "The Composition of Wealth in the United States," by the Democratic

Staff of the Joint Economic Committee. Published by the Joint Economic Committee, United States Congress, July 1986.

3. Congressional Joint Economic Committee press release, August 21, 1986.

4. Barbara Ehrenreich, "Is the Middle Class Doomed?" *The New York Times Magazine*, September 7, 1986.

5. *Federal Estate and Gift Taxes,* statement by James D. Smith. March 17, 1976, at Public Hearings and Panel Discussions before the Committee on Ways and Means, House of Representatives, 94th Congress, Second Session, Pt. 1 of 2, p. 1318.

6. Ravi Batra, *The Great Depression of 1990* (New York: Simon & Schuster, 1987), p. 118.

7. Jacqueline Thompson, *The Very Rich Book* (New York: William Morrow and Company, 1981), p. 414.

8. "The Second Most Powerful Man in America," *Newsweek,* February 24, 1986.

9. Richard Behar, "How Rich Is Bob Hope?" *Forbes,* October 1, 1984.

10. "Star Bucks," *People,* March 10, 1986.

11. Robert Simison and Karen Blumenthal, "Besieged Tycoon," *The Wall Street Journal,* November 2, 1985.

12. Thomas J. Bray, "Lammot du Pont Is Surviving Nicely in Wake of Financial Collapse," *The Wall Street Journal,* May 8, 1974. Also, "Riches to Rags," *The New York Times,* July 4, 1976; "Motsey Settles," *Time,* June 3, 1974; and "du Pont Scion's Plan to Settle Debt Is Cleared," *The Wall Street Journal,* November 15, 1974.

4. Wealth as an Extension of Self

1. "Simplot Flag Makes Waves in Boise," *The Wall Street Journal,* September 10, 1980.

2. "Market Shakers," *The Wall Street Journal,* June 1, 1976.

3. Charles J. V. Murphy, "Jack Simplot and His Private Conglomerate," *Fortune,* August 1968.

4. Ibid.

5. "The Great Potato Bust," *Time,* June 7, 1976.

6. See note 2.

7. Ibid.

8. See note 5.

9. "Damages Awarded over 1976 Default of Potato Futures," *The Wall Street Journal,* November 21, 1983.

10. "Idaho's Potato King Charged in 8 Cases of U.S. Tax Fraud," *The New York Times,* May 5, 1977.

11. See note 1.

12. See note 3.

13. "What Makes Jeno Paulucci Happy?" *People,* September 13, 1978.

14. "Jeno's Economic Ego," *Newsweek,* March 17, 1986.

15. Ibid.

16. Laurie McGinley, "Special Highway Project Funding in House Bill Stirs Pork-Barrel Charges, Could Block Measure," *The Wall Street Journal,* September 16, 1986.
17. Mark Andrews, "Paulucci Power — A Way of Really Making Things Happen," *The Orlando Sentinel,* May 31, 1987.
18. "Stranger Than the Remarkable Nautilus Exercise Machine Is Its Inventor, Arthur A. Jones," *People,* July 3, 1983.
19. Ibid.
20. Daniel Shannon, "The Man from Nautilus," *The New York Times,* July 25, 1982.
21. "Aching Back? Arthur Jones Says He Has the Answer," *Business Week,* December 14, 1987.

5. Wealth as a Problem to Be Escaped

1. "The Forbes Four Hundred," *Forbes,* Fall 1983.
2. Carol J. Loomis, "The Rockefellers: End of a Dynasty," *Fortune,* August 4, 1986.
3. *The Foundation Directory* (New York: The Foundation Center, 1983), items 2644–46.
4. Ellen Warren, "Home Sweet Home: Sen. Rockefeller's Estate," *The Miami Herald,* July 20, 1986.
5. Peter Collier and David Horowitz, *The Rockefellers: An American Dynasty* (New York: Holt Rinehart & Winston, 1976), p. 585.
6. Ibid., p. 621.

6. Wealth as an Ego Prop

1. Ronald Kessler, *The Richest Man in the World,* (New York: Warner Brothers, 1986), pp. 5–9.
2. "The Canadians Are Coming," *Time,* November 17, 1986.
3. "Sam," *The New Yorker,* May 12, 1986.

7. Wealth as a Way to Keep Score

1. Vance Packard, *The Pyramid Climbers* (New York: McGraw-Hill, 1962), chapter 13.
2. "Hard Times in Texas," *Forbes,* October 27, 1986.

8. Wealth as a Challenge
for True-Blue Capitalists

1. Doug J. Swanson, "Bright Still Afraid of Going Broke," *The Dallas Morning News,* March 25, 1984.

2. Jonathan Dahl, "Dallas Cowboys' Bum Bright Mixes Business Acumen with Some Wild Tactics," *The Wall Street Journal,* April 11, 1985.
3. Ibid.
4. Nancy Smith, "Bum Bright," *The Dallas Times Herald,* April 11, 1984.
5. See note 2.

9. Wealth as an Incidental
Aspect of Life

1. Tom Dowling, "Long Memories," *Forbes,* October 1, 1984.
2. Ibid.
3. Ibid.
4. Ibid.
5. Ronald Kessler, "A Real Estate Success Story," *The Washington Post,* August 11, 1978.
6. Harry Hurt III, *Texas Rich* (New York: W. W. Norton and Company, 1981), p. 21.
7. Ibid, p. 18.
8. Richard W. Stevenson, "The Hunts' Bid to Buy Time," *The New York Times,* September 2, 1986.
9. See note 6, pp. 131–134.
10. "The Forbes Four Hundred," *Forbes,* October 1985.
11. See note 6, p. 334.
12. Nancy Smith, "Nine Debs Take Their Bows at Idlewild Club's Ball," *The Dallas Times Herald,* October 25, 1982.
13. Thomas C. Hayes, "Dallas Cheers a Bank Merger," *The New York Times,* December 21, 1986.

10. Seeking to Live It Up

1. Interview by Harry Reasoner on *60 Minutes* (CBS), February 17, 1985.
2. Edith Evans Asbury, "Country Cousin to a Chateau," *The New York Times,* October 3, 1983.
3. "Guccione Son Defying Father over Magazine," *The New York Times,* August 10, 1987.
4. Marilyn Schwartz, "In the Money," *The Washington Post,* July 3, 1983.
5. Jeff Jarvis, "Reveling in the Lap of Luxury," *People,* March 21, 1983.
6. Ann Maier, "It's Show Business as Usual for Builder Harold Farb ..." *People,* October 24, 1983.
7. See note 5.
8. See note 7.
9. Jonathan P. Hicks, "Wheeling Chairman Sells Stake," *The New York Times,* January 7, 1987. See also *Times* article "Troika of Directors to Run Wheeling," February 12, 1987.

10. Jasper Dorsey, "Allen E. Paulson," *Sky,* March 1984.
11. "Ewing Kauffman Sold Self Rich in Kansas City," *Fortune,* October 1972.
12. Ibid.
13. Ibid.
14. Ibid.
15. N. R. Kleinfield, "Why Everybody Goes to the Mall," *The New York Times,* December 21, 1986.
16. Julie Baumgold, "The Bachelor Billionaire," *New York,* August 5, 1985.
17. Brian O'Reilly, "Leslie Wexner Knows What Women Want," *Fortune,* August 19, 1985.
18. "Parlaying Rags into Vast Riches," *Newsweek,* December 30, 1985.

11. Trying Elite Playgrounds and Pastimes

1. Source: Shannon Donnelly, society writer, *Palm Beach Daily News.*
2. Source: Archie Peck, Palm Beach realtor.
3. Source: Agnes Ash, publisher of the *Palm Beach Daily News.*
4. See note 1.
5. Malcolm Forbes, *Around the World on Hot Air and Two Wheels* (New York: Simon & Schuster, 1985), pp. 15–22.
6. "People," *Time,* April 14, 1986.
7. Source: Mark Masciarotte, Gilman Yachts, Palm Beach.
8. Steven Crist, "Spend a Buck Will Skip Preakness, Owner Says," *The New York Times,* May 8, 1985.
9. "Baseball's Big League Blues," *Business Week,* August 12, 1985.
10. "Once a Member of the Chorus, Georgia Frontiere Now Owns a Line That Goes 260 Pounds Per Man," *People,* October 19, 1981.
11. Ibid.

12. Living High but Craving Something Else

1. Emma Bugbee, "Electra Waggoner Bowman Pursues Career as a Sculptor," *The New York Herald Tribune,* May 3, 1937.
2. Kit Konolige, *The Richest Women in the World* (New York: Macmillan Publishing Co., 1985), p. 140.
3. "Estate Woes," *The New York Post,* August 27, 1981.
4. Dick Anderson, "Gamblin' Woman," *Hamptons* magazine, August 1, 1986.
5. Charlotte Curtis, "Theater Life, Second Love," *The New York Times,* June 19, 1984.
6. Claudia Cohen, "Queen of the Flops?" *The New York Daily News,* January 8, 1981.
7. See note 4.

13. Maintaining a Just-Folks
Life-style

1. Jim Atkinson, "The Caruth Saga," *D, The Magazine of Dallas,* September 1975.
2. Thomas C. Hayes, "The Wealthiest Woman in America," *The New York Times,* October 26, 1986.
3. See note 1.
4. Robert Levering, Milton Moskowitz, Michael Katz, *The 100 Best Companies to Work For in America* (New York: Signet, 1987), p. 165.

14. Playing the Power Game

1. Spencer Klaw, "They Don't Come Like Witt Stephens Any More," *Fortune,* May 1959.
2. David Stipp, "Despite a Low Profile, Stephens Inc. Thrives as Investment Banker," *The Wall Street Journal,* April 26, 1983.
3. Ibid.
4. Ibid.
5. See note 1.
6. See note 2.
7. Jeff Gerth, "The Stephens Empire Faces a Challenge," *The New York Times,* May 17, 1978.
8. See note 2.

15. Venturing for More Than Money

1. "The Man Behind a $5 Billion Dynasty," *Business Week,* October 20, 1986.
2. Kathleen Stauder, "How the Bass Brothers Do Their Deals," *Fortune,* September 17, 1984.
3. Scott McCartney, "Bass Family the 'Perfect Capitalists,'" *The Washington Post,* October 9, 1984.
4. "The Basses Stop Swimming in a School," *Fortune,* October 13, 1986.

16. Demonstrating Social Responsibility

1. Dan Rottenberg, "The Most Generous Living Americans," *Town & Country,* December 1986.
2. Eugene Steuerle, "The Charitable Giving Patterns of the Wealthy," draft report prepared for the Council on Foundations and the Yale Program on Non-Profit Organizations, January 31, 1986.
3. Kathleen Teltsch, "The Rohatyns Question the Glitter in Charity Fund Raising," *The New York Times,* January 5, 1986; Ron Rosenbaum, "Society Dissidents," *Manhattan, Inc.,* April 1986; "Giving When It Doesn't Hurt," *Newsweek,* May 26, 1986.

4. Dan Rottenberg, "Education of a Philanthropist," *Town & Country,* December 1984.
5. Ibid.
6. "The Forbes Four Hundred," *Forbes,* October 27, 1986.
7. Dan Rottenberg, "The Triumph of a Prodigal Son," *Town & Country,* February 1979.
8. Irwin Ross, "A View from Stewart Mott's Penthouse," *Fortune,* March 1974.

17. The Yearning for — and Problems of — Family Dynasties

1. The Editors of *The Wall Street Journal,* "American Dynasties Today, 1980" (Homewood, Illinois: Dow Jones–Irwin, Inc., 1980), p. xv.
2. Colin Leinster, "Business Dynasties Face the Raiders," *Fortune,* March 17, 1986.
3. Pauline Yoshihashi, "A Daughter's Quick Rise to the Top," *The New York Times,* December 16, 1984.
4. Michael Brody, "ComputerLand's Suddenly Poorer Boss," *Fortune,* April 15, 1985.
5. Ken Wells, "A Computer Tycoon and Saipan Discover They Are Incompatible," *The Wall Street Journal,* June 26, 1987.
6. Ellyn Spragins, "Houston to Dallas: Move Over, J.R.," *Forbes,* Fall 1983.
7. Ibid.
8. Charlotte Curtis, "A Baron and His Woes," *The New York Times,* April 17, 1984.
9. "Cullen Family Estate Suit Is Dismissed in Houston," *The Wall Street Journal,* May 29, 1984.
10. Alex S. Jones, "Bingham Family to Sell Louisville Media Holdings," *The New York Times,* January 10, 1986.
11. Alex S. Jones, "The Binghams, After the Fall," *The New York Times,* December 2, 1986.
12. Ibid.

18. The Fragmenting Effect of Modern Family Forms

1. "The Forbes Four Hundred," *Forbes,* October 27, 1986.
2. Barbara Mills, "It Sounded Like Dallas, Not Chicago . . ." *People,* December 2, 1983.
3. Andrew H. Malcolm, "Chicago Sun-Times Is up for Sale in Liquidation of Field Enterprises," *The New York Times,* April 16, 1983.
4. See note 2.
5. Leonard Samuel Shoen, *You and Me* (Las Vegas, Nevada: AMERCO, 1980), p. 2.
6. "U-Haul Hits the Skids," *Newsweek,* September 14, 1987.

19. Protective Strategies
While Still Alive

1. For a comprehensive analysis of changes created by the 1986 tax law, see Jonathan G. Blattmachr, "Tax Reform and Estate Planning," *The Chase Review*, October 1986.
2. "TRB from Washington," *The New Republic*, April 14, 1986.
3. Leonard Sloane, "Using a Trust to Ease Taxes," *The New York Times*, September 28, 1985.

20. Strategies for the Hereafter

1. Thomas B. Ripy, "Estate and Tax Revision: 97th Congress," Archived 11/18/82, Congressional Research Service, Library of Congress.
2. "Selected Statistical Services 1970–86," *SOI Bulletin*, Internal Revenue Service, vol. 6, no. 1 (Summer 1986).
3. George Cooper, *A Voluntary Tax?* (Washington: The Brookings Institution, 1979). See Introduction.
4. Gary J. Estep, "Fiduciary Income Tax Returns, 1982," *SOI Bulletin*, Spring 1985.
5. Eugene Steuerle, "The Charitable Giving Patterns of the Wealthy," prepared for the Council on Foundations and the Yale University Program on Non-Profit Organizations, January 31, 1986.
6. For a comprehensive explanation of how these valuation tables work with different types of trusts, see Jerry J. McCoy, "Tax Planning under the Revised IRS Actuarial Tables," *The Practical Accountant*, January 1985.

21. A Tycoon Who Would Crack Down
on the Super-Rich

1. "Fed-Mart Says Court Has Ruled in Its Favor in Suit by Ex-Chairman," *The Wall Street Journal*, October 25, 1979.
2. "The Forbes Four Hundred," *Forbes*, October 28, 1984.

22. The Lowering Rationality
and Increasing Consequences
of Great Private Fortunes

1. "The Forbes Four Hundred," *Forbes*, Fall 1983.
2. See, for example, the acclaimed book *Manufacturing Matters: The Myth of the Post-Industrial Economy*, by Stephen S. Cohen and John Zysman (New York: Basic Books, 1987).

3. Lester C. Thurow, "The Leverage of Our Wealthiest 400," *The New York Times,* October 11, 1984.

4. Griffin Smith, Jr., "Dallas," *The National Geographic,* September 1984.

5. TRB from Washington, "Boesky's Disease," *The New Republic,* November 10, 1986.

6. Richard I. Kirkland, Jr., "Should You Leave It All to the Children?" *Fortune,* September 29, 1986.

7. Jim Hightower, *The New York Times,* June 21, 1987, Op. Ed. page.

8. Robert Kuttner, "The Truth about Corporate Raiders," *The New Republic,* January 20, 1986.

9. Ravi Batra, "An Ominous Trend to Greater Inequality," *The New York Times,* May 3, 1987.

23. On Curbing a Moneyed Aristocracy

1. Carl S. Shoup, "Federal Estate and Gift Taxes," House Ways and Means Committee hearings, Ninety-fourth Congress, Second Session, Part 1 of 2, March 15–17, 1976, p. 1286.

2. See *The Washington Post,* May 8, 1982, p. A6, col. 2.

3. John Newman, "Foreign Taxation: New French Tax on Large Net Wealth," *Tax Management International Journal,* April 1, 1982.

4. For a sampling of the literature, see note 5 in John H. Davies's "Income-Plus-Wealth: In Search of a Better Tax Base," *Rutgers Law Journal,* Summer 1984.

5. "A Lament: All Work and Less Pay," *Time,* July 13, 1987.

6. Richard W. Lindholm, "A New Federal Tax System," *Tax Notes,* July 30, 1984.

7. Michael M. Thomas, "G.L.U.B., G.L.U.B.: (A Modest Proposal to Redistribute Wealth)," *The New York Times,* August 1, 1984.

8. Correspondence from Carl S. Shoup, authority on taxation previously cited.

9. Barry L. Isaacs, "Do We Want a Wealth Tax in America?" *University of Miami Law Review,* vol. 32 (December 1977).

10. Richard W. Lindholm, *A New Federal Tax System* (Westport, Connecticut: Praeger, 1984), p. 48.

11. See note 9.

12. George Cooper, *A Voluntary Tax?* (Washington: The Brookings Institution, 1979), pp. 46–49.

13. *Federal Estate & Gift Tax Reporter,* vol. 1, Internal Revenue Code and Regulations (Chicago, Ill.: Commercial Clearinghouse, Inc., 1983), pp. 5003–5005.

14. Alex S. Jones, "Dow Jones Insures Family Control," *The New York Times,* January 20, 1984.

15. Mortimer Hess Memorial Lecture by George Cooper, "Taking Wealth Taxation Seriously," Association of the Bar of the City of New York Records, vol. 34 (January–February 1979), p. 40.

16. See note 12, p. 89.

24. On Encouraging the Wealthy
to Shift Priorities

1. Robert Levering, Milton Moskowitz, Michael Katz, *The 100 Best Companies to Work for in America* (New York: Signet, 1987), p. 242.
2. "ESOPs: Revolution or Ripoff?" *Business Week,* April 15, 1985.
3. Ibid.
4. Mary Kuntz, "How the Other Half Gives," *Forbes,* October 1, 1984.

INDEX

Abdul-Jabbar, Kareem, 24
Above All Else (June Hunt), 128
Acapulco, Mexico, 170
Adams, John, 6, 7
Aga Kahn, 170
Alexander, Don, 277
Alger, Horatio, 8
Allen, Charles, 186, 187
Allen & Co., 186
American Civil War, 8
American Lawyer, The (magazine), 249
American Revolutionary War, 5–6, 324
American Stock Exchange, 329
AMERCO Co., 267
Annenberg, Mr. and Mrs. Walter, 169, 170
Antimony Corp., 113
anti-Semitism, 167, 264
arbitage, 214–215, 308, 316–317
Arkansas Louisiana Gas Co., 211
Arkansas Oklahoma Gas Co., 212
Arkansas Public Service Commission, 211, 212
artworks and taxes, 280
Astor, Brooke, 253, 337
Attica (film), 179
Autotechnicon, 225–226
Autrey, Gene, 22
Azurite Corp., 113

Bailey, Barry, 198
Baldwin, Dan, 67
Baldwin, Roger, 234

Bancroft, Christopher: entrepreneurship, 72, 73–76; personality and lifestyle, 72, 73–74; views on inherited wealth, 72–73, 74, 75, 76, 329; family, 73–76
Bancroft, Hugh, Sr., 73
Bancroft, Hugh, Jr., 73
Barcite, Corp., 113
Bar Harbor, Maine, 170
Barron, Clarence, 73
Barrons (magazine), 73
Bass, Anne, 213–214
Bass, Bob, 214
Bass, Edward, 213; homes, 214; wealth of, 216, 220, 308; Biosphere II project, 216–217, 218, 219–220; ranching and other interests, 217–219
Bass, Lee, 214
Bass, Perry, 214
Bass, Sid, 213–214
Bass Brothers Enterprises, 214, 308
Batra, Ravi, 16–17, 317–318
Battery Park City, New York, 90, 91
Bean, Andy, 24
Bechtel family, 242
Beckman, Arnold, 224
Bendel's, 158
Beryl Corp., 113
Bettencourt, Liliane, 26
Biddle family, 242
Biggs, Electra ("Electra III"), 183, 184, 185

Biggs, Electra Waggoner ("Electra II"),
  243; career as artist, 178, 180, 182–
  183; source of wealth, 179–180;
  personality and life-style, 180, 181–
  182, 184–185; home, 180–181, 184;
  family, 179–181, 183–184
Biggs, Helen, 184
Biggs, John, 183, 184
Biltmore House (Asheville, N.C.), 137
Bingham, Barry, Sr., 254, 255
Bingham, Barry, Jr., 254–255
Bingham, Eleanor, 254
Bingham, Mary, 254
Bingham, Sallie, 254–255
Biosphere II, 216–217, 218, 219–220
Bird, Larry, 24
Blattmachr, Jonathan G., 277, 285, 290
Blue Bell, Inc., 215
Boesky, Ivan, 209
bonds, 322
Boston Globe, 276
Braque, Georges, 116
Brazil, 26, 27
Brenninkmeyer, Godfried, 26
Bright, Harvey ("Bum"): personality
  and life-style, 108–109, 111, 114,
  115–116; source of wealth, 109, 111–
  113; political and social philosophy,
  110, 113–114; family, 110, 111, 114;
  homes, 110–111, 114–115
Bright, Peggy, 109, 110, 111, 114
Bright Banc, 112
Brinker, Norman, 172–173
Bronfman, Edgar, 13, 27, 190
Buffett, Warren, 193, 315–316
Bureau of Indian Affairs, 55
Busch family, 242
Bush, George, 168
Business Week (magazine), 20, 214, 335

Cabot, Cabot & Forbes, 260
Calcite Corp., 113
Caligula (film), 141
Camargo Penteado, Sebastiao Ferraz
  de, 27
Canada, 25, 26
Caplin, Mortimer, 277, 278, 280, 293
Caravan of Dreams (Fort Worth, Tex.),
  219
Carnegie, Andrew, 221
Carnegie family, 242
Carroll, Charles, 6
Carter, Gary, 24

Caruth, Bob, 200
Caruth, Mabel, 194, 196–202
Caruth, Walter W., Sr., 194
Caruth, Walter W., Jr.: background,
  193–194; personality and life-style,
  193–199, 200–202; family, 195–196,
  199–201; home, 195; problems of
  wealth, 198–200
Caruth, Walter W., III, 194, 200
Caruth Foundation, 201
Celebes Co., 113
Center for Science in the Public
  Interest, 47
chain operations as source of wealth,
  19, 247; *see also* Weis, Sigfried;
  Wexner, Leslie
Chalcopyrite Co., 113
Channing, Carol, 190
charitable lead trust. *See* trusts
charity. *See* philanthropy
charity remainder trust. *See* trusts
Chicago Sun-Times, 257, 258, 259, 260
Children's Defense Fund, 83
Chrysler family, 242
Chun King, 53, 54, 60
Clark, Ramsey, 323
ClayDesta Plaza (Midlands, Tex.), 96
Clifford trusts. *See* trusts
Coca-Cola, 25
Cohen, Sheldon S., 277
Columbus, Ohio, 230, 231
commodities speculation. *See* Hunt
  brothers; Simplot, Jack R.
Commodity Futures Trading
  Commission, 48
CompterLand, 21, 244, 247–251
Connors, Jimmy, 23
Cook, Jane Bancroft, 73
Coolidge, Calvin, 11
Cooper, George, 331
Copeland, Lammot du Pont, Jr., 28
corporate salaries and stock options,
  19–20, 21; *see also* profit sharing/
  employee stock ownership
Cosby, Bill, 23
Costa Smeralda, Sardinia, 170
Cox, Ed, 110
Cox, Jessie, 73
Crenshaw, Ben, 24
Cressy, Joseph, 292
Crow, Trammell, 222
Crown, Lester, 208
Cullen, Hugh Roy, 252, 253

Cullen, Lillie, 252
Curtis, Charlotte, 164–165

Dallas Cowboys, 109, 115
Dallas Social Directory, 34, 127
Dallas Times-Herald, 109
Davis, Marvin, 222
Davis, Peter, 245
DeBartolo, Edward, 105
debt: national, 12; as wealth-building strategy, 97, 278–279
Decisions Team Ltd., 219
Declaration of Independence, 5, 6
Democracy in America (Tocqueville), 7
Dick's Castle (Garrison, N.Y.), 138
Directory of Foundations, 51, 225
Discover (magazine), 217
Dixon, Fitz Eugene, Jr., 71
Domhoff, G. William, 10, 308
Donahue, F. Woolworth, 137
Donnelly, Shannon, 163, 164
Dorrance, John, III, 72
Dow Jones Co., 73, 74, 329
Drexel Burnham Lambert, 15
Duke, Doris, 169
Duke University, 228
Duluth, Minnesota, 53, 56–57
du Pont, William, Jr., 286
du Pont, Mr. and Mrs. Willis Harrington, 35
DuPont Corp., 20, 27
du Pont family, 27–28, 242
dynasty. *See* family

Edelman, Marian Wright, 83
Egypt, 27
Ehrenreich, Barbara, 16
Electra, Texas, 180
England, 26
entertainment industry, earnings in, 22–23
"estate freezing," 280–281
Evening with Harold Farb, An (record), 145
Exxon Corp., 20

family: within privately held companies, 49–50, 114–115, 141–143, 203, 242–243, 244–245; complications to companies caused by, 124–127, 193, 199–201, 251–258, 260, 265, 267–268, 270–271; dynastic tendencies, 241–

244, 307; effects of wealth on, 315–316; *see also* du Pont family; Rockefeller family
Fanning, Katherine, 260
Farb, Carolyn Shulman, 144–145, 146
Farb, Harold: source of wealth, 143; life-style, 143–147, 169; home, 144, 145
Faubus, Orval, 211
Federal Reserve Board, 15–16, 21
Fed-Mart Corp., 295
Fettuccini Co., 113
Field, Marshall, I, 257
Field, Marshall, II, 257
Field, Marshall, III, 257, 258
Field, Marshall, IV, 257, 258, 259
Field, Marshall, V: family and background, 257–260; life-style and philanthropy, 261–262
Field, Marshall, VI, 258, 259
Field, Ted, 258, 259–260, 262
Field Enterprises, 258, 260
Financial World (magazine), 14
Firestone, Cindy, 179
Fisher Brothers, 90
Fishers Island, New York, 81, 169–170
Flick, Friedrich Karl, 26
Floyd, Ray, 24
Forbes, Malcolm, 136, 171–172
Forbes (magazine)/*Forbes* 400, 11, 14–15, 18–19, 20, 21, 22, 23, 25, 27, 28, 222 and *passim*
Ford Corp., 20
Ford family, 242
foreign investments, 277
Fortune (magazine), 4, 26–27, 50, 78
foundations: as means to minimize taxes, 10; laws concerning, 51; major, 123, 201, 223–224, 226, 228–229; *see also* philanthropy
France, 26
franchises as source of wealth, 19; *see also* Millard, William
Freberg, Stan, 53
French Revolution, 6
Frontiere, Georgia: personality and life-style, 174, 176–177; involvement with L.A. Rams, 174–176; background, 175–176; homes, 176–177
Fund for Constitutional Government, 235
Fund for Peace, 235

Galbraith, John Kenneth, 9–10
Gallo, Ernest, 290
Gallo, Julio, 290
Gardini, Raul, 26
Gates, William, 244
General Electric Corp., 20
General Motors Corp., 20, 233
Getty, Gordon, 34
gifts: tax benefits of, 279–284, 289–290 (*see also* taxes (gift)); proposals to encourage social responsibility in, 333–334
Girls of Penthouse ("electronic magazine"), 141
Glimcher Co., 91, 92, 106
Goldwater, Barry, 110
Goodall, Jane, 220
Graham, Billy, 128
grantor retained income trust. *See* trusts
Great Crash, The (Galbraith), 9
Great Depression, 9–10
Green, Hetty, 31
greenmail, 214–215, 308, 316–317
Griffin, Merv, 23
Grimaldi, Prince Rainier, 170
Grosvenor, Gerald, Sixth Duke of Westminster, 26
Gstaad, Switzerland, 170
Guccione, Robert: home, 136, 138–140, 311; personality and life-style, 139–140, 141–142, 311; publishing career, 140–141, 142; family, 141–143
Guccione, Robert, Jr., 142–143
Guggenheim family, 242
Gulfstream Aerospace Corp., 147, 149

Hall, Barbara, 202
Hall, Donald, 202–203
Hall, Donald, Jr., 203
Hall, Elizabeth, 202
Hallmark Cards, 202
Hamptons (magazine), 188–189
Hancock, John, 6
Harvard Business Review (magazine), 243
Heathrow real estate development (Orlando, Fla.), 58, 59–62
Helmsley, Harry, 19, 206–207
Hewlett, William, 223–224
Hewlett-Packard Co., 35, 224
Heymann, C. David, 310

Highland Park, Texas, 110, 125
Hirshhorn, Mr. and Mrs. Joseph, 32
Holmes, Larry, 23
Hong Kong, 26
Hope, Bob, 22, 169
Hot Rod (magazine), 25
Hrudka, Joe, 137
Hudson, Mary, 193, 204
Hunt, Caroline, 125, 126, 127, 197
Hunt, Franie Tye, 125
Hunt, Franklin. *See* Hunt, H. L.
Hunt, H. L., 124–127, 128
Hunt, Hassie, 125
Hunt, Helen, 126, 127
Hunt, Herbert, 27, 125, 126, 127, 309
Hunt, June: personality and life-style, 123–124, 129–132, 308; family background, 124–128; evangelical work, 128, 129–132; home, 129
Hunt, Lamar, 125, 126
Hunt, Lyda, 125, 128
Hunt, Margaret, 125, 126, 127
Hunt, Nelson Bunker, 27, 110, 116, 125, 126, 127, 309
Hunt, Raymond, 126, 127
Hunt, Ruth Wright (Mrs. Raymond), 126
Hunt, Swansea, 126, 127
Hurt, Harry, III, 11, 124, 125, 126
Hutton, Barbara, 310

IBM Corp., 20–21
I Love My Wife (musical), 190
income cap, discussed in WW II, 10; *see also* tax (wealth); wealth
income tax. *See* taxes (income)
Indecent Exposure (McClintick), 186
Indiana Pacers, 107
Indian Wells, California, 169
Indonesia, 26
Industrial Revolution, 8
Information Management Science Associates, Inc., 246, 249
inheritance tax. *See* taxes (inheritance)
inheritance: as source of wealth, 18; managing, 27, 78–79, 84; *see also* taxes (inheritance); wealth; *specific names*
insurance: as source of wealth, 31–32; life, 291
Internal Revenue Service, 68–69, 280, 286, 289; *see also* taxes (income); taxes (inheritance)

irrevocable trusts. *See* trusts
Irwin, Hal, 24
Italy, 26

Java Co., 113
Jackson, Andrew, 7
Jackson, Michael, 22
Japan, 26
Jefferson, Thomas, 6–7, 11
Jeno Frozen Pizza Co., 55
Jobs, Steven, 244, 315
John Birch Society, 194, 200
Jones, Arthur: personality and life-
    style, 62, 63–64, 66–70, 330; interest
    in wild animals, 62–63, 64–66;
    exercise industry, 64, 65, 68; home,
    64, 66, 70; family, 63, 67, 68, 69; tax
    problems, 68–69
Jones, Eva, 64, 67
Jones, Terri, 63, 67, 69, 70
Jupiter Island, Florida, 81, 167–169,
    261, 310

Kansas City Royals, 153, 156, 173–174
Kapor, Mitchell, 244
Kauffman, Ewing Marion, 37, 315;
    personality and life-style, 151, 153,
    154, 155, 156, 173–174; source of
    wealth, 151–152, 154–155; homes,
    152–154, 155–156; family, 152, 232,
    243; philanthropy, 231–233; profit
    sharing plan, 151, 153, 334
Kauffman, Muriel, 151, 152, 173–174,
    231
Kauffman Foundation, 232–233
Keeton, Kathy, 139–140
Kelso, Louis, 334–335
Kennedy, John F., 6
Kennedy, Joseph P., Sr., 176
Khashoggi, Adnam, 85–86
kidnapping, fear of among wealthy, 35,
    36, 80–81, 147, 311
King, Rufus, 325
Kite, Tom, 24
Konolige, Kit, 11
Korein, Sarah, 204–207
Kramer, Irwin, 186, 187, 188
Kramer, Terry Allen: personality and
    life-style, 136, 185–189; career in
    theater, 189–191; family, 190, 191

La Jolla, California, 169, 297
Lapham, Lewis H., 315

Lasagna Co., 113
Lauder, Estée, 204
Leaders (magazine), 86
LeFrak, Denise, 93
LeFrak, Francine, 88, 93
LeFrak, Richard, 87, 88, 89, 94
LeFrak, Samuel: real estate empire of,
    85–87, 88–93, 106, 311; personality
    and life-style, 86, 87, 88–90, 93–94;
    homes, 87–88, 94; family, 88–89, 93;
    interests, 93–94, 194
LeFrak, Mrs. Samuel, 88
Lefrak City, Queens, New York, 89, 90
LeFrak family, 242
Lendl, Ivan, 23
Liem Sioc Liong, 26
life insurance, 291
Li Ka-Shing, 26
Limited, The, Co., 159, 229, 330
Lindbergh kidnapping, 80
Lindholm, Richard W., 300, 323, 325
living trusts. *See* trusts
London-American (magazine), 141
Long, Huey, 10
Lords of Creation, 11
lotteries, 12
Los Angeles Rams, 174–175
Louisville Courier-Journal, 254
Louisville Times, 254
Lundberg, Ferdinand, 308
Lyford Cay, Bahamas, 170, 186–187
Lynch, Denise, 34
Lyttlesdorf, Mr. and Mrs. Arthur, 165

MacArthur, Mr. and Mrs. John D., 31–
    32
McCartney, Paul, 22
McClintick, David, 186
McCormick family, 242
McCoy, Jerry, 277, 281, 289, 290, 291,
    293
McDonald Corp., 47
McEnroe, John, 23
Mackinaw Island, Michigan, 169
Madison, James, 6, 325
malls/shopping centers, 157; as source
    of wealth, 102, 104–105
Manicotti Co., 113
manufacturing a source of wealth, 19
Marbella, Spain, 170
Marathon Oil Co., 215
Marion Laboratories, 151–152, 153,
    232, 243, 330, 334

Marriner & Co., 249
Mars family, 242
Martin, Mary, 183
Massachusetts Institute of Technology,
    226, 228
Mattingly, Don, 24
Me and My Girl (musical), 191
media empires as source of wealth, 19;
    see also Bancroft, Christopher;
    Bingham, Barry, Sr.; Field,
    Marshall(s); Forbes, Malcolm;
    Guccione, Robert
MedX Co., 70
Meese, Edwin, III, 321
Mellon family, 242
Memorial Sloan-Kettering Cancer
    Center, 77
Miami Herald, 24
Micro-Vest Co., 249–251
Milken, Michael, 15
Mill, John Stuart, 332
Millard, Ann, 244, 246–247
Millard, Barbara, 244, 245, 246–247,
    248, 251
Millard, Elizabeth, 244, 246–247
Millard, William: background and
    wealth, 21, 241, 244, 246–248; family
    control of business, 244–245;
    business problems of, 245, 246, 247–
    251
Millard, Mrs. William, 244, 246–247
Miller, Ann, 190
Mills, Alice Frances du Pont, 310
Mills, C. Wright, 308
Mills, James, 19
Monaco, 170
Money (magazine), 11
Money and Class in America (Lapham),
    315
Morgan, J. P., 8, 138
Morse, Robert, 190
mortgages, tax benefits of, 278–279
Mott, Kappy, 234
Mott, Charles S., 233, 236, 237
Mott, Stewart: background, 233–234,
    235; philanthropy, 234–237; life-
    style, 234–237
municipal bonds, 277
Murchison, Clint, Jr., 27
Murdoch, Rupert, 209, 258, 260
Murphy, Dale, 24
Murphy, Eddie, 23
Murray, Eddie, 24

National Enquirer, 25
National Italian-American Foundation,
    52, 56
Nautilus (magazine), 67
Nautilus Sports Medical Industries,
    Inc., 62
Nederlander, James, 191
Netherlands, 25, 26
New Deal, 10
New Federal Tax System, A
    (Lindholm), 325
Newhouse family, 242
Newport, Rhode Island, 137, 169, 177
Newport City, New Jersey, 86, 90, 91–
    93, 106
Newsweek (magazine), 270–271, 316
New York Daily News, 190
New Yorker (magazine), 91–92
New York Mercantile Exchange, 47, 48
New York Stock Exchange, 329
New York Times, 19, 21, 24, 77, 92, 125,
    127, 223, 245, 255, 337
Niarchos, Stavros, 170
Nicklaus, Jack, 24
Novarro, Ramon, 182

Obey, David, 16
"October" gallery (London), 218
Oglala Indians, 55, 57
Ohio State University, 231
oil as source of wealth, 19; *see also*
    Hunt, H. L.; Waggoner, W. T.;
    Williams, Clayton
Olayan, Suliman Saleh, 26
Old Mountain Corp., 260
OMNI (magazine), 140
Orlando Sentinel, 58
Osman, Osman Ahmed, 27

Packard, David, 35, 223–224, 315
Packard, Virginia, 32, 170
Palm Beach, Florida, 137, 161, 162,
    164–167, 169, 172
Palm Beach Daily News, 164, 165
Palm Beach Post, 166
Palm Springs, California, 137, 169
Paulson, Allen, 35; source of wealth,
    147, 148–149; family, 147, 307;
    homes and life-style, 147–151
Paulson, Dick, 147
Paulson, Jim, 147
Paulson, Mike, 147
Paulucci, Cindy, 60

Paulucci, Gina, 56
Paulucci, Jeno: personality and life-
    style, 51–52, 54, 55–56, 59–60, 96;
    source of wealth, 52–53, 54–55; real
    estate development, 53, 58–62;
    family, 52, 54, 55; "hands-on"
    philanthropy, 55, 57–58; political
    clout, 58–59, 308; home, 59–60, 61–
    62
Paulucci, Mick, 55
Paulucci, Lois Trepanier, 54, 55, 59
Peale, Norman Vincent, 149
Peck, Archie, 166
Pennington, C. B., 224–225, 228
pension funds, 18
Penthouse (magazine), 25, 139, 141
People (magazine), 23
Perot, Ross, 315
Pew family, 337
philanthropy: lack of, among wealthy,
    44, 51, 221–223, 225, 307; as act of
    social responsibility, 57–58, 83, 229–
    230; major gifts, 77, 123, 223–225,
    226, 228–229, 230, 232–233; income
    tax advantages, 279–280, 283–284;
    and inheritance taxes, 287–288, 292;
    proposals to stimulate, 295, 299–300,
    331–333, 336–338; *see also*
    foundations
Picasso, Pablo, 94, 116
Pillsbury Corp., 53, 55
Placid Oil Co., 126
Planned Parenthood, 235, 237
Playboy (magazine), 139, 141
Poor Little Rich Girl (Heymann), 310
Porky's (film), 106
Portanova, Enrico (Nicky) di, 170, 252–
    254
Portanova, Paolo di, 252
Power Elite, The (Mills), 11, 308
Power of Positive Thinking, The
    (Peale), 149
Powers That Be . . . , The (Domhoff), 10,
    308
Price, Sol: life-style, 294, 297–298;
    attitudes toward wealth and the
    wealthy, 294–296, 298–301, 306, 323;
    source of wealth, 294, 296–297;
    philanthropy, 299
Price Co./Price Clubs, 296–297, 330
Pritzker, Jay, 170, 222
Pritzker, Robert, 222
Procter & Gamble Corp., 20

profit sharing/employee stock
    ownership, 151, 153, 203, 334–336
Prudential Insurance Co., 205
Public Finance (Shoup), 321
Pulitzer, Lilly, 179
Pyrite Corp., 113

qualified terminal interest property.
    See trusts
Quisenberry, Dan, 24

Rainwater, Richard, 214
Rancho Mirage, California, 169
Reagan, Ronald, 11, 321
real estate: as source of wealth, 4, 18–
    19 (*see also* Caruth, Walter; Farb,
    Harold; Korein, Sarah; LeFrak,
    Samuel; Paulucci, Jeno; Simon,
    Melvin; Tauber, Laszlo); tax
    advantages, 277–278
Reasoner, Harry, 137
Reed, Permelia, 168–169
Reichmann Brothers, 91
restructuring companies: for tax
    purposes, 279; to prevent takeover,
    329
Revlon Co., 160
Revson, Charles, 160
Rice, Jim, 24
Rich and the Superrich, The
    (Lundberg), 308
Richardson, Sid, 214
Richest Woman in the World, The
    (Konolige), 11
Rigby, Harry, 189, 190, 191
Roadway Services, 14
robber barrons (nineteenth century),
    8–9
robbery, fear of, among wealthy, 35, 36
Rockefeller, Abby, 78
Rockefeller, David, 78, 157
Rockefeller, Hope, 79
Rockefeller, John D., 77–78
Rockefeller, John, Jr., 78
Rockefeller, John, III, 78, 79
Rockefeller, John ("Jay"), IV, 79
Rockefeller, Larry, 79–80
Rockefeller, Laura, 4, 72; upbringing,
    76–77, 80–81; attitude toward
    inherited wealth, 76–77, 81–84; life-
    style and personality, 77, 79, 81–84,
    168; philanthropies, 82–83

Rockefeller, Laurance, 76, 77, 78, 84, 168
Rockefeller, Lucy, 80
Rockefeller, Marion, 80
Rockefeller, Michael, 81
Rockefeller, Nelson, 78, 79
Rockefeller, Sandra, 79
Rockefeller, Steven, 79, 80, 84
Rockefeller, Winthrop, 78
Rockefeller, Winthrop, Jr., 78
Rockefeller family, 242; trust fund organization, 78–79, 84
Rohatyn, Elizabeth, 223
Rohatyn, Felix, 16, 17, 223
Rooney, Mickey, 190–191
Roosevelt, Franklin D., 6, 10
Roosevelt, Theodore, 6, 9
Rosenbloom, Carroll, 176
Rottenberg, Dan, 236
Roush family, 14

St. Moritz, Switzerland, 169
Saudi Arabia, 26
Schmidt, Mike, 24
Schulz, Charles, 23
Scottsdale, Arizona, 137
securities investment, 18
Securities and Exchange Commission, 210
Sevan Co., 113
Shays Rebellion, 6
Sherman Antitrust Act, 9
Shoen, Jim, 270
Shoen, Joe, 270
Shoen, Leonard Samuel: life-style, 262–263, 268–270; family and business complications, 263, 264–267, 267–271, 315; background, 264, 266
Shoen, Mrs. Leonard, 269–270
Shoen, Mark, 270
Shoen, Samuel, 264, 265, 269, 270
Shoen, Paul, 270
Shopping Center World (magazine), 102
Shoup, Carl A., 321
Sibson and Co., 19
Simon, Brenda, 103, 104
Simon, Debbie, 104
Simon, Mr. and Mrs. David, 104
Simon, Herbert, 92, 105
Simon, Joshua, 103
Simon, Melvin: real estate/shopping mall empire, 91–92, 102, 104–106;

personality and life-style, 102–103, 104, 106–107; homes, 103–104; family, 103, 104, 282; other business interests, 106–107
Simon, Melvin, & Associates, 105
Simplot, Jack R.: personality and life-style, 43, 45–46, 50–51, 308, 315, 330; home and flag of, 44–45, 49; source of wealth, 44, 46–47, 49; legal difficulties, 47–49; family, 49–50, 51; organization of business, 50–51
Sinclair, Upton, 9
Singapore, 27
Skidmore, Thomas, 7
Smith, James D., 16
Smith, Ozzie, 24
Smith Kline Beckman, 224
Smithsonian Institution, 280
Social Pictorial (Palm Beach, Fla.), 164, 165
Southampton, Long Island, 188, 189
Southern Methodist University, 198
Spelman, Laura, 82–83
Spelman College, 82
Spin (magazine), 143
sports: salaries/earnings in, 23–24; as hobby and/or investment, 153–154, 156, 172–176
Springsteen, Bruce, 22, 23
Stallone, Sylvester, 23
Standard Oil Co., 77
status seeking, 136–137
Stephens, Jack, 208, 209, 211
Stephens, Wilton R. ("Witt"): business style, 208–212, 308; background, 209–211
Stephens Production Co., 212
Stern, Joan, 165
Stern, Leonard, 209
stock market: as source of wealth, 4; crash of 1987, 4, 20, 151, 157, 318, 330; crash of 1929, 9–10, 317–318; changes proposed, 329
Streisand, Barbra, 23, 93
Sugar Babies (musical), 190
Sulu Co., 113
Sulzberger family, 242
Sun Co., 337
Sunspace Ranch (Oracle, Ariz.), 216
Sutcliffe, Rick, 24

Taiwan, 27
takeovers, 243–244, 316–317; *see also* arbitage

Tarbell, Ida, 9
Tauber, Laszlo: medical career, 117–119, 120–121; real estate operations, 118, 119–122; background, 118–119; homes and life-style, 122; philanthropy, 122–123, 326
Tauber Foundation, 123
Taubman, A. Alfred, 159, 162, 190
taxes (gift): laws concerning, 11, 281–282, 285, 286; minimizing, 279–284, 292; generation-skipping, 290–291
taxes (income): introduced in U.S., 9, 10; 1981 tax law, 11; 1986 tax law, 11–12, 276, 277, 279; violations of, 49, 68–69; minimizing, 97, 237, 275–284, 292; inequities, 300, 321–322; as curb to wealth, 321
taxes (inheritance): introduced in U.S., 9, 10; 1981 tax law, 11; minimizing, 286–293; proposals to change, 299–301, 327–338
taxes (wealth), proposed, 300–301, 322–327
Technicon Co., 226, 227
Texaco Corp., 215
Texas A & M, 115
Texas Business (magazine), 101, 108
Texas Rich (Hurt), 11
Theory of the Leisure Class, The (Veblen), 9
Thomas, Lowell, 45
Thomas, Michael M., 324
Thompson, Jacqueline, 11
Thomson, Kenneth, 26
Thurow, Lester C., 318, 323
Time (magazine), 91, 126
Timor Co., 113
Tisch, Laurence, 305
Titanic expedition, 93
Tocqueville, Alexis de, 3, 7–8
Town & Country (magazine), 161, 221–222, 236
trade deficits, U.S., 12
Trevino, Lee, 24
Trump, Donald, 87, 316
trusts: to preserve dynasties, 78–79, 267, 286, 288; to minimize income taxes, 276–277, 282–284, 231; Clifford trust, 276; foreign-based, 277; irrevocable, 282, 291; living, 282–284; grantor retained income trust (GRIT), 284, 331; charity remainder trust, 284, 331; to minimize inheritance taxes, 286–

293, 331; qualified terminable interest property (Q-TIP), 287; charitable lead trust, 288, 289, 331; generation-skipping, 290–291; proposals regarding, 331
Trusts & Estates, 290
Tsutsumi, Yoshiaki, 26
Tyson, Mike, 23

U-Haul, 262, 266–267, 271
Ultra (magazine), 145
unions, 56–57
United States, billionaires in, 26
United States Congress: Joint Economic Committee, 17; Research Service, 285
United States Constitution, proposed amendment to, 324–326
United States Labor Department, 16
University Park, Texas, 195
U.S. Steel Corp., 215
utilities. *See* Stephens, Wilton R. ("Witt")

Valenzuela, Fernando, 24
Vanderbilt, George Washington, 137
Van Gogh, Vincent, 116, 280
Vanik, Charles A., 320
Veblen, Thorstein, 9, 36
Very Rich Book, The (Thompson), 11
Volker, Paul, 21–22

"W" (magazine), 88
Wadkins, Lanny, 24
Waggoner, E. Paul, 180
Waggoner, Electra ("Electra I"), 179
Waggoner, Guy, 179
Waggoner, W. T., 179–180, 181
Wall Street Journal: cited, 48, 58, 109, 211; ownership of, 73
Wal-Mart, 15, 297
Walton, Sam, 15, 26, 192–193, 222, 296
Wang, An, 224
Wang, Y. C., 27
Wang Laboratories, 224
Washington, George and Martha, 6
Washington Post, 280, 281
Waste Management, 20
Watson, Thomas J., Sr., 21
Watson, Thomas J., Jr., 20
Watson, Tom, 24

wealth: concentration of, 3–4, 9–10, 15–17; attitudes of wealthy toward, 4–5, 35, 37, 295, 299–301 (*see also* seen as a burden, *below*); life-styles and assumptions about life-styles created by, 4, 36, 44, 135–138, 171–174, 178–179, 192–193, 306, 310–312 *(see also specific individuals)*; historical background, in U.S., 5–12; concerns about undue influence of, 6–8, 10, 48, 58, 211–212; *Forbes* 400 as yardstick for, 11, 14–15, 222; reasons for increase of, 17–18; geographic distribution of, 18, 25–27, 163–170; sources of, 18–20, 25–27, 306–307; by professions, 20–24; fears raised because of, 30–31, 35–36, 80–81, 311; social responsibility resulting from, 44, 57–58, 83, 262, 307; seen as burden, 71–75, 76–77, 81–84, 132, 193, 198–201; "old" versus "new," 142; proposals regarding, 299–301, 321–338
wealth tax. *See* taxes (wealth)
Webster, Daniel, 7
Wee, Lee Seng, 27
Weis, Sigfreid, 86, 242–243, 312–313
Weis, Mrs. Sigfreid, 312
Weis Markets, 330

West Germany, 26
Wexner, Leslie, 37; homes, 136, 156, 157–158, 161, 278; source of wealth, 156, 157, 159–160; personality and life-style, 157, 158, 160–161, 162; philanthropy, 229–231
Wharton, Bucky, 180
Wheeling-Pittsburgh Steel Co., 149
Whitehead, Edwin: philanthropy, 225, 226, 228–229; background, 225–226; family and life-style, 226–228, 229
Whitehead Institute for Biomedical Research, 226, 228–229
Whitmore, Sue, 165
Who Is June Hunt? (tape), 132
Wild Cargo (TV series), 63
Williams, Senator, 9
Williams, Clayton, Sr., 98
Williams, Clayton, Jr., 95; attitude toward wealth, 96–97, 100–101, 278–279; source of wealth, 96, 98–99; personality and life-style, 97–98, 99–100; family, 96, 98, 100–101
Williams, Modesta, 96, 98, 99–100
Wolframite Co., 113
Working-Men's Party, 7
Wrightsman, Mr. and Mrs., 161

Zeckendorf, William, 31, 206